To Ni~

with love

gorgeous ~

Xmas '06

xxx

WOOLF
IN CEYLON

WOOLF
IN CEYLON

AN IMPERIAL JOURNEY
IN THE SHADOW OF
LEONARD WOOLF
1904–1911

Christopher Ondaatje

HarperCollins*PublishersLtd*

Woolf in Ceylon: An Imperial Journey in the Shadow of Leonard Woolf, 1904–1911

Published by HarperCollins Publishers Ltd

HarperCollins books may be purchased for educational, business, or sales promotional use through our Special Markets Department.

HarperCollins Publishers Ltd
2 Bloor Street East, 20th Floor
Toronto, Ontario, Canada
M4W 1A8

www.harpercollins.ca

Library and Archives Canada Cataloguing in Publication

Ondaatje, Christopher
Woolf in Ceylon : an imperial journey in the shadow of Leonard
Woolf, 1904–1911 / Christopher Ondaatje. — 1st ed.

ISBN-13: 978-0-00-200718-4 (bound)   —ISBN-13: 978-0-00-639525-6 (pbk.)
ISBN-10: 0-00-200718-5 (bound)   —ISBN-10: 0-00-639525-2 (pbk.)

1.Woolf, Leonard, 1880-1969—Travel—Sri Lanka. 2.Ondaatje,
Christopher, 1943- —Travel—Sri Lanka. 3.Sri Lanka—Description and
travel. I.Title.

DS489.O64 2005   915.49304'32   C2005-903208-1

HC 9 8 7 6 5 4 3 2 1

Typeset by Libanus Press, Marlborough, Wiltshire
Reprographics by Lyndale PhotoGraphic Ltd, Devon
Printed and bound by Butler & Tanner, Frome, Somerset

Literary Acknowledgements

Extracts from the autobiography of Leonard Woolf (*Sowing*; *Growing*; *Beginning Again*; *Downhill All the Way*; *The Journey Not the Arrival Matters*); and from other works by Woolf (*Diaries in Ceylon*; *Imperialism and Civilization*; *Letters of Leonard Woolf*; *Stories of the East*; *The Village in the Jungle*). By permission of the University of Sussex and the Society of Authors as their representative.

Extract from *On the Rocks* by George Bernard Shaw. By permission of the Society of Authors on behalf of the Shaw Estate.

Extracts from *The Diaries of Virginia Woolf*, edited by Anne Olivier Bell, published by the Hogarth Press. By permission of the Random House Group Ltd.

Extract from "A sketch of the past" by Virginia Woolf, published by the Hogarth Press. By permission of the Random House Group Ltd.

Extract from *The Letters of Virginia Woolf*, Volume 1, edited by Nigel Nicolson, published by the Hogarth Press. By permission of the Random House Group Ltd.

Extracts from *Virginia Woolf and Lytton Strachey: Letters*, edited by Leonard Woolf and John Strachey. By permission of the Society of Authors, as the literary representative of the Virginia Woolf Estate and of the Strachey Trust.

For Janet, Gillian, Michael and Susan
who grew up, as I did, in old Ceylon
and witnessed a way of life that
has now all but disappeared.

Photographic Acknowledgements

The author and publishers express their thanks to the following sources for permission to reproduce illustrated material. In the event that any omissions have occurred proper acknowledgements will be made in future editions.

National Portrait Gallery, London: front jacket, portrait (detail), pp.106, 252, 278, 285

Royal Geographical Society: pp. ii, iv, viii, 18, 26, 32, 36, 37, 38, 42, 43, 54, 55, 64, 67, 68, 69, 71, 72, 86, 108, 109, 118, 119, 143, 145, 147, 151, 153, 165, 169, 171, 172, 173, 190, 192, 193, 215, 314, 315

Estate of Henry Lamb, private collection, p. 14

Time & Life Pictures/Getty Images: pp. 17, 74, 238

Hulton Archive/Getty Images: pp. 92, 93, 237

John Plumer, JP Map Graphics p. 28

Ernest Macintyre: p. 301

University of Sussex and the Society of Authors as their representative: pp. 95, 103, 116, 117, 155, 157, 204, 208, 233, 241

Christopher Ondaatje (©The Ondaatje Foundation): pp. vi, vii, x, xii, 31, 33, 34, 41, 44, 52, 57, 59, 61, 62, 63, 75, 76, 78, 79, 80, 82, 84, 85, 87, 89, 90, 91, 113, 114, 123, 129, 130, 132, 133, 134, 135, 136, 137, 138, 139, 141, 148, 158, 177, 179, 181, 184, 187, 194, 195, 197, 199, 200, 202, 206, 217, 221, 222, 225, 226, 227, 229, 240, 257, 294, 298, 299, 300, 304, 310, 316

Contents

Author's Acknowledgements

Empire—in whatever phase of civilisation—is an eternally fascinating subject. It profoundly shaped my upbringing and career, as it did the life and work of Leonard Woolf, a successful imperialist who increasingly became an anti-imperialist. *Growing*, the second volume of Woolf's masterly autobiography, forms the foundation of this book, *Woolf in Ceylon*, which was then slowly constructed during a number of visits to Sri Lanka to excavate information and opinions about Woolf. At the same time, Joanna Macnamara and Susan Dyer helped me to research and digest hundreds of relevant articles about Woolf from all over the world. Theirs was an arduous task which they discharged with admirable patience and tenacity. Raj de Silva, my long-suffering travelling companion in Sri Lanka together with Lakshman Senatilleke, gave me invaluable historical advice in planning the book. Ernest Macintyre, Sri Lankan-born playwright, flew from Australia for our final journey to Hambantota district in search of Woolf's original "village in the jungle"; I have drawn upon many of his opinions and social observations. Michael Berry and Michael Mitchell helped with the book's design and production.

Lastly, I am indebted to Andrew Robinson for editing what must have been a confusing and long-winded draft manuscript. I will forever be grateful for his guidance, enthusiasm and encouragement.

Coastal scene off the Galle Road.

Foreword

There are few figures who are central to the cultures of two extremely different countries, still fewer who appeal deeply in both the East and the West. Leonard Woolf is one of this select band. As an English man of letters, publisher, political worker, journalist and internationalist, he remains a key figure in the Bloomsbury group of artists and writers, along with his more celebrated wife Virginia Woolf. Yet he is also deeply admired in Sri Lanka for his powerful novel *The Village in the Jungle* which was based on his devoted labours in Ceylon as a civil servant in the heyday of British imperialism a century ago. His life and work—in both Britain and Ceylon—are overdue for reappraisal.

Christopher Ondaatje, who was born in Ceylon, has been intrigued by Leonard Woolf ever since he read Woolf's unputdownable five-volume autobiography when it was published in the 1960s. *Growing*, the second volume, about Ceylon in 1904–11, resonated strongly with him, because he grew up in the waning years of the British Empire. *Woolf in Ceylon* is his homage to Woolf, in which he revisits his subject's former imperial haunts while considering afresh the wide range of his writings on Ceylon. In a jungle village, he encounters Woolf as a living legend, which allows him to explain the origin of *The Village in the Jungle* more convincingly than any previous writer. Rich in local detail and colour, subtle in analysis, and objective about Woolf's disturbing 'dark side', *Woolf in Ceylon* is a major contribution to understanding an aspect of Leonard Woolf that has been neglected in the West for too long. I personally regard it as Christopher Ondaatje's most valuable book to date.

ANDREW ROBINSON
Literary Editor, *The Times Higher Education Supplement*

Bathers, Tissamaharama.

Introduction

> In so far as anything is important in the story of my years in Ceylon,
> imperialism and the imperialist aspect of my life have importance and
> will claim attention ... I had entered Ceylon as an imperialist, one of
> the white rulers of our Asiatic Empire. The curious thing is that I was not
> really aware of this . . . I was a very innocent, unconscious imperialist.
> What is perhaps interesting in my experience during the next six years
> is that I saw from the inside British imperialism at its apogee, and that
> I gradually became fully aware of its nature and problems.
>
> LEONARD WOOLF, *Growing*

LEONARD SIDNEY WOOLF was born in London in 1880 into what is commonly known as the Age of Imperialism. This began in the early eighteenth century, reached its peak in the late nineteenth century, started to founder during the First World War, and was all but finished by the end of the twentieth century with the collapse of the Soviet empire and, symbolically, the British return of Hong Kong to the Chinese in 1997. Woolf was 17 years old in 1897, the year of Queen Victoria's Diamond Jubilee, a staggering display which was very much a celebration of empire. The British Empire was then the largest empire the world had ever known, controlling a quarter of the earth's land surface and nearly the same proportion of its people. On 22 June 1897, the old monarch sent a telegraphic message around the world thanking her subjects for their loyalty. Fifty thousand troops from the colonies marched through London to St Paul's Cathedral; the *Daily Mail* claimed there had never been a greater embodiment of energy and power. Sir Joseph West Ridgeway, governor of Ceylon, eulogised the jubilee's effect on the British people: "It dispelled the darkness of ignorance, the scales fell from their eyes, the sordid

Portrait of Leonard Woolf by Henry Lamb, 1912.

mists which obscured their view were driven away, and they saw for the first time before them, the bright realm of a glorious Empire."

Since the 1870s, the empire had expanded at such a rate that it was nearly impossible for atlases to keep up. There seemed to be no end to the acquisition of new territories (and new business opportunities), as more and more of the map of the world was coloured imperial British pink. Victorian society in Britain accepted this growth unquestioningly and did not bother itself much with the details. The general attitude in 1897 is summed up well by Jan Morris in her three-volume history of the British Empire known as the *Pax Britannica* Trilogy: "The infatuated British people did not greatly concern itself with the motives of the *Pax Britannica*. It had happened. It was splendid. It was part of that divine order which had made Britain supreme and Victoria sixty years a Queen." This remained the dominant domestic view of empire until the First World War, despite the unrest in some British colonies, such as Bengal, triggered by the Boer War of 1899–1902.

It is true that there was some British resistance to imperialism—from humanitarians who thought it sinful, and from radical politicians, including some socialists, who considered imperialism to be an expansion of capitalism. (Globalisation today attracts similar criticism from the left.) In 1902, J. A. Hobson published the first systematic critique of imperialism, examining its economics. But although his ideas were taken up and developed by Lenin— then a refugee from the tsar living in London—Hobson's work was largely ignored in Britain. As a rule, the British, even such highly educated and formidably intelligent young men as Leonard Woolf—unless they had actually worked in the colonies—either would have been unaware of any opposition to imperialism or would have considered it to be of little consequence.

Woolf worked in the Ceylon civil service from 1904 to 1911. This turned out to be the very period that marked the onset of the decline of the British Empire. How did the increasing anti-imperialism he felt there relate to the movement of imperial history?

I have been interested in the phenomenon of cycles of power since the mid-1970s, when I read "The fate of empires", an article by the diplomat Sir John Glubb (known as Glubb Pasha for his love of the Middle East). Of course cyclical patterns occur everywhere in human existence, from the respiratory cycle and our birth, life and death, to the growth, boom and crash of economies. But it would appear that the longest human cycles are those of empires, in which civilisations are born, expand, flourish, peak, decline, and eventually cease to be.

Glubb concludes that most historical empires have had a life cycle of around two hundred and fifty years, which is roughly true of the British Empire. It had its origins in the expansion of trade in the late seventeenth century, which led to military conquests in the eighteenth and nineteenth centuries. In India, the commercial ambitions of the East India Company led to territorial gains, which stimulated imperial ambitions in the British Government, which in turn led to a grand era of construction of palaces, bridges, roads, railways, hotels and communication networks. Woolf arrived in Ceylon at the tail-end of this explosion of confident activity generated by British imperial heroism, pride, courage, dedication and duty.

But with increased affluence, values like these invariably gave way to other values: the importance of protecting one's material assets rather than basking

in the glory of new acquisitions, and, among the more thoughtful of imperial rulers, the feeling that improving the conditions of life of the colonised was a more honourable activity than merely adding to the territory and wealth of the coloniser. Morris brilliantly defines the contradictions inherent in imperialism that would become steadily more troublesome in the twentieth century: "how to induce your coloured labour to work for you, but not live among you; spend money, but not earn profits; mend the public highway, but not vote in the public elections. In the tropical empire the pioneers, however humble their circumstances at home, soon came to regard themselves as a master race." Woolf, arriving in Ceylon on the

Sir John Glubb.
Overleaf: Village crowd, Ceylon, 1910.

cusp of this shift in attitude, began as a "model imperialist" (to quote the biographer and historian Peter Ackroyd, reviewing Woolf's letters), with a yen for action and a stern adherence to the law, but became converted, during his spell of duty, into a most thoughtful imperialist, almost an anti-imperialist, with an increasing conviction that to work for self-government by the Ceylonese was right and proper.

✳   ✳   ✳

For me, the final half-century of the British Empire is of particular interest since I was born in Ceylon in 1933 into a pampered colonial existence, the son of a tea planter. My family had lived in Ceylon for as long as the British had had their empire, and had made its mark on the imperial society of the island, first under the Dutch rulers and then under the British—as captured in the book *Running in the Family* written by Michael Ondaatje, my younger brother. (According to family lore, the first Ondaatje came to Ceylon in 1659 as a doctor summoned from the court of Tanjore in south India to cure the wife of the Dutch governor, Adriaan van der Meijden.)

My father Mervyn was by all accounts a quixotic character whose misadventures are one of the highlights of *Running in the Family*. He emerges there as a loveable maverick, but I remember that his exploits were not always as benign as we might have liked. He was a big man with sandy hair and blue eyes, bigger than his own severe father, and he was incredibly charismatic. He could lead anybody anywhere; he could sell anybody anything. A major in the Ceylon Light Infantry, he spoke Sinhala and Tamil fluently and was for a long time a successful planter, managing tea estates for Carson, Cumberbatch and Co. and helping on his father's estates. But eventually he was undone by alcohol. He would start drinking as soon as he woke up, then fall asleep from ten o'clock until three in the afternoon, do a little work until about six, then go back to sleep for the night. During a drinking bout, no one could predict what he would do, and we all—my mother and his four children—feared him then, just as he was feared on the estate. Still, I remember him as basically a kind man—but always someone given to the grand gesture, especially when he wanted to prove a point. He loved his family very much and was a broken man when my mother divorced him, as she was finally forced to do in the 1950s.

But before that happened he sent me away to a public school in England, Blundell's, which was the done thing for educating the sons of the English-speaking upper and middle classes in the colonies, if one could afford it. I left Ceylon for England in 1947, just before independence in 1948.

The next few years were years of both political and personal upheaval. While I was being turned into an Englishman at school in Devon, Ceylon was moving in the opposite direction, becoming nationalistic (and eventually changing its name to Sri Lanka). Independence meant increased government taxation and serious constraints on the ability of British companies in Ceylon to sell their tea into Britain. My father suffered badly. In fact the end of empire brought an abrupt end to my family's financial prosperity as my father sank into debt—so much so that I could not finish school. Just before starting my last year at Blundell's, I received a letter from my mother telling me that I could not continue because there was no more money. It was a shock: I had no idea of our family's financial troubles; like most privileged children, I did not think about things like money.

I was forced to start from scratch. My seventeenth birthday was spent in a London bank, learning the intricacies of finance. It was expected that I would soon return to Ceylon. But when, in 1956, I was offered a job in Colombo, I decided to decline it. I could see that Ceylon was coming to the end of an era, the end of the British imperial cycle, and I judged that there would be little in the way of opportunities for an entrepreneur. After comparing the gross national products of the industrialised countries, I decided to leave my bank in London and emigrate to Canada—in effect my first major financial decision. I did not return to Sri Lanka until 1990.

Looking back, I certainly view my colonial childhood with nostalgia for a lost age, but I take a philosophical view of the British Empire as a historical phenomenon. I regard it as the product mainly of unstoppable technological and economic trends in Europe in the eighteenth and nineteenth centuries, notably the industrial revolution and the accumulation of capital. For this reason, it does not make sense to me to say, today, that I am 'against' the British Empire. Yet it is equally clear to me that the dismantling of the British Empire was a desirable thing to have happened. There may be an element of genuine contradiction in these two attitudes of mine, but if so, it was shared by Leonard Woolf. In writing this book about Woolf in Ceylon, I have tried to explore his inner conflicts and have found myself largely in sympathy with his intellectual and emotional position on empire.

*　　*　　*

Woolf was the grandson of a Jewish tailor who had done extremely well in London's West End, and the son of a highly successful barrister, Sidney Woolf, who became a Q.C. and was said to have had an income of over £5,000 a year when he was 40. There was no hint of imperial service in the Woolf family, but both his grandfather's head for business and his father's knowledge of the law would prove important in Woolf's career in Ceylon and after.

Leonard considered himself very much his father's son—intelligent, reserved and quick tempered, unable to suffer fools gladly. His mother's sentimental optimism irritated him and they would always have a difficult relationship; Woolf thought she loved him the least of her ten children. However neither parent believed in harsh disciplinary methods, and Leonard was never beaten. His late Victorian childhood was a generally happy one.

But when he was eleven, in 1892, his father fell ill and died within weeks at the age of only 47, leaving the family in serious financial straits. They moved from a large house in Kensington to suburban Putney, where they were still living twenty years later when Woolf returned from Ceylon. From being a scion of privilege, Leonard almost overnight became a youth who would have to make his own way in the world.

Fortunately for him, at the age of thirteen, he won a scholarship to St Paul's, one of the country's top public schools, which was then a training ground for the imperial elite. The boys were taught the qualities necessary to rule others with confidence: self-discipline, teamwork and respect for the law. "This was the imperial class. Its members stood to gain directly from the existence of empire, in jobs, in dividends, or at least in adventurous opportunity," writes Morris.

Leonard did not entirely fit in at St Paul's—he was too intellectual, too close for comfort to the despised 'swot' (and perhaps too Jewish, though Woolf never mentions this). But he made a conscious effort to adapt to the ethos, as he would also do in imperial Ceylon, including learning to play sports at an acceptable level. In adjusting himself like this, he developed what he referred to as his "carapace", a shell or mask presented to the outside world as a protection and a concealment of what he always felt was his cowardice. Sensitive boys have done this at public schools ever since they came into existence, but in Woolf's case the mask seems to have become grafted on to his personality so that he could not easily remove it as an adult.

In 1899, he went up to Trinity College, Cambridge, where he stayed for five years. It was there that he made the friendships that would mature into the Bloomsbury group a decade or two later. Unlike St Paul's, Woolf's university education at Cambridge—especially his membership of the elite Apostles—became a vital ingredient in his entire outlook.

His greatest intellectual influence there was the philosopher G. E. Moore, who opened Woolf's mind to the pleasures and pains of hard thinking through his fastidious discussions of truth and reality. By his own admission, Woolf wanted to be a passionate and ruthless intellectual, and he chose his Cambridge group of friends on this basis. Moore, Lytton Strachey, Saxon Sydney-Turner and others encouraged the fiercely intellectual side of Woolf, though the friends did not neglect literature and music. Even so, Woolf did not shine academically by Cambridge standards, and also failed to achieve the high marks in the civil service exam in 1904 which were required to enter the home civil service. He had to make do with what he regarded as definitely second best: a cadetship in the Ceylon civil service, being too old for the Indian civil service at the age of 23. In the first volume of his autobiography, *Sowing*, he says: "Looking back I can see that the dismay was natural, but unnecessary. I am glad that I did not go into the home civil and did go into the Ceylon civil service. My seven years in Ceylon were good for me, and, though they gave me a good deal of pain, they gave me also a good deal of pleasure".

When he set sail for Ceylon in late 1904, there is no doubt that Woolf was, in his own phrase, an "unconscious imperialist". Yet he would never settle into a complacent acceptance of imperialism, because Cambridge had inculcated in him too many contrary values. Moreover, British society was beginning to become less rigid and hierarchical, with the death of Queen Victoria in 1901. The pace of social change was still quite slow, but it was easily perceptible. In 1904, when he left England, Woolf and his friends all addressed each other by their surnames; when he returned in 1911, this code had gone and they were on Christian name terms. The First World War would accelerate the process with the active encouragement of the Bloomsbury group, most notably through Lytton Strachey's satirical attack on Victorianism in his book *Eminent Victorians*, published in 1918. Imperialism was starting to go out of fashion in England.

In *Growing*, his autobiography about his years in Ceylon, Woolf describes how his voyage there on the P. & O. ship *Syria* gave him more than a hint of what life in imperial Ceylon would be like. The great steamship companies carried, deposited, and eventually returned the British ruling class to and from the colonies. The ships were in many ways microcosms of life on land. There were four fundamental imperial social classes Woolf observed among the passengers: civil servants, army officers, planters and businessmen. In the last three categories, he perceived "an embryonic feeling against the first"—in other words civil servants such as himself were considered the top dogs—

and he noticed that "relations between Europeans rested on the same kind of snobbery, pretentiousness, and false pretensions as they did in Putney or Peckham."

Almost everyone he saw on board seemed unlike his friends in England: "they were very ordinary persons with whom in my previous life I would have felt that I had little in common except perhaps mutual contempt." But, as at St Paul's School, so now on board ship, and later too in Ceylon—with both the British and the Ceylonese—Woolf overcame his instinctive reserve and made the effort to adjust. He was pleasantly surprised to discover "that there are practically no ordinary persons, that beneath the façade of John Smith and Jane Brown there is a strange character and often a passionate individual."

By way of example, he mentions Captain L., an army officer he got talking to who turned out to be "of some intelligence and of intense intellectual curiosity"—something which his family, school and regiment had done its level best to suppress. Woolf had heard shrieks and sobs from the officer's cabin near his own, as the captain beat his small daughter for wetting her bed. Eventually, while chatting to the captain one night in the smoking room, Woolf boldly told him that it was wrong and also ineffective to beat his daughter. Instead of getting a punch on the nose, Woolf won his point: "We sat arguing about this until the lights went out, and next morning to my astonishment he came up to me and told me that I had convinced him and that he would never beat his daughter again. One curious result was that Mrs L. was enraged with me for interfering and pursued me with bitter hostility until we finally parted for ever at Colombo."

In this relatively trivial incident, one can discern the outline of Woolf's work and attitudes in Ceylon: a dislike of injustice and the decisiveness and courage to act against it, combined with a certain insensitivity bordering on arrogance and ruthlessness. He undoubtedly was an intellectual, but he was also an intensely practical man. The combination would make for an imperial career in Ceylon of unusual interest and significance.

*   *   *

What makes Woolf virtually unique as a source for understanding British imperial rule in Ceylon is that he wrote so well. There are yards of memoirs of Ceylon by former British civil servants, but they mostly write like civil servants. At his best Leonard Woolf's writing matches the work of his wife

Virginia Woolf, especially in his non-fiction but even in his fiction. His five-volume autobiography, published in the 1960s, besides being highly enjoyable and often profound and wise, is indispensable as a social, intellectual and literary memoir of English life in the period from 1880 up to the 1960s; it has rightly been much admired.

The second volume, *Growing*, refers purely to the years 1904–11, when Woolf was in Ceylon, while the other volumes contain valuable references to his life there. Then there are his direct and pithy letters from Ceylon, which also preserve his experiences, edited by Frederic Spotts and published in 1989. Most of these, and by far the most outspoken, were written to Lytton Strachey, but there are also letters to John Maynard Keynes, Desmond MacCarthy, G. E. Moore, R. C. Trevelyan and Saxon Sydney-Turner. His correspondence was clearly an emotional lifeline for Woolf and it is unfortunate that his letters to his family have been lost, as they might have revealed something other than the mainly political and psychological issues of which he wrote to his Cambridge friends. Finally, there are the official diaries he kept while he was assistant government agent in Hambantota, his final posting. He was required to do this, but he chose to make the diaries far more revealing than most of those written by his colleagues. They were eventually published in 1962, at the behest of the Government of independent Ceylon, and form an intriguing complement to his novel about Hambantota based on many of the experiences documented in the diaries.

This novel, which was published in 1913 on the recommendation of E. M. Forster, is *The Village in the Jungle*. It was widely praised on first appearance in England and remained in print for many years but has now rather disappeared from view. In Sri Lanka, by contrast, it is part of the general culture of the island, available in Sinhala translation; in 1980 it was adapted for the cinema in Sinhala by Sri Lanka's leading director, Lester James Peries, with the part of Leonard Woolf played by Arthur C. Clarke. The original reputation of *The Village in the Jungle* deserves to be revived beyond the island because it is still one of the very few novels by a western writer with totally convincing Asian characters; indeed in this respect it is superior to Forster's later novel, *A Passage to India*.

In addition, there are three Woolf short stories about Ceylon, which were published in England in 1921 under the title *Stories of the East*. They too have subsequently been neglected, but at least one of them is of solid literary

worth—at the time of publication it led Woolf to be pursued by literary agents anxious that he should write for mass-circulation American magazines. All three stories shed much light on Woolf's reaction to different aspects of Ceylon: sex and romance, commerce and caste.

I first read Woolf's autobiography in the 1960s. For many years I have wanted to know as much as I could about him. At last, in 2004, the centenary of Woolf's arrival in Ceylon, I decided to follow in his tracks around the island. Accompanied by my local friends Lucky Senatilleke and Raj de Silva, and later joined from Australia by Ernest Macintyre, who was born in Sri Lanka, we drove, and sometimes went by train and boat, from Colombo, where Woolf landed, up north to Jaffna and the surrounding sea coast—his first posting in 1905—then on to Kandy in the centre of the island—his second posting in 1907–08—and finished up in the Hambantota district on the southeast coast of the island—his last posting in 1908–11, before he returned to England for good.

On the way we saw the landmarks Woolf had been associated with and talked about him to local officials, villagers and others who are interested in him. At the same time I read and reread Woolf's writings on Ceylon. My aim was to try to understand what these places were like in his time; what had happened to them since then; and what the colonial period means to us now. In the process I got to know Woolf better, though I still find him somewhat enigmatic. I also came to understand myself better, and my strange relationship with the rich and complex country where I grew up in the waning years of empire.

Ferry crossing, Kelani Ganga, outside Colombo.

1

Arrival in Ceylon

> To be born again in this way at the age of 24 is a strange experience which imprints a permanent mark upon one's character and one's attitude to life. I was leaving in England everyone and everything I knew; I was going to a place and life in which I really had not the faintest idea of how I should live and what I should be doing.
>
> LEONARD WOOLF, *Growing*

CEYLON OF A CENTURY ago, when Woolf reached Colombo, was a place of remarkable geographical, religious and cultural diversity, considering its small size. During his years there, Woolf was fortunate enough to be given postings that together directly exposed him to a wide range of landscapes and climates (from flat, arid and coastal to mountainous, verdant and central), to a variety of religions (Buddhism, Hinduism, Islam and Christianity, as well as folk religions), and to the island's two major cultures, those of the Sinhalese and the Tamils, not to speak of the colonial culture of the Europeans and the 'mixed' culture of the Burghers—my own community—which is the name given to the descendants of the Portuguese, Dutch and British settlers, some of whom intermarried with the Sinhalese and the Tamils during the centuries of colonial rule.

Because of its position on the sea routes of the Indian Ocean, Ceylon has long attracted visitors and settlers from near and far; the ancient Chinese knew it as Si-Lan and the Greeks and Romans as Taprobane. But it was the proximity of India that dominated Ceylon's way of life in antiquity and for many centuries after. (In prehistoric times, the island was even physically joined to India.) The strongest single Indian influence was Buddhism. The religion reached the

Leonard Woolf's journey 1904–11.

island from India well over two millennia ago—as chronicled in the Sinhalese epic the *Mahavamsa*, compiled by a Buddhist monk in the sixth century AD— and it established itself at all levels of society. Long after its disappearance from the Indian mainland, Buddhism continued to flourish in Sri Lanka, with centres today in the ancient city of Anuradhapura (site of a sacred bo tree), in the more recent city of Kandy (the location of the Temple of the Tooth), and on the sacred mountain Sri Pada (Adam's Peak). Buddhist society also created advanced technology, in particular irrigation systems for the dry zones of the island, which would be revived in the colonial period. This began in the sixteenth century. The Portuguese occupied the coastal areas from about 1505, until the Dutch ousted them in 1656. In 1796, the Dutch in turn gave way to the British, who in 1815 finally annexed the Sinhalese kingdom of Kandy, which had resisted every other invading power, and controlled the entire island until 1948, when Ceylon gained its political independence from Britain. In 1972, it became the Republic of Sri Lanka, while remaining within the British Commonwealth. Modern Sri Lankan society therefore exhibits the effects of nearly five hundred years of Portuguese, Dutch and British rule, superimposed on its ancient Indian-influenced culture.

Geographically speaking, the island is a 'teardrop' 270 miles from north to south and 140 miles wide in the middle. It is monsoonal, with hot, humid coastal plains and cooler inland hills, which can rise above 6,500 feet (the highest mountain, Pidurutalagala, is 8,281 feet high). The hill scenery is gentle, with forests, streams and waterfalls. Tea plantations abound, in contrast to the rubber trees, coconut palms and paddy fields that mark the lower plains. The flat stretches of coast contain many palm-fringed beaches, including the majestic sweeping shoreline at Hambantota, Woolf's last posting, in the southeast. To quote some pardonable purple prose of a kind that Sri Lanka has long tended to attract, "Caressed by warm waters, 770 miles of golden sand ring the island. Within those sands is green, lush-green, fertile land sculptured, towards the centre, into soaring mountains. An emerald, fringed by filigreed gold and set in aquamarine—truly a jewelled pendant."

It was a land of villages in Woolf's time, and it still is. Less than a quarter of the people live in urban areas. Ceylon's population, when I left the island in 1947, was under five million; today it is over 19 million. The majority is

Buddhism reached the island from India well over two millennia ago—as chronicled in the Sinhalese epic, the Mahavamsa, *compiled by a Buddhist monk in the sixth century AD.*

Ceylon was a land of villages in Woolf's time, and still is. Less than a quarter of the people live in urban areas.

Sinhalese, about 74 per cent of the population, and they are overwhelmingly Buddhists. The remaining 26 per cent are divided into Tamils (18 per cent), and Moors (7 per cent) and a large group of smaller communities (1 per cent). The Tamils subdivide into those who have lived in the north around Jaffna since ancient times, and those who the British imported from south India in the nineteenth century to work the coffee and tea plantations; the former group forms just under thirteen per cent of the total population, the latter just over five per cent (totalling 18 per cent). The Moors are descendants of Arab traders.

There are also a very small number of tribal Veddas, the descendants of Sri Lanka's earliest identifiable people, aboriginal hunter-gatherers whose traditional habitat was the jungle. According to the 1911 census, conducted while Woolf was in Ceylon, there were 5,342 Veddas, some of whom lived in a province north of Hambantota district, but by the time of the 1960 census, this figure had dropped to only 400. The Vedda language, a distinct linguistic synthesis of an original language mixed with Sinhala, is now virtually extinct. But in Woolf's time it was still spoken, and there are references to the Veddas in Woolf's novel, *The Village in the Jungle*.

More than most societies, Sri Lanka is therefore genuinely multicultural.

According to the 1911 census, when Woolf was in Ceylon, there were 5,342 Veddas, some of whom lived in a province north of Hambantota.

This has many advantages and attractions, but almost inevitably it has also led to trouble. The nation's stability has been militarily challenged since the 1980s by the minority Tamils. They were originally aggrieved by the majority Sinhalese decision, in the 1950s, to make Sinhala the country's official language; but this grievance soon became a focus for general Tamil discontent at Sinhalese dominance of government and politics. Many Tamils, led by the Tamil Tigers, came to want an independent Tamil state in the north of the island, and this now exists *de facto*, though officially unrecognised by the Government in Colombo. Another source of social and political breakdown was the rebellion in the 1970s of Sinhalese youth against the English-educated elite of Colombo in protest against their exclusion from positions of employment and power.

✶   ✶   ✶

The above sketch hints at Sri Lanka's cultural complexity. However to understand Woolf's imperial Ceylon of 1904—and Sri Lanka of today—it is necessary to go somewhat more deeply into the colonial history of the island.

The events that led to the Dutch surrender of Ceylon to the British in 1796 have their origins in the American War of Independence. At this time the people of the Dutch Republic sympathised with France and the American colonies, but the hereditary Dutch ruler, Prince William V of Orange, supported

the British. This led to the formation of the Patriot Party in Holland, whose ideas were influenced by the French radicals, and whose most eloquent rabble-rouser was my ancestor P. P. J. Quint Ondaatje; he had left Ceylon in 1773, intending to train in Utrecht for the church in Ceylon, but had never returned. It was the pressure applied by the Patriot Party that caused Britain to declare war and humiliate the Dutch Republic in 1781. The subsequent twists and turns of European alliances in the run-up to the Napoleonic Wars led to the British occupying the Dutch possessions in Ceylon. They had wanted to do this earlier but had feared upsetting the Dutch who had stayed neutral in the struggle between Britain and France. Essentially, the takeover finally occurred because the British wanted control of Ceylon while fighting the French-supported Indian ruler Tipu Sultan in southern India, and also so that they could bring direct pressure to bear on the recalcitrant kingdom of Kandy. About twenty years later, Kandy fell to the British. In 1818, the Kandyans rebelled and were again defeated. The whole island was now under British control.

P. P. J. Quint Ondaatje (1758–1818).

Immediately after the takeover, London viewed Ceylon as a useful military outpost with a thriving trade in cinnamon. Then in 1812 Europeans were permitted to own land, and this led to a plantation economy that would continue to grow throughout the nineteenth century and into the twentieth. Although Sri Lanka is now best known for tea, much of the early planting was of coffee. But obtaining labour for the plantations was a problem for the planters (many of whom were British civil servants, until this overlap between Government and business was banned so as to avoid corrupt practices in the administration). The traditional Sinhalese law of *rajakariya*, which required subjects to render service to the king—and after 1815 the British—had been abolished by the Government in 1833; but the Sinhalese refused to work on the coffee plantations for wages, considering wage labour a form of slavery and also naturally resenting the fact that their lands had been expropriated for the plantations. So the planters imported their labour from southern India, mainly from Tamil Nadu. Conditions were harsh in the early decades and many tens of thousands of Tamil labourers expired, either on the way to the plantations or while working on the estates.

In July 1848, there was a rebellion, principally in the Kandyan territories of Matale and Kurunegala, where plantations were widespread. The Government responded by making plantation labour compulsory unless a tax was paid. Such payments were impossible for already impoverished people, and an opposition movement arose under the leadership of Puran Appu, who lead a successful attack on Matale. However, other assaults failed and Puran Appu was captured, tried and executed. Though this rebellion was not as serious as that of 1818, it did force the Government to review some of its policies: some of the taxes that had alienated Sinhalese farmers were repealed and a more tolerant attitude to Buddhism prevailed in official circles.

In the second half of the nineteenth century, the economy grew steadily and working conditions improved somewhat on the plantations. From the 1870s, tea took over from coffee in the hill country as a result of a devastating coffee leaf blight, while in the lower areas of the island coconut and rubber were grown. The civil service began to control the traditional slash-and-burn clearing of the jungle for the growing of crops in the arid zones by issuing permits— a policy that would preoccupy Woolf—and attempted to revive the ancient irrigation system. The idea was to settle peasants on their own land, and the hope was that they would look upon their British rulers more favourably. Roads and railways were built—the major railway from the capital Colombo to Kandy was completed in 1867—using plantation and other revenues, for example from pearls and salt, initially in response to commercial needs, but then as an aid in the general administration of the island's various provinces. Colombo began to become a major port with the opening of its harbour in 1875 and the completion of a 4,000-foot breakwater in 1883. Education was introduced, partly through missionary schools but also through government schools and other schools set up by rich Sinhalese and Tamils. There was no political unrest and as yet no organised political consciousness among the Ceylonese, except marginally in the capital Colombo. It was into this quiet, essentially agricultural country, firmly ruled by the *Pax Britannica*, that Leonard Woolf arrived as a civil service cadet.

* * *

Woolf arrived in the Colombo harbour on 16 December 1904.

The P. & O. ship *Syria*, with Woolf on board, docked in Colombo on 16 December 1904. A few hours later—five-and-a-half hours, to be precise, Woolf noted—he sat writing a letter to Lytton Strachey from "an immense hotel with miles of corridors and thousands of rooms, a gallery in which I sit writing, a band playing, and the motleyest of motley crowds." In those days, the Grand Oriental Hotel was certainly a grand place, perpetually swirling with passengers arriving and departing from the magnificent harbour nearby. Today, in the age of air travel, the hotel has rather lost its *raison d'être*, even if it is still the best place from which to view Colombo's harbour. Those who seek colonial atmosphere now go to the Galle Face Hotel in central Colombo, also beside the ocean, where Woolf himself stayed on his return to Ceylon in 1960.

"I'm partially drunk, I think, with the complete unreality of it all and a very little whisky. I feel as if I were playing the buffoon in a vast comic opera. You *can't* exist, nor grey old Cambridge," wrote Woolf to Strachey.

This immediate sensation of theatrical unreality on arrival—of being an actor on the imperial stage—would never entirely leave him. Writing in his

Dhobis on the outskirts of Colombo.

autobiography more than fifty years later, Woolf remembered: "There was something extraordinarily real and at the same time unreal in the sights and sounds and smells—the whole impact of Colombo, the G.O.H., and Ceylon in those first hours and days, and this curious mixture of intense reality and unreality applied to all my seven years in Ceylon."

The main possessions he had brought with him were 90 large volumes of his favourite writer Voltaire and a wire-haired fox-terrier named Charles (acquired in his Cambridge days from an advertisement in *Exchange and Mart!*). Due to P. & O. regulations, the dog had to travel on a separate ship, where the ship's butcher overfed him and made him inordinately fat. Charles was ecstatic to see his master in Colombo and tore about on the great breakwater as they walked back from the docks. But the arrival in Ceylon disoriented Charles even more than it had Woolf. Opposite the Grand Oriental Hotel, the dog dashed up to a Sinhalese man standing on the pavement, cocked his leg and promptly urinated against the man's spotless white cloth "as though it were a London

Bathers, Colombo, around 1905.

lamp-post". Once inside the palm court of the hotel, the dog lay down at Woolf's feet, but then suddenly got up and vomited violently. "Three or four crows immediately flew down and surrounded him, eating the vomit as it came out of his mouth."

To both incidents, wrote Woolf, there was little or no reaction. The man in white seemed not to be "much concerned", and the hotel waiter looked impassive. No doubt waiters in the Grand Oriental Hotel were trained to tolerate all sorts of bad behaviour in guests, but in the case of the man in the street, it is hard not to see in the incident a minor and all-too-typical example of imperial life—very much a reality for the Sinhalese, even if unreal for Woolf. Probably the unknown man in white thought to himself something like: "Let me give this filthy dog a kick, but no, there is his white master across the road outside the big hotel, looking with a smile at the dog at my feet. Without moving at all I will turn my head the other way and pretend to keep looking for my friend, the lucky man whose cloth will really be clean when he arrives."

That very same day Woolf reported to the Secretariat, and was received by the principal assistant, Pagden, and the colonial secretary, Ashmore, who gave him a "short and cynical" lecture on his future life and duties in 'the service'. (Its general tenor can be imagined from the fact that Ashmore opposed the appointment of Ceylonese to government positions because they were "ordinarily lacking in that sense of duty and honour which the British Government expected.") Woolf was offered the choice of two 'outstations' as his first appointment: either Jaffna on the north coast or Matara on the south coast. He chose Jaffna. As he walked out of the Secretariat and into the Colombo sun, "which in the late morning hits one as if a burning hand were smacking one's face," he again felt the sense of unreality: "the whole of my past life in London and Cambridge seemed suddenly to have vanished".

The two weeks Woolf spent in Colombo over Christmas 1904 were a discouraging introduction to white colonial life. After only four days he told Strachey, "the English are hell, the Australians Sodom and Gomorrah", while the native people were "either Gods or animals". Probably his lack of intellectual and emotional companionship caused Woolf to view the hotel and Europeans in a negative light and Ceylon and its people more enthusiastically; the latter must have appeared so extremely exotic that they could not remind him of his loss. He told Strachey: "I have never felt so lonely in my life as I do at the present moment"—and a few days later: "Do you feel my isolation, the continual creeping of depression."

His view of the British in Colombo did not moderate with greater familiarity. If anything, Woolf became even more disenchanted as he got to know them better. A year or so later, after visiting Colombo for a week to take some exams, he told Strachey savagely:

> There has never been a lower depth of degradation than Colombo society. It is all 'sets' and exclusiveness. The level of the men rises, I think, from that of the haberdasher's assistant up to that of the lowest Cambridge pseudo-blood. The women—my God—they really give me, with their pale dried-up faces and drawling voices, the creeps. No one ever talks about anything more interesting than 'the service' or whether Mr A. is really engaged to Miss B. If you are in 'the service' you say 'what snobs the merchants are and really they only retail tin-tacks'; if you are a merchant, you say 'what snobs civil servants are'. The first hag you are introduced to at the Colombo

Garden Club can tell you what you had for dinner two weeks ago in Jaffna. And through the midst of them goes the unending stream of passengers.

By contrast, the passing scene among the Ceylonese struck Woolf as "heaven". "I went for a bicycle ride this evening, and it was absolutely superb—the sunshine, the streets, the myriads, even the smells which too I just saw my degradation in loathing." Pre-motor-car Colombo, as recollected in his autobiography *Growing*, was "a real Eastern city, swarming with human beings and flies, the streets full of flitting rickshaws and creaking bullock carts, hot and heavy with the complicated smells of men and beasts and dung and oil and food and fruit and spice."

✳ ✳ ✳

One can feel all these experiences of Colombo in the story Woolf wrote, "A Tale Told by Moonlight", which he published in his *Stories of the East* in 1921. Though it is not great literature, it is plainly true to its setting. It explicitly examines 'truth' and 'the real' in Ceylon, somewhat as Woolf and his Cambridge contemporaries had once explored truth and reality through the philosophy of G. E. Moore.

The story starts beside a river in England on a hot, moonlit evening in summer, a deliberately romantic setting. A small group of middle-aged men—perhaps partly modelled on the Bloomsbury group—take a walk after dinner and see a couple embracing. They start to talk about love and their passionate belief in it. But one of them, Jessop, who is not much liked, remains silent.

Then Jessop starts to tell his own story of love in Ceylon. He declares that most love of men for women is an ideal created by novelists, "not for her body or her mind or her soul, but for something beautiful mysterious everlasting". He qualifies this cynically:

> Oh yes, we've all been in love. We can all remember the kisses we gave and the kisses given to us in the moonlight. But that's the body. The body's damnably exacting. It wants to kiss and to be kissed at certain times and seasons. It isn't particular however; give it moonlight

Pettah market, Colombo.

Overleaf: Street scene, Colombo, around 1905.

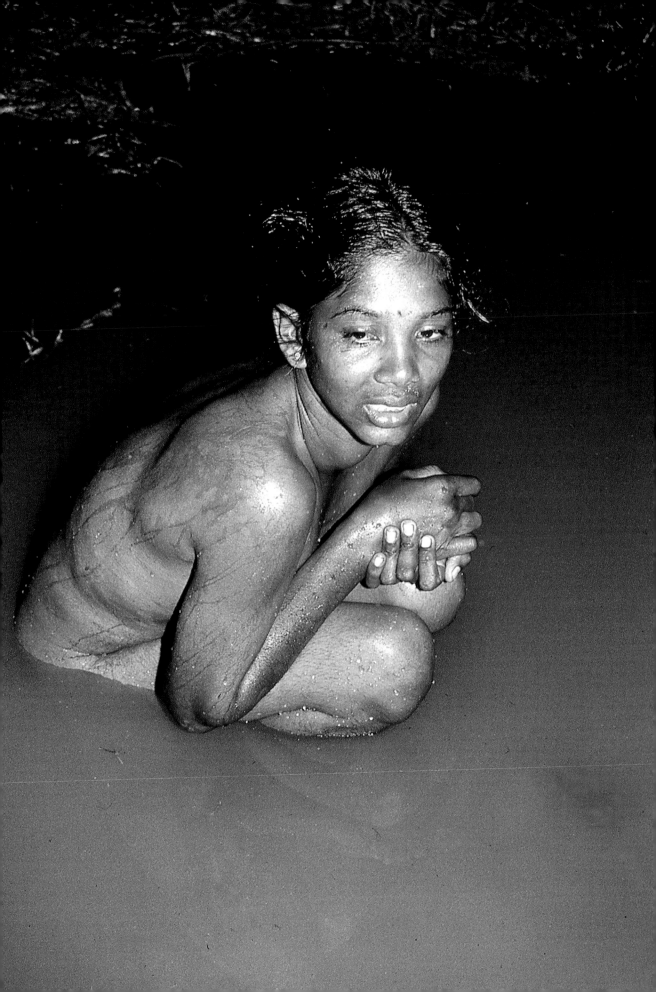

and young lips and it's soon satisfied. It's only when we don't pay for it that we call it romance and love, and the most we would ever pay is a £5 note.

Real love, he says, like other real things, is not predictable: it comes in strange ways and places, perversely and unreasonably.

Jessop recounts his time in the East where he truly saw life. His friend Reynolds, a novelist who writes of romance, remained at home in England, observing life but not feeling it. Jessop tells of how Reynolds finally comes to stay with him in his Colombo bungalow, where he is shy, "out of his element with these fat flannelled merchants, fussy civil servants, and their whining wives and daughters." Reynolds wants to feel and experience life at last, so Jessop—"I suppose the devil came into me that evening"—decides to take Reynolds to a brothel. He calls his servant to fetch two rickshaws and they bowl along dusty roads past the lake and into a red-light area with Tamil and Sinhalese girls. (This was either Slave Island or Maradana, near the Beira Lake; the Burgher girls were to be found elsewhere, on Reclamation Road.) "All the smells of the East rose up and hung heavy upon the damp hot air in the narrow streets."

Reynolds is at first awkward, but then he falls for Celestinahami, a Sinhalese girl. Her immense eyes "looked as if they knew and understood and felt everything in the world". Celestinahami differs from the other prostitutes: she wears white instead of coloured robes; she separates herself from the others so as to pay attention to Reynolds; and she is very beautiful. Reynolds pities her, looks into her eyes and thinks he has fallen in love. He tells Jessop that his feeling is the real thing, more than mere physical attraction. And part of Jessop agrees: "It was the real thing, I tell you; I ought to know; he stayed on in my bungalow day after day, and night after night he went down to that hovel among the filth and smells." But at the same time Jessop finds it unreal: "the chances were all against it. She was a prostitute in a Colombo brothel, a simple soft little golden-skinned animal with nothing in the depths of the eyes at all."

Reynolds becomes suicidal at the impossibility of his relationship, so Jessop encourages him to take a risk: buy Celestinahami out of the brothel and live

Woolf's short story "A Tale Told by Moonlight" explicitly examines 'truth' and 'the real' in Ceylon through a tragic mixture of sex and romance set in imperial Colombo. The story was probably based on Woolf's own experience of prostitutes in Ceylon.

with her. At first they are happy; he teaches her English and she teaches him Sinhala. Then Reynolds begins to see the "truth" of the situation. He wants to talk to Celestinahami about his new novel about the East, but she is uneducated and knows only how to pound and cook rice. "He was a civilised cultivated intelligent nervous little man and she—she was an animal, dumb and stupid and beautiful." In her desperation to please Reynolds she adopts European clothing but the divide between them is deeper than that: "when he looked into her patient, mysterious eyes he saw behind them what he had fallen in love with, what he knew didn't exist. It began to drive him mad." So Jessop induces Reynolds to leave her and get on a ship back to England, after offering Celestinahami a generous settlement with the help of a Burgher lawyer.

Two days after his departure, in Colombo Jessop attends an inquest and identifies Celestinahami's body. She had drowned herself, dressed in her "stays and pink skirt and white stockings and shoes."

At the end of the story, Jessop's English friends on the moonlit riverbank, though gripped, dismiss it as "sentimentality". One of them yawns, and says it's time for bed. The story was yet another melodramatic tale, they must have thought, of Western men falling in love with and then abandoning native women, already made over-familiar by Kipling and other English writers.

⁎ ⁎ ⁎

Woolf apparently worked through most of the two weeks he was in Colombo. Each day he went from the Grand Oriental Hotel to the Secretariat in the Fort area of the city, the centre of Government (once a Portuguese and Dutch fort, until that was demolished by the British in 1871). He wrote to Strachey on 20 December: "In the daytime I sit in a Kachcheri or Govt Office and sign my name to documents all of which say: 'Sir, I am directed to inform you that the Governor having considered the petition of X, H. E. refuses to interfere. By order L. S. Woolf for the Col. Sec.'" The *kachcheri* was a place that would feature constantly in Woolf's tour of duty in Ceylon. The word came into use in Ceylon from India. After the takeover from the Dutch in 1796, up to 1802, when the island officially became a Crown Colony, Ceylon was ruled by the East India Company from Madras, who appointed revenue collectors. *Kachcheri* was the Hindustani word for a revenue collection office in India (though it was normally spelt 'cutcherry' in Indian English). In Woolf's day, the term referred in Ceylon to the offices of the government agent or assistant government agent.

An insightful and judicious history of the Ceylon civil service by one of its number, S. D. Saparamadu, appears in the introduction to Woolf's *Diaries in Ceylon*. Established in 1802, with the colonial secretary at its head, the civil service was generally regarded as the virtual sole ruler of Ceylon until 1931. From the beginning it held not only administrative powers but was responsible for all legislative and judicial functions. Although the civil service reforms of 1832 changed this slightly by making the Supreme Court independent of the civil service, district judges and magistrates remained civil servants—and so legal work would form a large part of Woolf's duties.

An Executive Council of civil servants was established in 1832 to advise the governor on administrative and financial matters. The governor had the power to overrule its decisions, but he rarely did so, as this would have required him to provide a convincing reason for his decision to the secretary of state in London. Moreover governors as a rule served only about five years in Ceylon, unlike career Ceylon civil servants who generally spent their working lives there. Furthermore, in the nineteenth century, Ceylon was considered a somewhat obscure posting for a governor, and was often given to ex-politicians wanting to recoup their fortunes or to the younger members of the aristocracy. In the words of Saparamadu, "The powers of the civil service were thus supreme; they were the chief executors, the chief legislators and the chief judicial officers, except for the appellate powers and the major criminal jurisdiction held by the non-civil-service Supreme Court." So much so, that in his autobiography Woolf does not bother even to name the two governors of Ceylon in the period 1904–11.

Such untrammelled power could easily have led to corruption, but Saparamadu claims this did not occur. High salaries and strict regulations ensured that civil servants did not have conflicting business interests. There was also an *esprit de corps*: "the unifying bonds and traditions" which had built up over a hundred years prior to Woolf's arrival, based on known principles and shared goals of good government. Saparamadu lists these as being the establishment of the rule of law, the improvement of the economic conditions of the people and the introduction of western technology. The overall aim was to implement policies of benefit to Ceylon—even if these were not of benefit to Whitehall, says Saparamadu. An ethos of independence, even from the Government in London, meant that the civil service was not swayed by any particular caste, religion or ethnic group; nor were the 'unofficial' Europeans—

the Burghers and the business class—given preferential treatment. The over-whelming disadvantage, of course, was that good government was no substi-tute for self-government, as Woolf would increasingly come to accept while working in the Ceylon civil service.

To begin with, however, he conformed to what was expected of a civil servant. He applied the rule of law to the letter, even if he thought it bad law. And he went beyond the letter and conformed to the spirit too, by trying to adjust himself as much as possible to his imperial role. To conform was non-debatable, at least for those in the junior ranks of the service. Saparamadu cites the case of a nineteenth-century Ceylon civil servant who converted to Islam in order to marry a second wife. Although his duties were not affected and he had broken no official rules, he was dismissed from his government position.

✶   ✶   ✶

Colombo takes up only the tiniest fraction of the second volume of Woolf's autobiography, *Growing*—only a couple of pages in a book of some two-hundred-and-fifty pages. Even those two pages refer chiefly to Woolf's arrival and his dog Charles's arrival. There is not one word about the city's differ-ent areas, well-known buildings or tourist attractions, and nothing about its history or politics either. Clearly, Colombo's charms and history did not much attract or interest Woolf. At the very end of *Growing*, while describing his decision to leave the civil service, he notes: "I did not want to return to Ceylon and become a successful civil servant in Colombo and end eventually with a governorship and K.C.M.G." Again, in the last volume of his autobiography, writing at some length about his return to Ceylon in 1960, there are only the most passing references to Colombo, even though he stayed there for a few days at the Galle Face Hotel. For Woolf, Colombo meant chiefly officialdom, snobbery and mediocrity (and maybe some sex, judging from his letters to Strachey and his story "A Tale Told by Moonlight"). He never got to know any Sinhalese of note in Colombo since he never lived in the city. "He had no involvement or knowledge of local semi-political movements of national revival and working-class protests, and seems to have limited his social contacts to the expatriate group of 'white sahibs'," Kumari Jayawardena notes in a recent article published in Colombo.

There is, however, a lively picture of Colombo in Woolf's fiction, in his novel *The Village in the Jungle*. He imagines the capital as seen through the eyes of a sleazy, small-town, Sinhalese merchant and money-lender brought up in Colombo, who is trying to impress and seduce a simple woman living in a jungle village:

> I was only a little child when they brought me to Colombo to live there in the shop which my father kept. Ohé! what a town is Colombo. There we lived in a great building, and all around us were houses and houses, and people and people: no jungle or snakes or wild beasts; not even a paddy field or a coconut tree. Always streets and people walking, walking backwards and forwards on the red roads (and very few even known to you by sight), and bullock carts and carriages and rickshaws, hundreds upon hundreds. And there are houses, very high, as high as the hill at Beragama, full of white Mahatmayas and their women, always coming and going from the ships. How many times have I stood outside when a boy and watched them, always laughing and talking loud, like madmen, and dancing, men and women together. And how fair are the women, fair as the lotus flower as the tale says; very fair and very shameless.

Then the man describes the harbour:

> In the morning I went and walked on the stone road that has been built into the sea, and within is the harbour, full always of great ships bigger than villages. Always the Mahatmayas are coming and going in the great ships; from where they come and where they go no one can tell. You stand upon the stone road, and you see the great ship come in across the sea in the morning, filled with white Mahatmayas, and in the evening it carries them out again across the sea. They are all very rich, and for a thing that costs one shilling they willingly give five. Also they are never quiet, going here and there very quickly, and doing nothing. Very many are afraid of them, for suddenly they grow very angry, their faces become red, and they strike anyone who is near with the closed hand.

I personally can understand this childhood feeling of excitement about Colombo, because when I was a boy I went there only for short visits with my father and mother, when we were expected to do the rounds of our many relations (one of whom, my Uncle Noël, was attorney general of the island).

At this time we were living in the hills on my father's tea estate. Colombo seemed a very big and busy place indeed. It was certainly fun for a while, with lots of good food and drinks and visits to the zoo and the beach, but we were all, especially my mother, quite relieved to get back to the relative isolation of life on the tea estate and a wild, carefree existence for us children.

The Galle Face Hotel was my father's home from home in Colombo, and I remember being there on one of the last occasions I spent with my mother and father together. The three of us were having dinner in the Royal Dining Room, which was probably the most exclusive dining room in Ceylon at the time and a watering hole for wealthy planters and senior civil servants. It was a hot night and the fans were not working, so my father took off his jacket and draped it over the back of his chair. The waiter came over and requested him to put it back on—jackets were mandatory in the Royal Dining Room— but my father refused. Finally the very austere head waiter came over and said, "I'm sorry sir, but if you don't put on your jacket, you will have to leave." My father got up, grabbed his jacket from the back of the chair, and stormed off.

*   *   *

"We are to be sent to the outstations next week," a probably relieved Woolf wrote to Lytton Strachey on 28 December. On 1 or 2 January 1905, we can picture, with a little licence for the imagination, the following scene taking place in front of the Grand Oriental Hotel. A bullock cart has pulled up and the carter sits watching impassively. Woolf and his Sinhalese servant are supervising some labourers, known as coolies in those days, as they start to load a very heavy wooden crate into the back of the cart. The crate weighs so much because it contains 90 volumes of Voltaire (beautifully printed in the 1784 edition in Baskerville type, as Woolf informs us). An enormous tin-lined trunk follows the crate, containing clothes and sundry other items brought from England. Meanwhile Charles, Woolf's wire-haired fox terrier, restrained by a leash held in his master's hand, keeps baring his teeth at the waiting carter. Then Woolf's servant climbs into the back of the cart, avoids sitting on either the trunk or the crate of Voltaire, and squats down on the wooden floor of the cart. Woolf himself, accompanied by Charles, climbs into a rickshaw which is also standing by. The carter then hoists himself onto the small platform between the front shafts of his cart, takes his bull-thwacking stick in his right hand and the controlling ropes tied to the bull in his left, and stretches his left leg out so as to insert his foot just under the bull's crotch, in the time-honoured fashion of Ceylonese carters. The servant at the back relays a signal from his master, the carter pushes the top of his foot against the crotch of the 'engine', exhorting it with a shrill "Da! Ya! Hut!"—and Woolf is on his way to his first government posting in Jaffna.

A hundred years later, after a few days' adjustment in Colombo, I started along the same path—though in much greater comfort than Woolf. With my friends Lucky Senatilleke and Raj de Silva, we climbed into our vehicle, our driver Somasiri Liyanage gunned the engine, and we headed for the road that eventually leads to Jaffna.

2

Journey to Jaffna

> To Anuradhapura, the most famous of the island's ruined cities, which
> was just about half-way to Jaffna, one went by train. From there
> northwards the line was under construction, the only section so far
> opened being the few miles from Jaffna to Elephant Pass through
> the peninsula. The only way to travel the hundred odd miles from
> Anuradhapura to Elephant Pass was to use what was called the mail
> coach. The mail coach was the pseudonym of an ordinary bullock cart
> in which the mail bags lay on the floor and the passengers lay on the
> mail bags.
>
> LEONARD WOOLF, *Growing*

THE JOURNEY FROM COLOMBO to Jaffna in January 1905 took Woolf
three days in all—a whole day by train to Anuradhapura and then a
further two days' hard grind to Jaffna via Elephant Pass, mostly by 'mail
coach' and finally again by train. Less than a year later, when Woolf returned
to Colombo to take his law exam, the railway covered the entire route and
he would complete the journey by train in just fourteen hours.

Rail travel was however the exception to the generally slow pace of life
in Ceylon in 1905; motor cars only began to appear in any numbers after
Woolf departed in 1911. The main method of travel was by bullock cart. This
unhurried way of living and moving was something he easily fell in with,
making him more in tune with and sympathetic to the people than many of
his more insular British colleagues. In *Growing*, he wrote that something of the
rhythm and tempo of Ceylon, "like that of the lagoons and the jungle, crept
permanently into my heart and my bones."

During the first part of the journey, Woolf must have experienced for the

Hay gatherers on the road south of Anuradhapura.

Railway station, old Colombo.

first time, through the windows of his steam train, the landscape, villages and towns of lowland Ceylon. Unfortunately for us, he wrote nothing about what he saw; perhaps it was too quotidian or drearily mercantile to have stuck in his mind, after spending six or seven years in the island. Luckily Henry Cave's *Ceylon along the Rail Track*, published just five years later in 1910, comes valiantly to the rescue. Cave tells us that as the train left Colombo it passed through marshy land and backwaters, and crossed rivers with spectacular views. The agriculture was predominantly coconut and paddy up to Ragama junction (until very recently the site of a Boer prisoner-of-war camp), where tea and cinnamon were also grown. Further on at Veyangoda, there was a large coconut desiccating factory. But by the time one reached Mirigama, writes Cave, the traveller could not "fail to feel enchanted by the alternating scenes of primitive husbandry, glimpses of villages embosomed in palms, magnificent groups of tropical trees, and particularly with the effect of the masses of thick forest broken up at frequent intervals by deep recesses devoted to the cultivation of paddy."

About half-way between Colombo and Anuradhapura, the train enters the dry zone.

The first major town on the railway was Kurunegala. This was briefly the capital of the Sinhalese kingdom in the early fourteenth century after the abandonment of Anuradhapura and Polonnaruwa as capitals. The British had built a *kachcheri* on the site of the royal palace, since Kurunegala was a key coconut-growing area. In fact the railway owed its very existence mainly to pressure from coconut producers needing to transport their crop to the coast. Given this history, it is not surprising that Kurunegala was also a centre for the Sinhalese peasant rebellion of 1848.

Moving on, the land started to become less productive. After Ganewatta, about half-way between Colombo and Anuradhapura, the view from both sides of the railway would have been of waterless and uncultivated country. The train was now entering a dry zone. Apart from the artificial lakes and tanks that are a feature of the dry zone from Galgamuwa onwards, in the second half of their journey train travellers would have seen very little natural water right up to their arrival in Anuradhapura.

The latter part of Woolf's train journey was along a line very roughly parallel to (though outside of) the western side of what Sri Lanka now calls its "cultural triangle", so designated by the Government and Unesco in 1980, with its three corners at Anuradhapura, Polonnaruwa and Kandy—the three successive major capitals of the Sinhalese. Within this triangle lie the most important remains of the island's earlier Sinhalese civilisation, in the shape of palaces, temples, cave sanctuaries, statues, paintings and great man-made channels and reservoirs for diverting and containing scarce seasonal rainwater.

There was no possibility of Woolf's seeing any of these remains from the train, except at his destination at Anuradhapura. But he does not seem to have minded very much. It is a surprising fact that throughout his time in Ceylon Woolf made virtually no mention of the art-historical aspect of the island, though he could hardly have been ignorant of it—not least because it strongly interested some of the more cultured of his civil-service colleagues— as witness his brief comment at the head of this chapter, that Anuradhapura was "the most famous of the island's ruined cities". Given his silence on the subject, we can only speculate on the reasons for his apparent indifference.

On the whole, during his long life, Woolf did not show himself to be particularly sensitive to the visual arts and, perhaps more important, he displayed more interest in art and culture when viewed from an anthropological or sociological angle than from a purely aesthetic one. His single significant reference to Anuradhapura's ancient heritage in *Growing* confirms this:

> I once in Anuradhapura saw a man sweeping the courtyard round one of the *dagobas* [Buddhist stupas]. He was dressed like a sweeper, but there was something rather strange about him. I got into conversation with him and found that he had been a wealthy businessman in Colombo; he was highly educated and spoke perfect English. Suddenly at the age of about fifty he had felt an irresistible desire to throw it all up and to follow the path of the Buddha which led him, not to penance or mortification of fakirs, sanyasis, dervishes, or monks, but to the life of gentle contemplation sweeping the courtyard of a *dagoba*. It is not a withdrawal and occupation which would ever appeal to me personally, but I respect the man to whom they appealed and the religion which inspired him.

Perhaps another clue to Woolf's attitude lay in that wooden crate of Voltaire that he insisted on carting to Jaffna. Voltaire travelled all over Europe in the eighteenth century, but he is said never to have made any special effort to see a great cathedral, a classical statue or a beautiful picture.

✳ ✳ ✳

As a dedicated art lover myself, at this point I decided to ignore Woolf (and Voltaire) and divert from his route into the cultural triangle. I was encouraged in this by my travelling companions Raj and Lucky, as well as by our driver Somasiri Liyanage.

Raj—Dr Rajpal de Silva—had come on the trip partly for research purposes. He was in the midst of updating W. A. Nelson's *The Dutch Forts of Sri Lanka*. Formerly a hospital doctor practising in London, Raj is now retired from medicine and concentrates on his passion for historical research. He is the author of three books: *Early Prints of Ceylon (Sri Lanka) 1800–1900*, *Illustrations and Views of Dutch Ceylon 1602–1796* and *19th Century Newspaper Engravings of Ceylon*. These books are wonderful examples of painstaking research. This makes Raj an informative travelling companion who is both full of curiosity and thoroughly entertaining. He and I do not always agree on colonial history, but he would often suggest new ways of looking at Woolf.

Lucky—Lakshman Senatilleke—is also well educated. He went to St Thomas College in Gurutalawa, where I also went to school, and then studied for a law degree. Afterwards he started to teach mathematics in a school but abandoned it to practise industrial law independently. He is a brilliantly incisive lawyer with an attraction to gambling, bridge and gin rummy, in which he excels. His passion for the outdoors, wildlife and travel make him an easy target for the hungry adventurer and a good person to have around when in a scrape. He is one of my favourite travelling companions.

Dr Rajpal de Silva.

Lakshman Senatilleke.

Lucky accompanied me on my first long journey around Sri Lanka in 1990, picking up pieces of my childhood, which resulted in my first book about the island, *The Man-eater of Punanai*. We argue a great deal, but he is a firm friend.

In the mid-morning, we reached Dambulla, the site of spectacular rock caves containing hundreds of Buddha figures, ceiling paintings and wall paintings. But we had seen them before and decided to pass through without stopping. We stopped only twice on the way to Anuradhapura, first at a place 30 miles south-east of the ancient capital in the direction of Kekirawa, close to the great tank of Kala Wewa, in order to admire the Aukana Buddha. This colossal upright statue, 46 feet tall, is over thirteen hundred years old and is truly magnificent; each ankle is about the height of a man and each toe the size of a human arm. Carved out of the hill it faces eastwards in honour of the sun, as befits the name Aukana, which means 'sun-eating'. As I gazed at it, the sun fell on the statue creating a fascinating pattern of light and shade. The face, with closed eyelids, was blissfully serene. When it rains, water is said to drip from the forehead to land on a sacred lotus leaf between the feet, where a rock temple has been excavated. Nearby there was a monastery surrounded by sacred bo trees and dense jungle. The statue lay hidden for centuries, but when it was rediscovered, a single priest and his pupil were found guarding it.

The second place we stopped was Sasseruwa, seven miles west of Aukana, where Buddhist monks lived between the third century BC and the second century AD inside more than a hundred caves, amidst what would then have been jungle. We climbed 280 steps to the *vihara* (temple). There was not much left to see except a Buddha statue, 40 feet tall but incomplete and of inferior workmanship. The story goes that the Aukana Buddha and the Sasseruwa Buddha were carved at the same time in a competition between a master and his pupil. The master at Aukana won, and the pupil at Sasseruwa abandoned his own carving.

Arriving at the ruins of Anuradhapura, our route reconnected with Woolf's journey—though not, as already mentioned, with Woolf's true interests. This is a pity because, well before the birth of Christ, Anuradhapura was the capital of a great civilisation. Its name probably derives from Anuradha, a constellation of stars under which the city was founded, but there is also a persistent legend about a Prince Anuradha who crossed over from India into Lanka with

The Aukana Buddha is 46 feet tall and over thirteen hundred years old.

five companions around 500 BC and founded the settlement. However its pre-Buddhist ruler Pandukabhaya is generally regarded as the founder, probably in the fourth century BC. The area then grew into a kingdom with well-ordered cities, major roads and a fine irrigation system, and was a centre for trade. But because only religious structures were considered worthy of stone, little remains of the secular kingdom.

Ancient Anuradhapura was in a dry zone—as it is now—and so its civilisation was dependent on the effective functioning of huge tanks for irrigation. These were constructed with a sophisticated knowledge of hydraulics and trigonometry. It was probably the collapse of this system that eventually caused Anuradhapura to be abandoned. The site disappeared under the jungle, until it was officially 'discovered' by a British government official in 1823. The clearing of the ruins began in 1840 when the government grudgingly gave £40 for the purpose. A later administration, under Governor Sir William Gregory, was appalled at the lack of progress and preservation, and in 1872 ordered the first archaeological work, including the restoration of some of the irrigation system. Subsequently, a combination of Sinhalese nationalism and Buddhist fervour created a new passion for the island's ancient heritage, and politics and pilgrimages revived the fame of the site. Anuradhapura is now the headquarters of the Sri Lanka Archaeological Survey.

Tissa Wewa, in the southwest sector of Anuradhapura, is the largest of the tanks of Anuradhapura. Its name commemorates its original builder, Devanampiya Tissa, the king who ruled in the period 250–210 BC. It must have been a wonder of the ancient world, and in 1905 its languid atmosphere inspired Woolf to this description in *Growing*:

> Nothing in the universe could be more unlike a London street than
> the bund of the tank in Anuradhapura. Everything shines and glitters
> in fierce sunshine, the great sheet of water, the butterflies, the birds,
> the bodies of the people bathing in the water or beating their wash-
> ing upon the stones, their brightly coloured cloths. Along the bund
> grow immense trees through which you can see from time to time
> the flitting of a brightly coloured bird, and everywhere all round the
> tank wherever you look are shrubs, flowers, bushes, and trees, tree
> after tree after tree.

We visited the tank in the early evening. Women were bathing in the

Women bathe in the shallow waters of the Tissa Wewa.

shallow water. Near the bund is the attractive and peaceful Issurumuniyagala rock temple, also built by Devanampiya Tissa, and probably the oldest extant Buddhist temple in Sri Lanka. Carved out of solid rock, it houses a large statue of a seated Buddha. Some of its other sculptures, especially that of a baby elephant and a hunter, are wonderfully alive. There are steps to the top of the rock which gives a good view of Anuradhapura and its many ancient *dagobas*, modern temples and monasteries.

In the evening light, I photographed two magnificent examples of *Dagobas*. The Ruwanweliseya Dagoba was completed in 137 BC. Priests from all over India were said to have attended when its relics were enshrined. The Jetavanarama Dagoba is much later in date, built by Mahasena (274–301 AD). It boasts the highest stupa ever built: some 400 feet to the tip of its spire and 370 feet in diameter across its base. A Victorian writer calculated that the bricks in the stupa were enough to build a wall a foot thick and ten feet high between London and Edinburgh, a distance of some four hundred miles. This was then the highest brick structure in the world, and its mass was exceeded only by the biggest pyramids in Egypt. I wondered whether Woolf would have seen the Jetava-

Ruwanweliseya and Jetavanarama Dagobas, Anuradhapura.

narama Dagoba on his way to dinner during the evening he spent in Anuradhapura. But it seemed unlikely he would have, because in 1905 there was as yet no system of lighting to display the wonders of Anuradhapura at dusk.

✳ ✳ ✳

Woolf stayed at the Anuradhapura Rest House near the Tissa Wewa. His dinner engagement that night was with the government agent, C. T. D. Vigors, at the British Residency (now the residence of the district secretary). This was Woolf's first plunge into outstation social life in Ceylon. He found Vigors to be "an athletic, good-looking English gentleman and sportsman", Mrs Vigors "very genteel maternal", and Miss Vigors "the tennis-playing, thoroughly good sort, belle of the civil service". The guests, apart from Woolf himself, were the office assistant and archaeological commissioner, and probably the district judge and police magistrate. Everyone was very friendly but the conversation revolved around "shop, sport, or gossip". Perhaps the archaeological commissioner made some references to his work of restoring the ruins of the ancient civilisation not far from the Residency, but if he did, Woolf made no mention of them.

Tissawewa Rest House, Anuradhapura.

Post office, old Anuradhapura.

Also present at the dinner table was the same feeling of unreality Woolf had experienced in Colombo. People seemed to be playing a role rather than being themselves: somebody rather grander than they really were at home, in London or Edinburgh, Brighton or Oban. "We were grand because we were a ruling caste in a strange Asiatic country; I did not realise this at the time, though I felt something in the atmosphere which to me was slightly strange and disconcerting." In due course Woolf recognised the truth: "The stage, the scenery, the backcloth before which I began to gesticulate at the Vigors's dinner-table was imperialism."

Back at the rest house after dinner Woolf was distressed to discover that his dog Charles had gone missing: his servant had ignored the strict instruction not to untie him and Charles had gone looking for Woolf—trotting resolutely back down the railway line to Colombo! Woolf discovered what had happened to him only because Charles was spotted early the next morning by two English missionaries from Jaffna, Miss Beeching and Miss Case, as they arrived by train from Colombo at the last station 15 miles before Anuradhapura. They got a porter to catch Charles and bring him back to their carriage. "The result was that, as I sat dejectedly drinking my early tea on the resthouse verandah, suddenly there appeared two English ladies leading Charles on a string . . . In their stiff white dresses and solar topees, leading my beloved Charles frantic with excitement at seeing me again, on a string, they appeared to me to be two angels performing a miracle."

The Anuradhapura Rest House is now called the Tissawewa Rest House and I was looking forward immensely to returning there. It is a small place with an intimate feel—partly because of its antique colonial furniture and the period prints on the walls, which have been kept in place since it was taken over in 1965 by Quickshaws, a specialist Sri Lankan travel agency. We arrived there in time for lunch. Having eaten and dropped off some things, we went into Anuradhapura, so that I could photograph the railway station where Woolf had arrived a century before me. I also had one of my Ceylonese knives sharpened in a shop.

Our evening in the rest house was enchanted. After returning from the *dagobas* and the Tissa Wewa, we drank some coconut arrack (distilled from toddy) and *thambili* (coconut water) on the upstairs verandah before eating a first-class dinner of rice, curry and tilapia, a coarse fish caught in the Tissa Wewa. I have always thought that some of the best rice and curry meals on the island are served in the rest houses. Sri Lanka's cuisine is as varied as the country itself is multi-ethnic, nevertheless most of its curries are spiced with a fairly generous quantity of chilli and are cooked in coconut milk. The plain boiled rice is always accompanied by six or seven different curries containing vegetable, meat, fish and sometimes egg, plus a variety of *sambols* in which the main ingredients are grated coconut and chilli.

After dinner, Raj, Lucky and I had three comfortable old chairs placed on the upstairs verandah of the rest house. Then, in the warm semi-dark, beneath a sky of a million stars, I prompted my two companions to discuss the history of the north of the island, beginning with the history of Anuradhapura. I wanted to compare my knowledge of the ancient Sinhalese civilisation, refreshed by the day's visit to the site, with their deeper knowledge. I also wanted to hear more of the complicated history of the Sinhalese-Tamil relationship, which has led to the current conflict in the north centred on Jaffna, where we were planning to go the next morning.

We began with the idea of the dry zone in Sri Lanka, which covers roughly three quarters of the island, as opposed to the wet zone in the southwest of the island, which includes Colombo and the Western Province, as well as the hill country in the centre of the island around Kandy. The contrast between the two zones—as experienced in Woolf's train journey from Colombo to Anuradhapura—is unbelievably sharp, compared to the gradual transitions in climate to be found in temperate lands like England.

Raj and Lucky confirmed my general notion that in ancient times the thick, impenetrable tropical jungles of the wet zone would have resisted attempts at agricultural settlement; only in the dry zone would humans have been able to clear the sparser vegetation and introduce cultivation. However Lucky quickly added, with a touch of lawyerly precision:

> There was a proviso. They would have had to build large reservoirs to catch the lower seasonal rainfall and create an intricate and sophisticated system of sluices and channels to irrigate rice growing. The one exception in the dry zone, not requiring reservoirs, was the Jaffna area in the far north which possesses water-bearing strata, making possible the irrigation of crops by means of wells, denied to the rest of the dry zone for geological reasons.

Both the Sinhalese and the Tamils were originally migrants from India. At different times they apparently crossed the Palk Strait and settled at first in the nearest habitable part of the island, the northern dry zone. Later the Sinhalese alone moved into other parts of the island and established the Rohana, or Ruhuna, kingdom in the southeastern dry zone (where Woolf would have his third posting) on the far side of the hill country—probably by journeying down the east coast of the island or sailing around the island in boats.

However the two groups came from different parts of India. According to a somewhat improbable legend, the Sinhalese hail from northwestern India, whereas the Tamils unquestionably come from southern India. Though the Sinhalese origin myth contains fantastical elements, like all such myths, it is a thought-provoking fact that the language of the Sinhalese, Sinhala, is descended from Sanskrit and belongs to the Indo-Aryan group of languages of northern India, while Tamil belongs to the totally separate Dravidian group of languages of southern India.

Early temple ruin, Anuradhapura.

In the legend, as told in the *Mahavamsa*, the Sinhalese are the progeny of Vijaya, the grandson of a lion (hence their name: *sinha* means 'lion') who mated with a princess. Vijaya was so wild and rebellious he was banished by his father from northwestern India and came to Lanka with 700 followers. There he lived with a woman of the indigenous people and later married a princess of India. Around the same time as his arrival, the Buddha was entering the state of nirvana in far-away north India. As he departed this life, the Buddha prayed for Vijaya: "In Lanka, O Lord of gods, will my religion be established, therefore, carefully protect him with his followers, and Lanka." Thus Buddhism came to Sri Lanka. Historians, on the other hand, date the arrival of Buddhism to the conversion in the third century BC of Devanampiya Tissa and his Brahmin

Lankarama Dagoba, Anuradhapura.

court at Anuradhapura by Mahinda, who was either the son or the brother of the great Indian emperor Asoka, an early convert to Buddhism.

We do not know when the Tamils, who are of course almost exclusively Hindus, arrived in Sri Lanka. By the time that the *Mahavamsa* was written by the Sinhalese monk Mahanama Thera in the sixth century AD, Tamils had long been living in the northern part of the island. One of the epic's greatest sections, if not the greatest, tells of how Duttagamini (161–137 BC), the Sinhalese ruler of the southern dry zone kingdom, saved Lanka for Sinhalese Buddhism by expelling the invading Tamils, led by Elara, from the northern dry zone after a war lasting 15 years.

The Tamils returned, however, and a long history of war and peace between the two groups unfolded. During the reign of the Sinhalese king Datusena (460–78), the Tamils were again in possession of Anuradhapura, until they were defeated by Datusena, who re-entered the ancient capital. In the eleventh century, the Sinhalese, under Vijayabahu I, defeated the Tamil Chola kingdom of south India, which had ravaged Anuradhapura and occupied Polonnaruwa for five decades, in a battle at Polonnaruwa in 1070. This place, southeast of Anuradhapura, now became the Sinhalese capital, where Sri Lanka's greatest medieval ruler, Parakramabahu I (1153–86) built extraordinary monuments and irrigation works; he even sent armies into south India to fight the Cholas and as far afield as Burma. But the Polonnaruwa kingdom did not last. Regular outbreaks of warfare with the Tamils, who had settled and firmly established a kingdom in the northwest around Jaffna, and wars between the Sinhalese themselves, devastated the Sinhalese irrigation systems of the northern dry zone. The royal capital had to be shifted progressively further south into the wet zone—at one point, as we know, it was in Kurunegala—and eventually into the hills at Senkadagala, a mountain fastness above modern Kandy, where the Sinhalese court settled until its defeat by the British in 1815. The once-magnificent tanks of the dry zone—such as the Tissa Wewa of Devanampiya Tissa at Anuradhapura and the Parakrama Samudra of Parakramabahu I at Polonnaruwa—became breeding grounds for the anopheles mosquito. Malaria would defeat all attempts to resettle this part of the northern dry zone until as late as the 1930s.

By the mid-fourteenth century, the Jaffna kingdom had effective control over the northwest. From there the Tamil rulers made occasional forays against the Sinhalese, but any major territorial ambitions of the Jaffna kingdom were thwarted by their own kith and kin, the Vijayanagar Empire, then dominant in south India, which had designs on the Jaffna kingdom and drew it irresistibly into its orbit from across the Palk Strait. This fact, amongst many others, reveals how these ancient conflicts were not always over race, nationality and religion, as propounded by partisan commentators today on both sides of the Tamil-Sinhalese conflict.

No one, however objective and detached from the current conflict they may be, denies that there has always been a conflict. But history shows that it is not straightforwardly racial or ethnic in nature. Even in the pages of the most important Sinhalese literary work, the *Mahavamsa*, the Tamil king Elara is said to have ruled "with even justice towards friend and foe." Moreover, he is said to have been "a protector of Buddhist tradition" and to have had miraculous powers because, although he had not put aside "false beliefs", he had "freed himself from walking in the path of evil". After Elara is slain by Duttagamini in the epic, the Sinhalese ruler personally celebrates the dead king's funeral rites, and builds a monument to him which he ordains should be worshipped by his fellow Sinhalese. "Even to this day," says the *Mahavamsa*, "the princes of Lanka, when they draw near to this place, are wont to silence their music because of this worship." In later historical times, we find that the Buddha's sacred tooth relic was once guarded by Tamil soldiers at Anuradhapura; that the Tamil stronghold of Jaffna has place names of Sinhala origin; and, most surprising of all, in its last years Kandy was ruled by Tamil-speaking kings. One of these Kandyan kings was responsible both for the revival of the Buddhist monastic order and for the restoration of Hindu temples. Facts such as these have led a number of scholars to conclude that "pre-colonial and most of colonial Sri Lankan history does not conform to the model of two opposed nations, imposed on it today by present-day Tamil and Sinhalese rhetoricians."

⋆ ⋆ ⋆

Happily reunited with his dog Charles, Woolf and his Sinhalese servant boarded the 'mail coach' near the Tissa Wewa, along with a single fellow passenger, a Sinhalese who was the Jaffna district engineer, and the coach set out for Elephant Pass. In *Growing*, he recorded: "I left Anuradhapura at nine o'clock in the evening of Tuesday, 3 January, and the bullock cart with its broken and battered passengers arrived at Elephant Pass at nine o'clock in the morning of Thursday, 5 January."

The road had been cut straight through solid jungle, and so visually, as well as rhythmically, the journey was monotonous. The jungle on either side was completely silent and Woolf saw hardly any birds or animals except very occasionally large grey monkeys. If the bullock cart stopped, or if he got out to walk beside it, so as to relieve his aches and pains and escape the "unending ejaculations" of the carter to his bullocks, he could see that the road in front and the road behind were absolutely identical, "a straight ribbon of white or grey between two walls of green." These walls were high enough to prevent even the slightest stirring of the hot air at ground level.

There is no doubt that Woolf was in deep misery while on the coach. Apart from the physical discomfort, he had a splitting headache and was also brooding anxiously about what awaited him in his first posting. Immediately after his arrival in Jaffna, he wrote to Strachey:

> I have just endured 40 hours of hell ... The coach was just a springless old waggonnette with a cover on it and the place between the seats filled with board. On this surface hard as stone and scored with

Leonard Woolf travelled by bullock cart from Anuradhapura to Elephant Pass—an excruciatingly uncomfortable 36-hour journey.

mounds and ridges you and your servant and any other black or white passengers lie. For 36 hours I underwent jolting indescribable, flung now against an iron railing, now on a mail bag or box, now on Charles or a passenger. I could neither sit up nor lie down and every muscle and bone in my body was and is aching. We went on day and night only stopping to change bullocks, and you can imagine how I slept.

At half a century's remove, in *Growing*, he manages a bit of wry humour also:

Each time that the rolling of the cart flung the D. E. [district engineer] towards my side and therefore on to Charles, there was a menacing growl and once or twice, I think, a not-too-gentle nip.

As I left Anuradhapura in the morning with Raj and Lucky—travelling in sybaritic luxury compared to poor Woolf a hundred years before us—I found myself brooding on the Tamil-Sinhalese conflict. We had just visited the world-famous bo tree in Anuradhapura. The tree is supposed to have grown

from a cutting taken from the original bo tree under which the Buddha attained enlightenment, which had been gifted to Devanampiya Tissa by the Emperor Asoka through his emissary, Mahinda (who had converted the Sinhalese king to Buddhism). The Anuradhapura bo tree may be the oldest documented tree in the world. Certainly it is among the holiest places in Sri Lanka and among Buddhists generally, and is always busy with pilgrims. It is therefore particularly shocking to learn that in May 1985 the Tamil Tigers chose to massacre 146 pilgrims and priests at this spot and to shoot at the holy tree itself.

The conflict between the Tamil Tigers (known formally as the Liberation Tigers of Tamil Eelam, LTTE) and the Government in Colombo dates back to 1972, when the country changed its name from Ceylon to Sri Lanka and Buddhism was given prime position as the national religion. As we know, the Tamil minority was already feeling marginalised by the growth in Sinhalese nationalism after independence in 1948. The LTTE was established in 1976, but the bloodshed took some years to get going.

In 1983, thirteen government soldiers were killed in an LTTE ambush, sparking anti-Tamil riots in Sinhalese areas and the deaths of several hundred Tamils. Open conflict between the LTTE and the Sri Lankan army began in the north of the island. In 1985, the first attempt at peace talks failed. In 1988, though, the Government, under President Junius Jayewardene, signed an accord with the Indian Government—under Prime Minister Rajiv Gandhi—to create a federal structure for the island with a new North-Eastern Provincial Council to govern the Tamil areas. But the LTTE rejected the accord and the Indian peace-keeping force sent by New Delhi to guarantee the accord and to persuade the LTTE to disarm. The Indian forces became embroiled in the violence and left the island in 1990, leading to an escalation in the war between the Tamil separatists and the Sri Lankan army. During the next few years, the LTTE arranged suicide bomb attacks that assassinated Rajiv Gandhi in Madras in 1991 and Ranasinghe Premadasa, the president of Sri Lanka, in Colombo in 1993. With the failure of more peace talks in 1995, the Government launched a huge military offensive to drive the separatists out of Jaffna. The fighting, at times intense, continued until 2002, when a ceasefire was brokered by the Norwegian Government. But there is still no final political resolution of the conflict.

Woolf left Ceylon more than seventy years before the start of the current

Villagers on the road to Jaffna.

Young Tamil Tiger militants.

clash. But he had the foresight, from his personal knowledge of the Tamils and the Sinhalese and of their history in the north of the island, to understand the need for a political solution to their historic conflict. In 1938, he first proposed a federal structure for Ceylon. His recommendation to the Labour Party's advisory committee on imperial questions, "Memorandum on the demands for reform of the Ceylon Constitution", states that in regard to the protection of minorities such as the Tamils, "Consideration should . . . be given to the possibility of ensuring a large measure of devolution or even of introducing a federal system on the Swiss model." He went on to compare, numerically speaking, the German-speaking Swiss with the Sinhalese, the French-speaking Swiss with the Tamils, and the Italian-speaking Swiss with the Moors. He continued to press his case for either federalism or devolution in the run-up to the granting of independence in 1948. According to a Sri Lankan academic and writer, Dayan Jayatilaka, in an article published in Colombo in 2000, Woolf showed "an uncanny grasp of this country's reality".

We were now heading north on the A9 road following pretty much the

Our first checkpoint at Medawachchiya, manned by a Village Protection Unit of the Sri Lankan army.

exact route that Woolf travelled by bullock cart in 1905, through the area that had earlier witnessed centuries of conflict between Sinhalese and Tamil armies, beginning with Duttagamini and Elara in the second century BC.

Only twenty minutes out of Anuradhapura we arrived at Medawachchiya, a small place with a mainly Tamil population together with a smattering of Muslims and Sinhalese. Here was our first checkpoint, manned by a so-called Village Protection Unit of the Sri Lankan army wearing dark-brown battle fatigues. No problems: after a brief halt we passed through.

Nearby is a war memorial built by the soldiers of the Gajaba regiment of the Sri Lankan army, which we decided to take a look at. According to the inscription, it was completed on 19 September 2001. It lists the names of 2,898 soldiers, each with the location and date of the soldier's death, and the name of his regiment, his regimental number and his rank. Not a single private is listed because every soldier was given a posthumous promotion. There is also a symbol: a blue lotus flower, representing the Motherland, protected by the hands of the people and a gun.

LTTE checkpoint near Periyamandu, 77 miles from Jaffna.

Only fifteen minutes later, at another small place, Irataperiyakulama, came a second Sri Lankan army checkpoint. From there it took us half an hour to reach the town of Vavuniya. This is a predominantly Tamil town and has suffered from the years of separatist fighting. Although Vavuniya is controlled by the Sri Lankan army, its proximity to the rebel-controlled Vanni area has made it subject to attack. In 1999, three quarters of the population fled following a warning broadcast by the Tamil Tigers, and became refugees. The following year there was a suicide bomb attack, in addition to bombs in buses and landmine explosions. It was reported that Tamil Tigers had ordered children off a school bus before setting it on fire. Human rights groups have criticised the LTTE for targeting children as young as ten years old as potential recruits.

Six miles north of Vavuniya we reached Omantai, the last checkpoint under Sri Lankan government control. We would shortly enter LTTE-controlled territory. The car was certainly going faster than Woolf's bullock cart, but we were careful to hold our maximum speed to only 40 miles per hour, the limit stipulated by the LTTE. Lucky pointed out that motorists in LTTE areas are far more reluctant to break the speed limit than motorists in the rest of the island. They know that if they are caught, there is a chance of receiving a more severe punishment than the fine required by law. After all, the LTTE is answerable only to itself. As a lawyer, Lucky was ambivalent about this, but he admitted that the LTTE had reduced the level of traffic accidents.

Beyond the checkpoint there was a no man's land for just over a mile and then, half an hour beyond this, the first LTTE checkpoint. The soldiers thoroughly examined the vehicle and our documents, and we began to feel somewhat uneasy. But in the end they made no demands on us. Things were more difficult at the next checkpoint at Periyamandu, 77 miles from Jaffna. All the notices and signs were now in Tamil, and I was thankful that our driver was fluent in Tamil. There were four soldiers, using computers, and we were quizzed thoroughly in a fairly menacing manner for an hour, before being taxed 65 rupees for a single unopened bottle of arrack costing 280 rupees.

Noon brought us to Kilinochchi, which as a result of the war has attained the status of a political 'capital', where meetings have taken place between the Norwegian monitoring force, the LTTE and the Government, and between the LTTE and foreign ambassadors, ministers and other emissaries from countries including Norway, Japan, Canada and the UK. Here we made a short detour to see the Mahavire (Great Heroes) cemetery built by the LTTE. There were about two thousand graves. I thought of the Gajaba war memorial we had seen earlier that morning and the memorial built by Duttagamini, the Sinhalese ruler, for Elara, the Tamil king, over two thousand years ago, and a fanciful thought crossed my mind: perhaps, as in ancient times, each of today's two warring groups should build a memorial for the other side. The peaceful monotony of Woolf's journey also came to mind. Were he to travel the same route now, he would probably be depressed by the violence, but he surely would not be much surprised by the war and its memorials, having lived through two world wars himself.

Not far from Elephant Pass, I stopped to photograph an official building badly scarred by bullets and shells. Numerous signs warned us of mines.

In the Dutch period, Elephant Pass was famous—hence its name—for being the narrow place through which elephants that had been captured on the island of Ceylon were driven into stalls on the Jaffna peninsula beside the Jaffna lagoon, in preparation for their export by boat. Before being shipped abroad, the elephants were trained for war: made accustomed to manoeuvring

Destroyed tank, Elephant Pass.

in battle and inured to the explosion of firearms.

Today the elephants are gone, but war remains. A signboard riddled with bullet-holes in front of a tank greeted us at Elephant Pass, which is a location of vital strategic importance to both the Government and the LTTE. It has seen terrible battles in recent years and is famous for being the site of a heroic act by a Sri Lankan army officer. In 1991, the LTTE made a surprise attack on a Sri Lankan army camp at Elephant Pass using a bulldozer converted into a tank. They intended to ram this contraption, stuffed with explosives, into the camp. But as the bulldozer approached, Corporal Gamini Kularatne ran up to it under fire, climbed the steps and dropped two grenades inside. This act destroyed the tank and its suicidal occupants and their nemesis Corporal Gamini, and saved the camp. To honour his bravery, the army, with the blessings of the Government, has erected a monument in Hasalaka, the place where the soldier came from. Kularatne is known as the 'Hasalaka hero'.

The Dutch fort at Elephant Pass was almost completely destroyed by the LTTE in 1991, leaving only small signs of its foundations; a man was distinctly hostile as I searched for remains. It was originally one of three forts close

Signboard riddled with bullet-holes, Elephant Pass.

together at the southeastern end of the Jaffna peninsula, which were intended as small control and customs posts. Their design, as Raj informed me, differed somewhat from other forts in Ceylon in being almost square with two bastions placed at diametrically opposite ends. Before its destruction, the fort at Elephant Pass had been converted into a rest house and was popular with naturalists and fisherman. The railway station, too—from which Woolf once took the train to Jaffna—had been destroyed.

"As we approached Elephant Pass in the early morning, the country gradually changed," writes Woolf in *Growing.*

> The thick jungle thinned out into scrub jungle and then into stretches of sand broken by patches of scrub. Suddenly we came out upon the causeway. On each side of us was the sea and in front of us the

peninsula, flat and sandy, with the gaunt dishevelled palmyra palms, which eternally dominate the Jaffna landscape, sticking up like immense crows in the distance. Everywhere was the calling and crying and screaming of the birds of the sea and the lagoons.

The road to Jaffna has no choice but to follow the railway along the peninsula. Exhausted though he was by the 'mail coach', Woolf was fascinated by the views from the train window. From the landscape and the look of the people he immediately sensed a significant difference between Jaffna and the parts of Ceylon he had already seen. As I looked out of my car window, I felt the same difference as he did—with the additional factor of the presence of the military and the relative absence of the palmyra palms with their crow-like tops. For sadly, many of them have been uprooted and used for guard posts and watch-towers, while the dishevelled heads of those that remain have been shot off by flying shrapnel.

At last, we arrived in Jaffna. And I felt shell-shocked by the devastation all around us.

Official building near Elephant Pass badly scarred by shells and bullets.

3

Jaffna

It was characteristic of our rule in Ceylon that there was practically nowhere any sign of a military occupation. There was not a single soldier in Jaffna or in the Northern Province.

LEONARD WOOLF, Growing

THE FIRST PLACE we wanted to see when we entered Jaffna on the A9 road was the *kachcheri*. In Woolf's day, this government office, headed by the government agent, was the seat of imperial authority in the Northern Province. In *Growing*, Woolf describes the building:

> The *kachcheri* is separated from the road by a small courtyard and adjoining it at the back is the G. A.'s Residency. Both are solid grey buildings with broad verandahs and date, I think, from Dutch times. Attached to the Residency is what in England we would call a garden, but in Ceylon is called a compound. It was in fact almost a park, with great trees planted so that they gave the whole place an air of beautiful stillness and, what was so rare in the blistering dry heat of Jaffna, of coolness even in the middle of the day.

And he also catches the working atmosphere:

> We sat all day in the office working, except for the hour we took off when we bicycled back to the bungalow for lunch or tiffin. I rather doubt whether any European ever really understands an important side of the East and of Asia, ever gets the feel of its castes and classes and individuals into his brain and his bones, unless he has sat hour after hour in a *kachcheri*, watching from his room the perpetual coming and going along the verandah of every kind and condition of human being,

Decapitated statue, Jaffna.

transacting with them the most trivial or the most important business,
listening to their requests, their lies, their fears, their sorrows, their
difficulties and disasters.

We looked at the Jaffna *kachcheri* in front of us now. It had been blasted to
smithereens in the various battles for Jaffna of recent years. All that remains
are its oval-shaped ruins.

After the *kachcheri*, the short road into Jaffna curves south and then straight-
ens up to join with the town's main street. This road was Woolf's route to and
from the office on his bicycle, chased by Charles, his wire-haired fox terrier.
At the other end of the street is the Jaffna fort, which in 1905 had long been in
civilian hands and contained the bungalow where Woolf put up on first arrival
in Jaffna. The fort was our next stop.

Raj negotiated with a sentry, who finally granted permission for us to visit
and take photographs. The fort, too, is in an appalling state of devastation, with
only its outside perimeter recognisable. In the civil war between the Tamil
Tigers and the Government, the fort was occupied in turn by both sides. Until

The once magnificent Jaffna fort is in an appalling state of devastation.

Railway station, old Jaffna.

then, said Raj, it had been the best-preserved fort in the island. Built by the Portuguese in the sixteenth century, it was captured by the Dutch in 1658 and rebuilt to their own design. They replaced the Portuguese square shape with five bastions forming a pentagon, and in the following century—undeterred by the stone and lime shortages of the late 1700s—they added a circuit wall. W. A. Nelson, in his book on the Dutch forts of Ceylon, describes the Jaffna fort as the Dutch ideal of a fortress and the strongest fortress in the East. Completed in 1792, it passed into British hands, without a shot being fired, a mere three years later, in 1795. Thus, from the beginning to the end of its use as a fortress, its strength was never really tested—until the fearsome weaponry of a modern war virtually flattened it.

Considering the fort's entire history, including that of the past decade or two, it is poignant to read Woolf's comment written in the 1960s: "The Portuguese had built out of blocks of grey stone an enormous fort commanding the sea. I suppose the area which it covers must be nearly equal to that of Trafalgar Square; it has a rather beautiful solidity and austerity; it is perfectly intact . . ."

The Jaffna railway station today is wrecked beyond belief and is still mined.

While this was still true, in 1978, my uncle Milani Claude Sansoni, then the chief justice of Sri Lanka, lived in the fort, occupying what had once been the governor's house. He was in Jaffna to conduct an inquiry into some riots in 1977 that later proved to be antecedents of the civil war that would destroy the house. When he was there, my brother Michael came to stay, as he describes in the evocative chapter, "Jaffna afternoons", at the start of his book on the Ondaatje family.

We now visited the railway station, Woolf's terminus on 5 January 1905, and found it wrecked beyond belief. It is still mined, and with extreme care I picked my way through the danger areas, avoiding several stones marked with red paint, and took some photographs.

Then we looked around the rest of the town before finding our way to a hotel. Nearly every building had been shelled, and many were damaged beyond repair. Churches were smashed, statues decapitated. Many of the 750,000 residents who fled the chaos after 1983 and the big battle of 1985, have returned, and there are cars and trucks on the road again, yet the general atmosphere is quiet, without the hustle and bustle of a typical Sri Lankan town. The scars visible everywhere cannot but make the visitor feel that the peace is tenuous. Except for the town's relative quietness, which Woolf regarded as typical of Jaffna, it would be hard to imagine a greater contrast with the Jaffna described by him in his autobiography.

The Old Park Restaurant, which is also a tiny hotel, was our base for the next four nights. The place is run by Sothilingam—known as Sothi—a Tamil who preserves the charm of the world before the civil war. Sothi loves Jaffna, despite its battered condition, and has taken a gamble on it by opening his hotel, which is really a bed-and-breakfast 'motel'. He was a very attentive host, generous with both his time and his food. Dinner was a delicious mix of fried prawns and cuttlefish. All the food was extraordinary and spicy, reminiscent of the food in Kerala, the coastal state in southwestern India. Unlike the food in the rest of Sri Lanka, the curries in Jaffna are seldom, if ever, cooked in coconut milk, as there are relatively few coconut trees in the area. Local fish is used, and sometimes wild boar. The bread, or *roti*, comes in a variety of forms, including *pittu*, a steamed cylinder-shaped dough. There are also *vadais*, round and doughnut-shaped lentil croquettes, a snack originally from Tamil Nadu, that has become part of Sri Lankan cuisine; and there are *iddlis*, the rice-flour cakes also eaten in southern India.

*   *   *

The population of Jaffna has always been predominantly Tamil and Hindu, mainly Sivaite Hindus. Owing to its geographical position, just 21 miles from south India, Jaffna has been subject to invasion for at least two millennia, as already discussed, but the independent Tamil kingdom there was not established until the thirteenth or fourteenth century, and it was not until the fifteenth century that it developed sufficient cohesion and confidence to hold its own against the rulers of the mainland.

In the 1540s, it was threatened by the arrival of Portuguese missionaries seeking converts to Catholicism. The Hindu ruler was furious and had a large number of the converts killed. The Portuguese were keen to avenge this act, and were also interested in Jaffna as a strategic base and in controlling the pearl fishery south of the town in the Mannar district. So they attacked Jaffna in 1591, killing the Hindu king and placing a Portuguese on the throne. Twenty-six churches were now built in the district and a seminary founded at Nallur. Under the Dutch, conversion to Christianity continued. Philippus Baldeus, a Dutch priest, and the author of *A Description of the Great and Most Famous Isle of Ceylon* (1672), exerted a major influence. At Point Pedro, on the northeastern coast of Jaffna district, there was a tamarind tree named after Baldeus, under which he preached in 1658. It was blown over by a cyclone in 1952, and a stone marks the spot. The Dutch, like the Portuguese, administered the Jaffna area separately from the rest of Ceylon. But the British, after they took over from the Dutch in 1796, merged the district (in 1833) with the administration of the rest of the island.

A Tamil gives us directions in Jaffna.

However Europeanisation was never as strong in Jaffna as in other parts of Ceylon. In the town itself, only a few places ever looked European: chiefly the main street (known as Parangi Theru—Burgher Street—to the Tamils), the fort and the *kachcheri*. "Europe has made a deep and wide impression upon the face of all the big towns of Ceylon which I know except upon Jaffna," Woolf remarks. He saw Jaffna more as a collection of connected villages than as a European town with a centre and suburbs. It was hard to determine where the town ended and the countryside began, which, he says, "increased, in a curious way, one's sense of imperialist isolation from the life of the surrounding country".

The Jaffna peninsula is peculiarly flat; Woolf could not recall cycling up even the slightest slope. This enables the Jaffnese to live in compounds divided from each other by endless high *cadjan* fences, a feature unique to the area, constructed out of the plaited leaves of the coconut palm. W. T. Keble comments in *Ceylon Beaten Track*:

> These *cadjan* fences are famous. It is said that the people of Jaffna spend much of their time waiting for their neighbour to go out, so that they may shift the dividing fence a few inches on to his land. This of course leads to a lawsuit if somebody is careless enough to be

Jaffna's kachcheri *has been blasted to smithereens.*

caught; but as the practice is said to be practically universal, the only result would seem to be a perpetual oscillation of the fences; and a sense of satisfaction on each side of them.

The tall trees towering above these fences generated a tunnel of heat for Woolf on his bicycle. The contrast between the hot, airless town and the stretches of totally flat open country beside the sea were part of the melancholic charm of Jaffna district for him, though this feeling took time to get a hold. He writes in *Growing*: "Everywhere the lone and level sands stretch far away, interrupted only occasionally by a few black palmyra palms. Out of the enormous sky all day long the white incandescence of the sun beats down upon the earth; towards evening it changes slowly to a flaming red or a strange delicate mixture of pink and blue."

In his short story "The Two Brahmans", which we shall come to a little later, Woolf gives the compounds and *cadjan* fences of Jaffna a literary existence in the shape of 'Yalpanam', which is actually the Tamil name for Jaffna. This is from the story's beginning:

Most major buildings in Jaffna have been shelled, and many damaged beyond repair.

Yalpanam is a very large town in the north of Ceylon; but nobody who suddenly found himself in it would believe this. Only in two or three streets is there any bustle or stir of people. It is like a gigantic village that for centuries has slept and grown, and sleeps and grows, under a forest of coconut trees and fierce sun. All the streets are the same, dazzling dusty roads between high fences made of the dried leaves of the coconut palms. Behind the fences, and completely hidden by them, are the compounds; and in the compounds still more hidden under the palms and orange and lime trees are the huts and houses of the Tamils who live there.

As I too got to know Jaffna better, I began to see not only the destruction caused by the war but also a few signs of reconstruction as a result of the 2002 ceasefire. Some rebuilding has started, in the hope that the ceasefire will be permanent. Jaffna's clock tower was constructed in 1875 to commemorate the visit of the Prince of Wales (the future Edward VII), and it suffered damage

Tamil Tiger officer with young LTTE recruits.

in the recent hostilities. Now it has been generously restored with the help of Prince Charles, the current Prince of Wales, who visited Sri Lanka in 1998. Unfortunately, when we looked at it, all four clock faces were showing different times!

Another, more potent restoration is that of the public library. In 1981, it was set alight by policemen from Colombo. They had been provoked by the killing of two police constables at a Tamil United Liberation Front election meeting in Jaffna. The official report of the International Commission of Jurists states:

> a large group of police (estimated variously from 100–200) went on the rampage on the nights of 31 May–1 June and 1–2 June burning the market area of Jaffna, the office of the Tamil newspaper, the home of the Member of Parliament for Jaffna and the Jaffna Public Library . . . The destruction of the Jaffna Public Library was the incident which appeared to cause the most distress to the people of Jaffna . . . the 95,000 volumes of the Public Library destroyed by the fire included numerous culturally important and irreplaceable manuscripts.

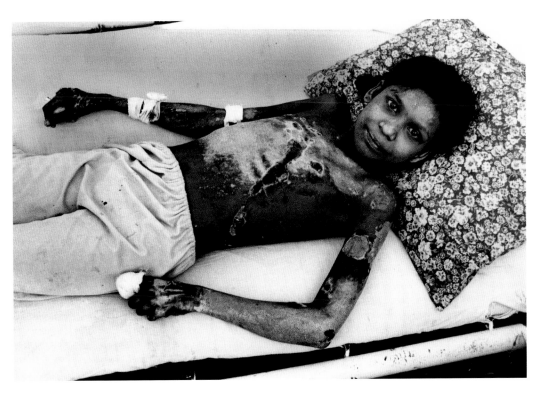

A burned Tamil refugee, casualty of the war.

The money for the restoration has come from the Government in Colombo, and books are being donated from different quarters, including the collection of a former Sri Lankan cabinet minister and president of the Cambridge Union, the late Pieter Bartholomew Keuneman.

Commerce in Jaffna seemed to me quiescent, however, though I am sure it will revive if the ceasefire holds. My visit to Kasthuria Road, famous for its gold and filigree shops, proved to be worthwhile for digging up antiques. Curiously, bronze and brassware are still sold there by the ounce. But visits to several other rundown antiques shops arranged by our helpful hotel landlord Sothi, were less productive. However I did find an old 'CEYLON PRISON' belt buckle, perhaps dating from the period when Woolf used to visit Jaffna's prison on official work.

* * *

The "curious mixture of intense reality and unreality" which struck Woolf on landing at Colombo, and the theatricality of his evening dinner with the government agent in Anuradhapura, give way in his autobiography to something bleaker on his arrival in Jaffna—at least so far as his contact with British society was concerned.

For one thing, the Europeans in Jaffna numbered only about two dozen people. They were some ten serving civil servants like himself, a retired civil servant with a daughter and two grand-daughters, ten missionaries and "an appalling ex-army [captain] with an appalling wife and an appalling son". For the first time in his life, Woolf was surrounded by individuals, with perhaps two passable exceptions, who had nothing in common with his Cambridge friends. For example, there was a hard-drinking assistant superintendent of police named Bowes who was furiously contemptuous of 'natives', and a police magistrate named Dutton who was a reclusive misfit, "A bloody unwashed board school bugger, who doesn't know one end of a woman from the other" (said Bowes). A grim Woolf told Strachey a few weeks after his arrival: "The 'society' of this place is absolutely inconceivable; it exists only upon the tennis court and in the G. A.'s house; the women are all whores or hags or missionaries or all three; and the men are, as I told you, sunk." In general, as at his public school St Paul's, Woolf found that signs of intelligence aroused uneasiness, suspicion and dislike. He was perhaps being a bit arrogant here, since many of his colleagues were intelligent men in the sense of being good at exams, and a few had wider interests, such as the government agent Lewis who wrote articles on the castes and archaeology of Ceylon. But no doubt Woolf was thinking of a higher form of intelligence than this, of the kind he had found in the philosopher G. E. Moore and his circle.

So he began concealing his intelligence and adjusting his public face, or rather wearing his 'carapace' or mask, in order to survive. And he quickly found that he was quite popular. An unsuspected asset were some bright-green flannel collars in his large tin-lined trunk. He had bought them a while back in a fleeting moment of bad taste and Thoby Stephen (Virginia Woolf's brother) had been horrified to see him actually wearing them. Now these collars, along with his brown boots derided by Strachey, convinced the white population of Jaffna that the young civil servant just arrived from London was a fashionable, daring young man.

He was unexpectedly fortunate, too, in his redoubtable dog Charles. This affectionate and intelligent animal had only two real faults—fighting and hunting—but these were to bring Woolf acclaim. On his first day in Jaffna, Charles,

Woolf in Jaffna with his dogs, around 1906.

while walking through the fort with Woolf, Bowes, the superintendent of police Dowbiggin, and a civil servant called Southorn, spotted and gave chase to a tabby cat. "In England Charles was well aware that he was not allowed to chase cats, but, I suppose, the imperialist Anglo-Indian spirit had already got hold of him and he thought that in any case a native cat was different." After a terrific scrap, Charles killed the cat and brought its corpse to Woolf. Then, up on the ramparts of the fort, Charles unearthed a very large snake which he seized behind the head and battered to death in a second titanic struggle. Woolf concluded with some irony: "My reputation as a good fellow, a Sahib, a man not to be trifled with, was therefore established within three hours of my arrival, for a civil servant, wearing bright-green flannel collars and accompanied by a dog who within the space of ten minutes had killed a cat and a large snake, commanded immediate respect."

That evening he partnered the government agent's wife Mrs Lewis at bridge against Dowbiggin and Southorn. Unknown to Woolf, Dowbiggin was a bad bridge player who had bullied the others into letting him have his way. Dowbiggin revoked, and Woolf openly accused him of this at the end of the hand, to the fury of his opponent; and then proved his point with the cards. "Silence fell upon the bridge table and I felt that something had happened . . . I was accepted as one of them by the Sahibs of the Northern Province and therefore of Ceylon."

At first, Woolf shared a bungalow on the ramparts of the fort with Southorn, the office assistant. (He later married Woolf's sister Bella and in due course, as with others of Woolf's colleagues, was elevated to Sir Wilfrid Southorn, governor of the Gambia.) Their bungalow was overshadowed by a huge banyan tree said to be inhabited by a devil and avoided by the servants at night. Superstition abounded: from his bungalow window Woolf could see a place near the fort where sacrifices were made—headless chickens flapped around, and on important days goats were slaughtered.

It did not take him long to work out the hierarchy of the civil service, how to fit in with its requirements and use them to his advantage. He knew it was better to be an office assistant like Southorn than someone in a judicial position like Dutton, because this ensured rapid promotion to assistant government agent. However, promotion did not necessarily follow from competence; one had to be thought a 'good fellow' or a 'gentleman', too. Woolf may have developed anti-imperialist ideas later on, but from the very start he knew how to play the imperialist game. This was especially true of his time in Kandy, as we shall see later, but even in Jaffna, when he was forced to make preparations for the official visit of the governor and his wife, Sir Henry and Lady Blake, he knew how to charm Lady Blake with his knowledge of Jaffna's Hindu temples—despite his low opinion of both the husband and the wife. (He told Strachey privately that: "H. E. is, I think, the crassest man to whom I have ever spoken. Lady Blake is an old bearded hag".) Woolf ascribed his official success to a psychological insight: he would always try to imagine what another person was thinking or feeling—which, he believed, caused people to think he was rather pleasant and prompted them to help him out.

Every evening was spent on the tennis courts at the fort. The tennis club was exclusively white, except for the Tamil ball boys and the keeper of the courts, Sinnatamby, who also looked after the drinks. Any attempt at racial integration in the club was severely dealt with. Woolf mentioned an occasion when the district judge put forward a European married to a native for membership; the judge was forced to resign. Conversations at the club almost always consisted of "the same incongruous mixture of public school toughness, sentimentality, and melancholy." Woolf liked to watch Sinnatamby's reactions. The Tamil was a big man, stoutish, who dressed in voluminous white with a towering maroon turban.

> He was extremely respectful, but I sometimes thought that I caught in his eye a gleam which belied the impassive face when some more than usually outrageous remark of the captain or of Jimmy Bowes echoed up into the heavy scented immense emptiness of the tropical evening sky. He might have been a character in a Kipling story, and I could imagine generations of Sinnatambys standing respectfully behind their white masters in India right back to before the Mutiny—and some of them with that gleam in the eye getting their own back during the Mutiny.

Woolf often found himself wondering if Kipling had modelled his Anglo-Indian characters on the actual society, or whether in reality it was the other way around: the society surrounding him in Ceylon was somehow modelling itself on Kipling's fictional characters.

Bowes epitomised the displaced, melancholy imperialist for Woolf. Though only 33, he felt he was a failure in comparison to his brother Freddy, a high-flying civil servant. He drank too much, frequented prostitutes and hated Ceylon. His bitterness came out in his abuse. Woolf told Strachey (the language was too salty for his autobiography, though) about riding through Jaffna with Bowes in his gig while he ranted at his fate and, between rants, cursed the natives in the street. He offered Strachey this sample:

> I didn't ask for much, a little house in an English shire, with plenty of hunting and six or seven horses and enough money to run up to London for a week when the frost comes—Get out, you ugly stinking fucking son of a black-buggered bitch; you black bugger you—I don't

ask for much, I'd be as happy as a king—you greasy fat Jaffna harlot,
get out of the light, you black swine—and I don't get it.

Dutton, the police magistrate, was pathetic in a different way, which Woolf was forced to confront when he had to share a bungalow with him after leaving his first bungalow, which was required by the family of Southorn's replacement. A small, bespectacled, sunken-cheeked man, Dutton was without doubt a failure in the civil service, who had literary pretensions and a penchant for writing terrible poetry about fairies and elves. "His roots began and remained in Peckham, while his mind was full of Keats, the Gaiety Girl, Shakespeare, and fays… His lower-class origin superimposed upon his timidity a deep inferiority complex which burst out in the most grotesque intellectual arrogance." *Growing* gives chapter and verse in support of this character analysis. It says something for Woolf's success in Jaffna society, despite all his inner anxieties, that his sharing of a bungalow with 'dirty' Dutton did not jeopardise his reputation.

Dutton's lack of judgement caused him to act in an inappropriate manner in the courtroom, as Woolf recounted in his autobiography, while not hiding his own role in the revealing incident. One day, not long after his arrival in Jaffna, Woolf was riding back to his bungalow by horse when he happened to see a Burgher girl on her verandah. They exchanged smiles, and a few moments later Woolf was pestered by a minute boy who said: "Sah! Sah! That young girl ask whether she come to your bungalow tonight." Woolf agreed—"very foolishly", he says—and lost his virginity to the girl that night. Then he discovered that she was the niece of one of his own, very respectable, clerks at the *kachcheri*. Subsequent gossip revealed that she was being kept by a Tamil lawyer and was known to all Jaffna as a 'loose liver'. When the lawyer now brought a case against the girl for abuse and indecent language, claiming she had come to his home where he lived with his wife and family and hurled insults at them from the street, it was Dutton who tried the case. He ruled that although the girl was guilty of the abuse, her morality and purity had been wrongly impugned by the lawyer. And to demonstrate his belief in her innocence, Dutton gave her a nominal fine and immediately paid it himself in the courtroom. "The whole incident and Dutton's little speech gave the Jaffnese immense pleasure and amusement."

Nevertheless, it was Woolf who coaxed Dutton into the pukka circle at the tennis club, and there introduced him to the missionary Miss Beeching (one of the two 'angels' who had rescued his dog Charles in Anuradhapura). A romance developed, and they married; but perhaps predictably it was a sad affair. Woolf happened to encounter Mrs Dutton again a few years later, after he had moved to Hambantota. She was alone because her husband was away on police business. Eventually, she broke down and told Woolf that the marriage was a complete failure because Dutton was basically a homosexual ("so queer that he ought not to have married", writes Woolf). Not long after he left Ceylon in 1911, Woolf heard that Dutton had died in Ceylon from tuberculosis.

A larger-than-life character, and the matriarch of white society in Jaffna, was Mrs Lewis, the wife of the government agent John Penry Lewis. Woolf found her more attractive than the other women. She talked non-stop, often in a deliberately outrageous way. Her husband enjoyed her vulgarity and accepted her typical greeting: "O Pen dear, you really are *too* fat, with your great ugly paunch sticking out before you." Like some character from Jane Austen, thought Woolf, matchmaking was uppermost in Mrs Lewis's mind, an inveterate habit with her, and she took great delight in embarrassing people with suggestive, though not malicious, remarks. She tried one on Woolf at the tennis club by asking in a loud voice, "I hope you kissed Mary goodbye?"—behaviour that was rare in public in the Ceylon of 1905. But after this one attempt Mrs Lewis gave up and treated Woolf with a caution he found complimentary. In fact they got on rather well, both in Jaffna and later in Kandy.

* * *

When he first arrived, Woolf's work as a cadet was dull and repetitive: issuing licences, answering petitions and fining "miserable wretches". After some weeks of this he lost patience and told Southorn that he must be given some interesting and responsible work. This was overstepping the mark for a cadet, and Woolf admits he was "an arrogant, conceited, and quick-tempered young man". But Southorn must have been impressed by him, because instead of dismissing the request he complied with it.

Woolf was also helped by the fact that Lewis, the government agent, was more interested in archaeology and anthropology than in administration. He was glad to delegate some responsibility. Woolf thought Lewis typical of many older civil servants in higher administrative posts who had spent so many years in hot and inhospitable places they had lost their drive, but in saying this he overlooked the genuine importance of Lewis's scholarly work. Even today

Lewis's research into the caste system of the Tamils is cited along with the work of modern scholars like Bryan Pfaffenberger, Michael Banks and David Kenneth—somewhat as Woolf himself is best remembered in Sri Lanka for his novel, *The Village in the Jungle*, rather than for his professed anti-imperialism. Moreover Lewis's research while in office was encouraged by his superior, the colonial secretary in Colombo. Perhaps Woolf was at least slightly biased against recognising its importance by his own lack of interest in the archaeology of Ceylon, which was apparent when he passed through Anuradhapura.

Right at the beginning, even before his request, Woolf was doing work that took him outside of the office routine. In late January, he accompanied the government agent in the exemption of sick people from work. The Government forced everyone of a certain age to do some annual labour on the roads, but not all were fit enough. This work must have been a disturbing experience for Woolf since he confided to Strachey: "You have no conception of what degree of foulness a naked body is capable until you have done that: mere skeletons covered in sores, deformities in every part of the body". Yet he also remarked on the "extraordinarily beautiful" men—and how sodomy was apparently rampant. In another letter he mentioned a rape case in which an old woman had charged a boy of 18. It was "the most astonishing and sordid thing I have yet seen out here". He described the woman as "an old hag" who had plainly let the boy copulate with her. His crass assumption that the old woman was guilty, not the boy, is typical of his arrogance and of the attitudes towards rape at this time.

But such experiences also gave him the first inklings of a humane interest in the people he ruled, that would gradually mature into the sympathy he expressed for them in his final work in Hambantota, in his short stories, and especially in his novel.

The concept of caste was ingrained in the Tamils, and it soon began to interest Woolf. He would have been aware, as he cycled back and forth from the *kachcheri*, of the countless pariah-dogs in Jaffna. The word comes from the Tamil word *pariah*, which refers to a large drum used in India. The *paraiyar* caste is a drummer caste in southern India, who play the drums at certain religious festivals. Many of these *paraiyars* violated concepts of purity by working as domestics for Europeans and performing other duties regarded as polluting. Thus they ranked very low in the caste hierarchy.

In Jaffna, the Brahmins were technically the highest caste, but they had no social control. Their role was limited to well-defined ritual duties in the temples. Instead, the *vellalar* caste (agriculturists and landowners) exerted real social control, but as to exactly how this operated, it would depend on the region. For instance in Velvettiturai, the coastal village where the Tamil Tiger leader Velupillai Prabhakaran comes from, it is the *karaiyars* (fishing people) who are the dominant caste. Some other significant castes in the Jaffna district are the *ampattars* (barbers), the *taccars* (carpenters), the *kollars* (blacksmiths) and the *tattars* (goldsmiths).

Though Woolf would never show any serious interest in Hindu philosophy (unlike Buddhism), he clearly became quite knowledgeable about the caste system in Jaffna, and indeed elsewhere in Ceylon. He gained this knowledge from his work in the *kachcheri* and especially from listening to court cases as a magistrate. Unlike many of his contemporaries, he quickly moved beyond the usual European feelings of irritation and contempt for caste and began to observe how it worked in practice. His attitude was, in a sense, connected with his discovery about the British social classes on board the P. & O. ship that brought him to Ceylon, which we quoted earlier: that social class co-exists with the fact that "beneath the façade of John Smith and Jane Brown there is a strange character and often a passionate individual."

The clash between caste values and the individual's values is at the heart of Woolf's short story, "The Two Brahmans", which he published in *Stories of the East* in 1921. As we know, it is set in Jaffna, though the town is given its Tamil name Yalpanam. The two central characters, Chellaya and Chittampalam, being Brahmins, know that they and their fathers and their fathers' fathers have lived in the same way by the side of the blue lagoon under the palm trees for many thousands of years. They do no work, for there is no need to work. The *dhobi* or washer caste man, who washes the clothes of the Brahmins and of no other caste, washes their white cloths and in return is given rice and allowed to be present at weddings and funerals. And there is the barber caste man who shaves the Brahmins and no other caste.

Woolf explains that a member of one caste cannot eat with or marry into another caste, or work at the work of another caste, for their own caste will then be defiled and they will lose their status.

But the two Brahmins of the story are not content with the time-honoured caste traditions. Chellaya spends almost all of his time watching the fishermen cast their nets in the lagoon and capture "the great leaping twisting silver fish".

The beauty of the act gradually makes him hate his slothful Brahmin's existence. He becomes convinced that fishing is the only thing in life that can bring him pleasure, even though it would be utter pollution of his caste.

Using his status as a Brahmin, Chellaya persuades a reluctant fisherman to teach him to fish, saying that he needs to do this in order to lift a curse on his grandson. He learns fishing in secrecy but the rumour of his transgression spreads. Soon the whole town is talking about it behind their *cadjan* fences. "Everyone began to believe in it, the lower castes with great pleasure and the Brahmins with great shame and anger."

Then the other Brahmin, Chittampalam, also pollutes his caste by carrying earth on his head. His reason has nothing to do with beauty: he is too much of a miser to pay a man of the appropriate caste to dig a well, and so digs it himself.

Both Brahmins are "cast out" from the Brahmin caste by the other Brahmins. Chittampalam does not care and dies soon after. Chellaya tries to stop himself from fishing, but it is no use because the other Brahmins still ostracise him.

Years pass and the community forgets exactly what transgressions the two Brahmins in these families committed, but people retain the memory that they did something wrong. "Only it was known in Yalpanam that no Brahmin could marry into these two families."

Then a young man and woman, descendants of the two families, fall in love and want to marry. The man is the son of Chellaya, who is the great-great-great-grandson of the earlier Chellaya; the woman is the daughter of Chittampalam, the great-great-great-grandson of the earlier Chittampalam. Negotiations for the wedding go well until an argument over the dowry causes old resentments to emerge. Each family finally accuses the other of polluting the caste. "'Fisher! Low-caste dog!' shouted Chittampalam." "'Pariah!' screamed Chellaya."

The quarrel is eventually healed, only to flare up again. This happens several times and at the end of the story, Chittampalam is left contemplating the need to go to distant villages to find a husband for his daughter. "Chellaya's son is very unhappy; he goes down every evening and sits by the waters of the blue lagoon on the very spot where his great-great-great-grandfather Chellaya used to sit and watch the fishermen cast their nets."

When Woolf wrote the story, Christian missions (especially in the Jaffna area) and the introduction of English education by the Government were

Fisherman on Jaffna lagoon, around 1905.

already eroding Ceylonese caste barriers. Mechanisation has subsequently been another contributing factor; jobs like lorry driving, not to mention computing, cannot fit into caste occupations. Employment practices in the cities and later the exodus to work in the Middle East has continued the erosion. And of course in the armed forces, caste regiments and military rank reserved for particular castes would be an impossibility. Notwithstanding all this, everyone in Sri Lanka today knows that caste remains a significant element in politics and marriage, as it does across the water in India.

*   *   *

Whatever Woolf's growing feelings for the people of the district may have been, his general reputation with them was for strictness and on occasions arrogance. He admitted this in *Growing*:

> My unpopularity in Jaffna was not undeserved. I meant well by the people of Jaffna, but, even when my meaning was well, and also right— not always the case or the same thing, my methods were too ruthless, too much the 'strong man'. The difficulties and the friction made me for the first time dimly perceive the problems of the imperialist.

My own impression, judging from the long chapter on Jaffna in Woolf's autobiography, is that the friction was mainly with the best-educated people, not with the vast majority, the village cultivators and fisher people of the coast. Imperialism grated on the feelings of the professional men, educated in English, much more than on those of the poor and unlettered—just as it did in imperial India. The friction was inherent in the famous *Minute on Education* written in 1835 by Thomas Babington Macaulay when he was a civil servant in Bengal. This laid down the future aim of the colonial system of education in the subcontinent: to create "a class of persons Indian in blood and colour, but English in opinions, in morals and in intellect". Not unnaturally, this class of Indian persons, having been created by the British, resented being treated as inferiors by white English persons.

A relatively minor example of the friction was a complaint against Woolf by the Jaffna Tamil Association. He had posted an order in the verandah of the *kachcheri* forbidding spitting. "The amount of spitting which went on in the verandah was extremely unpleasant." The office peons were ordered to turn out anyone who spat. One day one of his own clerks spat and Woolf told him to clean the spot. "He refused", Woolf wrote at the time in his official explanation to the Government in Colombo, "but when he saw I meant it, he did it. Of course I knew he was of a caste to hate doing it, but he was also a person who wanted a lesson given to him." And he added, concerning the complaints of the Tamil Association in general: "They don't like the 'strong measures'. . . , and so of course they take the paying line that [I am] anti-native. In my case they have pitched on things which are of course not anti-native but in the main true." In *Growing*, Woolf confessed that the way he handled the spitting incident was, "of course, crudely wrong", but defended himself as fair-minded, not 'anti-native'.

A second, more serious accusation against Woolf appears to have been completely untrue. A well-known lawyer in Jaffna, Harry Sanderasekara, complained that Woolf had deliberately lashed out at him with his whip when they passed in the street. Given the virulently 'anti-native' attitude of a policeman like Bowes, such an incident was plausible, but deeply wounding for a liberal like Woolf, especially as he knew and liked Sanderasekara. It turned out that the misunderstanding arose as Woolf, mounted on a restless, dancing horse, had been in the street with the new government agent Price, pointing out to him with his whip where verandahs were encroaching on the highway, when Sanderasekara's trap happened to ride past. The Government accepted Woolf's explanation, but he doubted if the Tamil Association and Sanderasekara himself ever did.

> It shocked me that these people should think that, as a white man and a ruler of Ceylon, I should consider the brown man, the Tamil, to be one of the 'lesser breeds' and deliberately hit him in the face with my riding whip to show him that he must behave himself and keep in his place. For that is what all this meant. And perhaps for the first time I felt a twinge of doubt in my imperialist soul.

Woolf even questioned whether his mere presence on the street in an official capacity was tantamount to the Tamils to a slap in the face. To this day, there are those in Jaffna who think Woolf did not tell the truth about this notorious incident.

A hundred years after Macaulay, in 1933, George Bernard Shaw gave amusing and still-pointed expression to such racial friction in his political play, *On the Rocks*. Woolf knew Shaw well at this time, and Shaw had visited Ceylon and thought it "the most beautiful country in the world". His play contains a wealthy character from Ceylon named Sir Jafna Pandranath. He was very likely based on a Tamil public figure and scholar, Sir Muttu Coomaraswamy, who married an Englishwoman (and whose son became the internationally famous scholar of Sinhalese art, Ananda Coomaraswamy). And his name may well have been an echo of Woolf's experiences in Jaffna. "It seems entirely possible," says Shaw's biographer Michael Holroyd, "that Shaw's close association with Leonard Woolf, and Woolf's related experiences in Ceylon, and particularly in Jaffna, resulted in Shaw's using Jafna as the first name for Sir Jafna Pandranath in his play."

The crucial scene takes place in the cabinet room.

It is probable that George Bernard Shaw was influenced by Woolf when he wrote his political play On the Rocks.

Sir Jafna Pandranath: Hello! Am I breaking into a cabinet meeting?

Sir Arthur Chavender (Prime Minister): No. Not a bit. Only a few friendly callers. Pray sit down.

Sir Dexter Rightside (Foreign Secretary): You are welcome, Sir Jafna; most welcome. You represent money; and money brings fools to their senses.

Sir Jafna: Money! Not at all. I am a poor man. I never know from one moment to another whether I am worth thirteen millions or only three.

Sir Bemrose Hotspot (First Lord of the Admiralty): I happen to know, Sir Jafna, that your enterprises stand at twenty millions today at the very least.

Mr Glenmorison (President of the Board of Trade): Fifty.

Sir Jafna: How do you know? How do you know? The way I am plundered at every turn! (*To Sir Dexter*) Your people take the shirt off my back.

Sir Dexter: My people! What on earth do you mean?

Sir Jafna: Your land monopolists. Your blackmailers. Your robber barons . . . You were quite right at the Guildhall last night, Arthur. You must nationalise the land and put a stop to this shameless exploitation of the financiers and entrepreneurs by a useless, idle, predatory landed class . . .

This is too much for Rightside. He loses his temper and calls Sir Jafna, "a silly nigger pretending to be an English gentleman". His contemptuous remark sends Sir Jafna into a fireworks display of Shavian "irreverent wit" (to quote Woolf on Shaw in the third volume of his autobiography). An extract:

> *Sir Jafna*: I am despised. I am called nigger by this dirty-faced barbarian whose forefathers were naked savages worshipping acorns and mistletoe in the woods while my people were spreading the highest enlightenment yet reached by the human race from the temples of Brahma the thousands fold who is all the gods in one . . .
> . . . you call me nigger, sneering at my colour because you have none . . . I should dishonour my country and my race by remaining here where both have been insulted… But I now cast you off. I return to India to detach it wholly from England and leave you to perish in your ignorance, your vain conceit, and your abominable manners.

Exit Sir Jafna, and Sir Dexter, after which the remaining characters continue their conversation:

> *Sir Arthur*: That one word nigger will cost us India. How could Dexy be such a fool as to let it slip?
> *Sir Bemrose*: Arthur! I feel I cannot overlook a speech like that. After all we are white men.
> *Sir Arthur*: You are not, Rosy, I assure you. You are walnut colour, with a touch of claret on the nose. Glenmorison is the colour of his native oatmeal, not a touch of white on him. The fairest man present is the duke. He's as yellow as a Malayan headhunter. The Chinese call us pinks. They flatter us.
> *Sir Bemrose*: I must tell you, Arthur, that frivolity on a vital point like this is in very bad taste. And you know very well that the country cannot do without Dexy… I must go and see him at once.
> *Sir Arthur*: Make my apologies to Sir Jafna if you overtake him. How are we to hold the empire together if we insult a man who represents nearly seventy per cent of its population?
> *Sir Bemrose*: I don't agree with you, Arthur. It is for Pandy to apologise.

In Jaffna Woolf began by living with Wilfrid Southorn in a gloomy bungalow overshadowed by an immense banyan tree.

> Dexy really shares the premiership with you; and if a Conservative prime minister of England may not take down a heathen native when he forgets himself there is an end of British supremacy.
> *Sir Arthur*: For heaven's sake don't call him a native. You are a native.
> *Sir Bemrose*: Of Kent, Arthur: of Kent. Not of Ceylon.

Incidentally, Woolf records that at a meeting with Shaw in 1915, Shaw gave him the "only serious dressing down I ever had from him"—for using the word native in referring to the Indians.

However, not all upper-class Hindus in Jaffna were against Woolf, as he was keen to point out in *Growing*. There he reproduces an entire letter from another lawyer well known in Jaffna, V. Casippillai, written after Woolf left Jaffna for Kandy in 1907; the motive of the writer therefore cannot have been flattery. Casippillai observed:

> Very few here worked as hard as you have done or earned a reputation

Dhobis washing under palmyra trees, Jaffna.

for more conscientious discharge of duties and I can bear testimony to the fact that very many of your subordinates who had evinced much displeasure at your relations with them at the outset had to confess that they had never had a superior who exacted so much work and at the same time treated them so kindly, holding the balance between all parties—justice being your motto.

Even after his return to London, Woolf was still in contact with some of his clerks at the Jaffna *kachcheri*. A letter of April 1913 from K. Naganath, office assistant, expresses thanks for a monetary gift for the Hindu new year: "I can never forget the kindness you cherish towards me a poor insignificant peon and am at a loss to know how to be grateful for such unique kindliness of heart in you . . . the money has been of great use to me at this festive occasion and I thank you once more for the present."

Woolf's sense of justice, of what was right and wrong, was one of his defining characteristics. And he had plenty of opportunities to put it into action. A case in Jaffna, which he thought typical of his time in Ceylon, involved a murder at Kankesanturai on the north coast of the district in 1905. A small boy had disappeared. He had last been seen travelling in a bullock cart with a young man who was known to keep a dancing girl and therefore to be badly in debt. Woolf, who was then acting as the superintendent of police, was informed in Jaffna by a police constable. He set off on his bicycle for Kankesanturai, but before reaching there he was directed to the chief headman's house by another policeman, where they found a young man and the child's family. When the child went missing, his relatives had stopped every bullock cart they could find until finally, at two in the morning, they came across the suspected young man whose cart contained the boy's jewellery. They took him to the headman's house where they tortured him with sticks and whips and pushed pins down his fingernails until he confessed to the murder. He had taken the young boy to the sea in Kankesanturai and knelt on him until he drowned, then stolen his jewellery.

Woolf cycled off to Kankesanturai and together with thirty villagers scoured the sands. He spent two days in the place looking for the body. He even contacted the captain of a nearby ship and requested his assistance. (*Growing* reproduces a letter from the master of the vessel with a matter-of-fact PS: "We give a drowned man from seven to nine days to float but he must have weighed the child down.") Woolf could not recall whether the body was ever found, but he remembered his horror at the methods of the police and headmen in dealing with criminals.

In another typical homicidal incident, we get an idea of what a hospital was like from a letter to Strachey. Woolf had accompanied the police magistrate Dutton to the Jaffna hospital to take the dying deposition of a man whose head had been cracked open in a brawl. He described the scene:

> The hospital consists of two long rooms bare and whitewashed, with rows of plank beds down each wall. Horrible looking dishes lay scattered about and on the planks lay three or four natives without any covering but the clothes in which they had arrived, their heads and bodies bandaged, groaning grunting and spitting on the floor. Outside and on the verandah and therefore to all intents and purposes in the room, squatted a crowd of patients and their friends talking, quarrelling, chewing betel and spitting it out upon the floor. Among these

sat the dying man eating curry and rice out of a big dish, and quarrelling with the man who is accused of having broken his head.

The description brings to mind some grotesque caricature by Hogarth or Rowlandson. Woolf added: "The whole thing was exactly what I imagine the eighteenth-century hospitals were like."

Another time he told Strachey of how he had to bicycle about 35 miles to inspect the stumps of two trees near a big temple. "A violent dispute had arisen between two priests and one accused the other of cutting down trees on crown land. I had to decide whether it was crown land or not in the midst of a yelling mob of some hundreds of people."

More pleasant was the occasion when a headman came to the *kachcheri* to report that a hole had appeared in a field about five miles from Jaffna and that the size of the hole kept increasing. Woolf got on his bicycle and went to see for himself. The hole was already a large pond and it was getting bigger, as every ten minutes or so a crack appeared at the edge, then the crack widened and the earth toppled into the water. Each time another foot of ground disappeared, the crowd of watching Tamils shouted "Aiyo! Aiyo!" The water was salty and was coming from the sea about a mile away. There was nothing a mere civil servant could do about it and so Woolf joked to Strachey: "I expect that it means that Jaffna peninsula is going to return to the sea bed from which it came . . . If so, this is my last letter to you".

*　*　*

In addition to his work in the *kachcheri* and his police work, Woolf was responsible for visiting the customs houses on the islands off Jaffna. He loved the solitariness and beauty of these islands. From Kayts, the nearest one to Jaffna, he wrote to Strachey: "Can you see it all? The sun and blue water, the boats with their great square sails, the quay crowded with people in their wonderful clothes, the melancholy islands we glided by, with their low deserted sandy beaches and the palm trees coming almost down to the sea."

In the next chapter, we ourselves will follow him to the islands by boat. But first I want to describe how Woolf nearly met an untimely death at the end of 1905.

It happened while he was making visits to supervise famine relief works and to ensure that the people were paid in rice. On one of these trips, across the Jaffna lagoon to Punakari near Pooneryn, a place then inaccessible by road (which became a strategic crossing point in the war between the Sri Lankan army and the Tamil Tigers), the wind dropped and the boat was becalmed. Remembering the experience in *Growing*, Woolf could not help but quote Coleridge's ancient mariner:

> *All in a hot and copper sky*
> *The bloody Sun, at noon,*
> *Right up above the mast did stand,*
> *No bigger than the Moon.*
>
> *Hour after hour, hour after hour,*
> *We stuck, nor breath nor motion,*
> *As idle as a painted ship*
> *Upon a painted ocean.*

In the meantime flies swarmed over the foul bilge water in the bottom of the boat. The waiting Woolf ate a little food he had brought with him. It infected him with typhoid.

Back in Jaffna, now with a bad headache, that afternoon he moved into yet another bungalow (Dutton was about to marry and needed more space) with a government surveyor called Shipton, and after a wretched night he valiantly forced himself to the breakfast table. Confronted with a dish of fried egg and greasy hoppers (*appa* in Sinhala, *appam* in Tamil: a thick pancake made of rice or wheat flour with a soft centre), Woolf thought he might die. Shipton took his temperature and, fortunately for Woolf, did not assume he had malaria—a diagnosis "which almost certainly saved my life". Since there was no decent doctor and no decent hospital in Jaffna for a European, Shipton immediately went off to the American Mission Hospital at Manipay, six or eight miles away, and fetched the doctor. (Known as the Green Hospital, it was founded in the 1840s by an American missionary Samuel Fisk Green, and was the first medical college in Ceylon.) Woolf was placed on a stretcher and taken by bullock cart to the hospital. There, for lack of any place suitable for a sick European, he was housed in a completely bare outhouse with only a small window about ten feet from the floor.

The hospital had only one trained nurse, a Tamil girl who was too shy to touch a white patient. So Woolf was forced to take his own temperature and was nursed by his servant Appukutty. He slept endlessly as his body

American Mission Hospital, Manipay.

battled with the dread disease, waking up on one occasion to see three white-robed, turbaned headmen standing beside his bed. They salaamed and then one stepped forward and said: "Sir, we heard that you are ill and dying, so we have come to pay our respects to you." After three weeks, his temperature returned to normal, as the doctor had said it would. There followed ten days to two weeks' further rest at the hospital, and then he returned to Jaffna to convalesce. But Woolf was still weaker than he knew, and he collapsed by the side of the road while returning from an unwise evening visit to watch tennis at the fort.

What really cured him was three weeks' leave, first in Kandy, then in a hotel in the tea-planting area of Hatton, near Adam's Peak, and finally in the small hill station of Bandarawela (which remains a favourite resort in the hot weather). On 28 January 1906, he received a telegram in Bandarawela from the government agent in Jaffna asking him if he was well enough to take up a special appointment as a superintendent of the pearl fishery in Mannar. "It was obviously an extremely interesting job, so I wired back 'Yes', and next day set out to Jaffna."

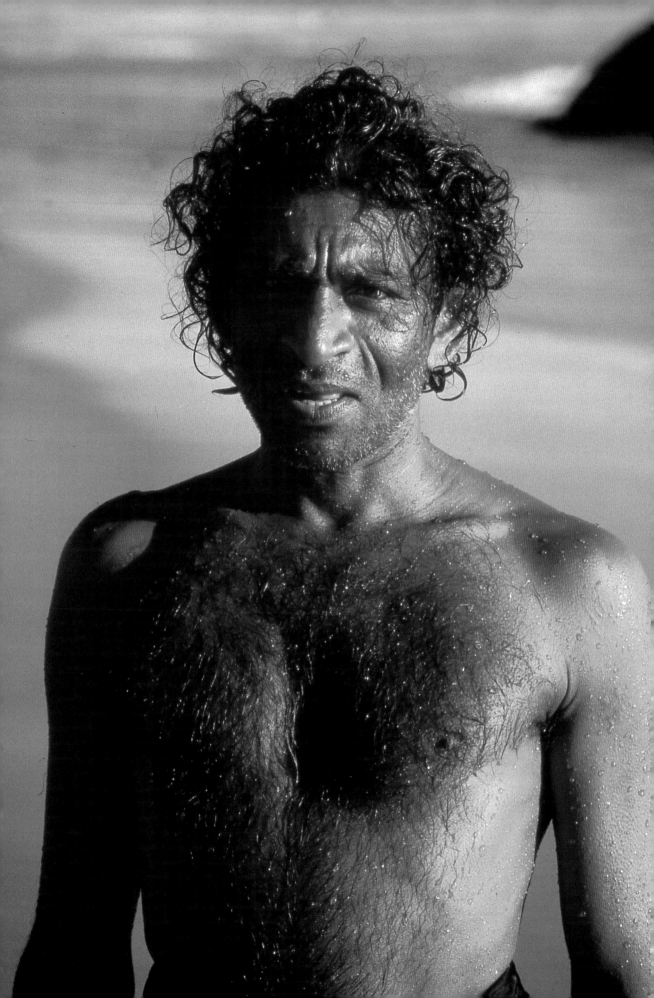

4

Pearls and Swine

The pearl fishery camp was always at Marichchukaddi, which as the crow flies is about eighty miles from Jaffna. When there is no fishery, Marichchukaddi is merely a name on a map, a stretch of sandy scrub jungle with the thick jungle beginning half a mile inland. There was no road to it, only a rough sandy track along the coast to Mannar, so that the only way to reach it was by sea … About twenty to thirty thousand people came from all over Asia to the fishery, divers, jewellers, dealers, merchants, traders, financiers, shopkeepers, dacoits, criminals.

LEONARD WOOLF, *Growing*

ABOUT TWO WEEKS after his return to Jaffna from sick leave, Woolf found himself on a small boat sailing haltingly around the northwest coast of Ceylon, starting from the Jaffna lagoon, skirting the long peninsula of Mannar Island, passing between the islands of Adam's Bridge that crosses the Palk Strait to India, and mooring south of Mannar at Marichchukaddi, the site of the pearl fishery. He had been seconded there for seven weeks by Lewis, the Jaffna government agent.

Although it was a short distance on the map, only 80 miles or so, the journey took a day and a half. "It really was as though time stood still." He relished the solitude, the star-strewn heavens at night and the romance of being cut off from civilisation. "When they ran my boat up on to the sandy beach at Marichchukaddi and I jumped down into the sand, I felt that, though my body was unwashed and unshaved, my mind had been curiously cleaned and purified." The spell did not last long: the first person he encountered was the jolly Mrs Lewis, sitting beside a wind-up gramophone which was blaring out Neapolitan songs.

Migrant coastal fisherman south of Mannar.

Preparing to dive at the pearl fishery, 1906.

The Marichchukaddi pearl fishery was said to date from very ancient times. Under the British, it existed erratically, dependent on enough pearls being dredged up from the oyster banks by the superintendent of pearl fisheries for him to declare a fishery in the following February. The diving was of a very primitive kind. Arab divers came from the Persian Gulf in dhows, Tamil and Moor divers from India in their boats—8,667 of them were registered for the fishery of 1906. They plunged from their vessels down to the oyster banks wearing no equipment other than a nose clip and a rope, which was used to haul them up with their basket of oysters. Occasionally, they were hauled up drowned, and the body would be brought ashore for the cause of death to be certified by the Government; Woolf gave a graphic and moving description

Arab divers with nose clips, 1906.

of one such death of an Arab diver in *Growing*.

His exhausting task at the pearl fishery, which went on day and night, was to supervise the landing of oysters, their transfer to a large stockade known as the *koddu*, their sorting into piles, and their distribution and sale: one third went to the divers, two thirds to the Government. As the divers rushed out of the *koddu* with their share of oysters, they were besieged by dealers and merchants, who then hurried off to open what they could buy. The number and quality of the pearls they discovered would determine their bids at the auction of the government's share every evening. Around this central activity, a temporary town of perhaps thirty thousand people sprang up—all of it under the control of a mere four Europeans: the government agent, his assistant, a superintendent of police, and Woolf, who had been designated 'assistant koddu superintendent'.

He liked the Arab divers most, finding them less distant than the Tamils:

> The Tamil treated one as someone apart; he would never dream of touching one, for instance. The Arabs, on the other hand, although extremely polite, treated me as a fellow human being . . . They would surround me and make long eloquent guttural speeches, and often if one of them got excited, he would put his hand on my shoulder to emphasise the torrent of his words.

Divers carry oysters into the koddu, *Marichchukaddi, 1906.*

Probably the difference in religion was influential here: there was no direct
equivalent among the Arabs of the caste feeling among the Hindu Tamils.

At any rate, the Arab sense of 'equality' was used by Woolf to justify some
rough-and-ready methods. He told Strachey: "the Arabs will do anything if you
hit them hard enough with a walking stick". According to him, they were vastly
amused by his "beatings", which he employed mainly to clear a passage through
them into the *koddu*. One Arab gave him a camel-hair headdress and a nose clip,
so it would seem that Woolf's rather aggressive policing did not provoke much
resentment. He himself noted that he never dared to strike the non-Arab divers.

Pearls were extracted from the oysters for their purchasers by leaving the
oysters to rot in the sun for several days. Therefore an overpowering stench
hung over the pearl fishery, along with a cloud of millions and millions of flies.
It was essential to cover every morsel of food thoroughly until the moment it
was put into the mouth—a rule that Woolf scrupulously obeyed, having just
recovered from typhoid. How very different it all sounds from the extremely
exotic and lyrically beautiful Ceylon pearl fishery in Bizet's nineteenth-century
opera *The Pearl Fishers*!

As the divers rushed out of the koddu *with their share of oysters, they were besieged by dealers.*

Though he felt physically fit again, Woolf's melancholy and depression seem to have returned in an extreme form at the pearl fishery as a result of the punishing schedule, the lack of sleep and the bad food. He even wrote to Strachey from Marichchukaddi:

> I sometimes wonder whether I shall commit suicide before the six years are up and I can see you again; at this moment I feel as near as I have ever been. Depression is becoming, I believe, a mania with me, it sweeps upon and over me every eight or ten days, deeper each time. If you hear that I have died of sunstroke, you may be the only person to know that I have chosen that method of annihilation.

✳   ✳   ✳

Pessimism is the dominant note of Woolf's finest short story, "Pearls and Swine", about the pearl fishery, which he published in *Stories of the East* in 1921. There is little sign in it of the exotic elements found in his two other stories, "A Tale Told by Moonlight" and "The Two Brahmans". Besides capturing the strangeness of the pearl fishery and the gritty texture of colonial life, "Pearls and Swine", with its perfectly judged title, is a literary achievement that is almost, though not quite, on a par with the classic Kipling stories of India that Woolf admired.

As in "A Tale Told by Moonlight", the eastern setting is distanced by the story's starting in England. Five Englishmen—an archdeacon, a stockjobber, a retired colonel, an Anglo-Indian district commissioner (the Indian equivalent of a government agent in Ceylon), and the narrator—find themselves together by chance in the smoking room of a seaside hotel in Torquay late in the evening, when the conversation turns to the subject of the East. The commissioner is the only one of them who has worked out East, running the Indian empire for 30 years. As the archdeacon and the stockjobber spout their views on how to rule the millions of Indians, the commissioner, who has been fidgety but silent, suddenly speaks up. "*Kasimutal Rameswaramvaraiyil terintavan.*"

"I beg your pardon," said the archdeacon.

The commissioner offers a mock apology for voicing a Tamil proverb, which just happened to come to his mind. It means: "He knows everything from Benares to Rameswaram." In other words, from one end of India to the other. (Rameswaram is a great Tamil temple town at the Indian end of Adam's Bridge, opposite Sri Lanka.) "Last time I heard it, an old Tamil, seventy or eighty years old—he looked a hundred—used it of one of your young men. The young man, by the bye, had been a year and a half in India. D'you understand?"

The archdeacon is still puzzled. He knows of Benares, he says, but does not recollect the name Rameswaram. So the commissioner openly explains that the old Tamil was commenting on the presumption of a young British missionary in claiming to 'know' India. He adds:

> Perhaps you also don't recollect that the Tamils are Dravidians? They've been there since the beginning of time, before we came . . . Uncivilised, black? Perhaps, but, if they're black, after all it's *their* suns, through thousands of years, that have blackened them. They ought to know, if anyone does: but they don't, they don't pretend to. But you two gentlemen, you seem to know everything between Kasimutal—that's Benares—and Rameswaram, without having seen the sun at all.

(A comment that, incidentally, seems to have influenced a passage in Woolf's friend E. M. Forster's slightly later novel, *A Passage to India*.)

The temperature in the smoking room has risen, but the archdeacon emolliently invites the commissioner to give his own views on India, since he has worked there. "I won't give you views," he says somewhat fiercely. "But if you like I'll give you what you call details, things seen, facts. Then you can give me *your* views on 'em." They agree to hear what he has to say.

The scene is now set for the commissioner's story of the East. He launches into a description of a pearl fishery somewhere on the south coast of India which closely resembles the one Woolf had known in Ceylon.

He was in virtually sole charge, he says. "It would have taken fifty white men to superintend that camp properly: they gave me one, a little boy of 24, fresh-cheeked from England, just joined the service." His name was Robson. "He had views, he had been educated in a board school, won prizes, scholarships, passed the civil service 'exam'. Yes, he had views; he used to explain them to me when he first arrived. He got some new ones I think before he got out of that camp."

Then he mentions that there was one other white man, apparently come to "deal" in pearls. He appears out of nowhere from a boat and gives his name as White. His background is sketchy but it seems to be public school followed by failure at home as a gentleman, tea planting in Assam, and then a long succession of jobs all over the Asian empire. He looks "unhealthily fat for the East" and has a red face and a red nose. "I noticed that his hand shook, and that he first refused and then took a whisky and soda—a bad sign in the East." In the second week White has his first attack of DT's. The commissioner and Robson pull him through it, in the intervals between watching over the oysters.

The commissioner describes the way oysters are fished, with sharp-edged comments on the Government. "You'd think being progressive we'd dredge for them or send down divers in diving dresses. But we don't, not in India. They've been fishing up the oysters and the pearls there ever since the beginning of time, naked brown men diving feet first out of long wooden boats . . . They were doing it centuries and centuries before we came." The only difference now, he says, is that "we—Government I mean—take two thirds of all the oysters fished up: the other third we give to the diver, Arab or Tamil or Moorman, for his trouble in fishing 'em up."

Then he mentions the flies and the stench of rotting oysters. And the evenings, after the boats have gone out to fish, with Robson and White, who lay before him their certainties on how India must be governed. White is in favour of "the strong hand" of "rule". Robson says it is important that one should "get hold of India" and not "let India get hold of you".

White's D.T's become very bad and he has to be knocked cold with a rifle butt. When he comes to, they tie him with cord to a camp bed. White is now delirious, imagining things, such as hundred of birds, snipe, rising out of the bed from beside him, with their shrill "cheep! cheep!" and their feathers against his bare skin, and he goes into paroxysms of fear and agony. Seeing this, Robson breaks down abjectly. So the commissioner decides that he must take White out into the open enclosure—the *koddu*—and tie him to a post, so he himself can watch him while also watching over the divers and oysters. Soon hundreds and hundreds of Arab and Tamil divers will arrive from the boats. While he writes up some urgent paperwork into the early hours, the commissioner hears White confessing the history of his life, a very sordid tale of exploitation of both whites and natives all over the colonial East.

Then, about 4 a.m., the first divers arrive. "They burst with a roar into the enclosure: they flung down their sacks of oysters with a crash. The place was full of swaying struggling forms: of men calling to one another in their different tongues: of the smell of the sea." And over their babel come the screams and prayers of White, the madman tied to his post. The divers gather around him, in the light of a few coconut-oil flares in the enclosure. "They seemed to be judging him, weighing him: calm patient eyes of men who watch unastonished the procession of things." And White thinks the blacks are not real but devils from hell sent to plague and torture him. He curses them and howls with fear. "I had to explain to them that the Sahib was not well, that the sun had touched him, that they must move away. They understood. They salaamed quietly, and moved away slowly, dignified." This scene is repeated over and over again in the night as the boats keep coming in.

"As dawn showed grey in the east, he was suddenly shaken by convulsions horrible to see. He screamed for someone to bring him a woman, and, as he screamed, his head fell back: he was dead. I cut the cords quickly in a terror of haste, and covered the horror of the face. Robson was sitting in a heap in his chair. He was sobbing, his face in his hands."

But there is more death to come. The commissioner is told that he is wanted beside the shore. He goes quickly. "A solitary boat stood out black against the sky, just throbbing slowly up and down on the water close in shore. They had a dead Arab on board, he had died suddenly while diving, they wanted my permission to bring the body ashore."

A Jaffnese fisherman casts his net in the shallow lagoon.

Four men wade slowly back from the boat, the body placed high on their shoulders, its feet sticking out, "toes pointing up, very stark over the shoulders of the men in front". The corpse is laid out on the sand. Its bearded face looks very calm, very dignified in the faint light. The dead man's brother sits down on the sand near its head. "I heard him weeping. It was very silent, very cold and still on the shore in the early dawn."

A tall Arab sheik steps forward, the leader of the fishing boat. He lays his hand on the head of the weeping man and speaks to him calmly, eloquently. The commissioner senses what he is saying: that the dead man had lived and worked and had died working, without suffering, as a man should desire to die. "I heard continually the word *khallas*—all is over, finished."

The dawn breaks red in the eastern sky. The sheik stops speaking, motions silently to the four men. They lift the dead man on to their shoulders once more. The small group moves off. Over their shoulders the toes of the dead man again stick up. "Then I moved away too, to make arrangements for White's burial: it had to be done at once."

As in "A Tale Told by Moonlight", at the end the story reverts to England. "There was a silence in the smoking room." The colonel has fallen asleep, the stockjobber tries to appear bored, but the archdeacon is, it would seem, quite discomforted. "Dear me, dear me, past one o'clock"—he gets up. He allows himself one view: "Don't you think you've chosen rather exceptional circumstances, out of the ordinary case?" But the commissioner does not let him off the hook. "There's another Tamil proverb," he says, not too cryptically: "When the cat puts his head into a pot he thinks all is darkness."

* * *

On return to Jaffna in early April, after the pearl fishery, Woolf moved into yet another bungalow, this time on the shore of the lagoon. He shared it with the assistant conservator of forests, G. D. Templer; and they also shared a love of animals. Together they kept something of a menagerie in and around the bungalow: a leopard, five dogs, a monkey and a deer. The leopard had been found in the jungle and given to Templer. As a cub he was very affectionate and playful, but this playfulness became a problem as he acquired adult strength; he could send one of the dogs flying with a swipe of his paw. The servants became frightened, especially after the leopard badly wounded the monkey (which survived only because it was bravely defended by the forest head clerk using a broom)—the only creature for which the leopard showed any animosity. He had to be tethered to a coconut tree; but a week or so later he was found hanged by his rope. Woolf thought it conceivable this was the result of an accident while the leopard was clambering on the tree, but much more likely that his death had been contrived by the clerks and servants in the bungalow. The deer, too—which had a strange passion for tobacco—came to a bad end. Though affectionate with Woolf, he attacked a latrine coolie, wounding him badly in the thigh, and had to be shot.

"I do not know why I am so fond of animals", Woolf commented in *Growing*. "They give me the greatest pleasure both emotionally and intellectually." Lytton Strachey condemned him for being sentimental and Woolf agreed with the criticism "to some extent". But, he explained, he was fascinated by animals' "cosmic strangeness". He had no use for sentimentality about the universe, as found in the human cosmological fantasies of the major religions, and this lack of sentimentality was actually reinforced by knowing animals deeply: "their strange minds, fears, affections—their souls if there is such a thing as a soul" made "nonsense of all philosophies and religions". Some stories in his autobiography—notably his unique confrontation with Nazi storm-troopers in Germany in 1935 while he was in the company of a marmoset (see chapter ten)—confirm Woolf's wisdom about animals.

His new living circumstances seem to have lifted his mood somewhat; his letters became less melancholy. Another reason may have been a relationship with a woman called Gwen, a young English girl who had arrived in Jaffna with her sister and widowed mother. In the evenings, Woolf and Templer would walk on the beach with the two sisters, which was highly improper in Ceylon in 1906. Woolf wondered why her widowed mother allowed it, but he was grateful for the time they spent together on the beach where Gwen would lie "platonically" in his arms. He described her in *Growing* as "pretty, lively, sweet-natured", but was far more explicit in a letter to Strachey: "Among other things I have been in love lately… I am beginning to think it is always degraded being in love: after all 99/100ths of it is always the desire to copulate, otherwise it is only a shadow of itself". Long after Gwen had married and had a family, they continued to exchange occasional letters. In *Growing*, Woolf wrote: "whenever I suddenly get the strong smell of seaweed, as in the town of Worthing, I get a vivid vision of Gwen and the sands of Jaffna."

In August, Woolf was able to get away from Jaffna again. The assistant government agent in Mannar (the district north of the pearl fishery) was taken ill, and Woolf was sent temporarily in his place by Price, the new government agent in Jaffna, who had taken over from Lewis. He was thrilled to be given such a post, not only because it was an unusually responsible one for so inexperienced a civil servant but also because he could escape Jaffna and its society for a while. Mannar was quiet and isolated, a town amidst thick jungle. Woolf was the only white man in a district of 400 square miles.

Woolf spent most of his time there riding around Mannar Island—18 miles long by roughly two miles wide and connected to the mainland by a causeway—dealing with local affairs. At Talaimannar, the outermost tip of the island, he came upon an amazing sight: two mounds of sand purporting to be the graves of Adam and Eve, covered with white sheets. Three Muslims were looking after the graves and invited Woolf to view them. Everyone was delighted by his interest. Luckily, he had the presence of mind to stop Charles just as his dog was about to follow him into the enclosure. "Thus were the graves of our first parents saved by a hair's breadth from defilement by the dog of an infidel." Woolf was disappointed when his month in Mannar came to an end. In a sense, it was a trial run for his final posting in Ceylon, the nearly three years he would spend in the solitude of Hambantota.

Back in Jaffna—having ridden all the way along the coast for the challenge and then through Elephant Pass—Woolf worked closely with the government agent, Ferdinando Hamlyn Price. Although he found Price exceptionally cold and even ruthless, he admired his intelligence and administrative skill, which taught him two useful lessons: to answer 99 out of 100 letters on the day of receipt, and never to use two words where one would do. He also liked Price's wife, who invited him to stay with them at Christmas. In fact a routine developed between Woolf and the Prices, involving lunch, always at 1 p.m. sharp and usually the same food taken with an unsuitable glass of Madeira, dull conversation, and a daily sweepstake where the three of them would guess the previous day's rainfall, with a prize of three rupees. "As the rainfall for day after day between the monsoons was always nil, the routine was nearly always crazy."

In early 1907, while Price happened to be away, Woolf was delighted to learn from a telegram that the post of assistant government agent in Mannar was now vacant and the Government wished him to go there immediately. He decided to wait for Price's return so he could secure his blessing. However Price had other ideas: he wanted to keep Woolf in Jaffna, and he manipulated the situation so that another man was sent to Mannar. Woolf was not surprised; knowing Price, he had half-expected this and was even rather fascinated by the psychological games involved in the manipulation. But it meant, as he told Strachey in March 1907, that "I suppose I shall have another year in this accursed place." In the event, it was only five months before he was ordered to go to Kandy to join Lewis, the previous government agent in Jaffna. Price now had no choice but to acquiesce.

Judging from the letters Woolf wrote while stationed in Jaffna in the years 1905-07, his time there was a generally melancholy experience. Looking back on it in *Growing* over fifty years later, he himself observed that the "passions and prejudices of youth" may have distorted the picture. But the numerous and vivid details in his letters suggest that on the whole the picture he gave was a true one. Life really was tough, monotonous and lonely for a young imperialist in the outstations, most of the time, even if he was not as intelligent and sensitive as Woolf. And there were few women to ameliorate it, other than the wives of senior colleagues—and those there were, were unlikely to suit an intellectual. The boredom and lack of like-minded company drove Woolf to visit prostitutes, not caring if he got syphilis. He told Strachey in a letter that the pleasure of sleeping with prostitutes was grossly exaggerated but desperation had driven him to it. He undoubtedly knew, at first hand, of the feelings of simultaneous attraction and revulsion that he attributes to his character Jessop, who takes his English novelist friend to a brothel in "A Tale Told by Moonlight".

The famous poet Pablo Neruda had a comparable experience while he was in Ceylon as a Chilean diplomat in the late 1920s. Neruda fitted in neither with the British nor with the Ceylonese, as he recalled in his memoirs. While inhabiting a bungalow in an isolated part of Colombo, by the sea at Wellawatte, Neruda suffered from acute loneliness. He became obsessed with a Tamil woman of the pariah caste who emptied his latrine each day. "She was so lovely that, regardless of her humble job, I couldn't get her off my mind. Like a shy jungle animal she belonged to another kind of existence, a different world." Eventually, he led her to his bedroom and raped her:

> One morning, I decided to go all the way. I got a strong grip on her wrist and stared into her eyes. There was no language I could talk with her. Unsmiling, she let herself be led away and was soon naked in my bed. Her waist, so very slim, her full hips, the brimming cups of her breasts made her like one of the thousand-year-old sculptures from the south of India. It was the coming together of a man and a statue. She kept her eyes wide open all the while, completely unresponsive. She was right to despise me. The experience was never repeated.

Neruda's account implies that his loneliness compelled him to rape. But he must certainly also have known—from the scathing way he describes colonial Colombo society in his memoirs—that his power as a white man in Ceylon, and the woman's low-caste status, left her with no option but to submit to him. Indeed Neruda goes so far as to praise Woolf's anti-imperial novel *The Village in the Jungle* as "one of the best books ever published about the Orient" and even to claim—with breathtaking inaccuracy—that Woolf was dismissed from his post in Ceylon and sent back to England because he refused to burn down a Sinhalese peasant's hut on the orders of his imperial bosses! Whatever kind of imperialist or anti-imperialist he may have been, Woolf was never a subscriber to Neruda's version of political correctness.

✱   ✱   ✱

Having seen the town of Jaffna, following Woolf's trail I wanted to visit the rest of the Jaffna district, then the islands off Jaffna, then Mannar district and the area of the pearl fishery, before finally heading back towards Anuradhapura and then on to Kandy.

As we were about to leave, it suddenly rained, which was very unusual for March in Jaffna. The main rainy season there is October to January, when the northeast monsoon arrives. Its effect, in such a dry place, is startling, as Woolf recalls in *Growing*: "you hear it coming from miles away in the breathless evening, the patter patter patter of the rain on the palms and trees, creeping slowly towards one until suddenly the sun is blotted out and with a rush and a roar of wind it is upon one, a deluge of water from heaven." Within hours, the dusty earth would become lush green land, ditches would become rivers, and one would be deafened by a million frogs.

When the shower stopped, we went first to the American mission hospital in Manipay, where Woolf's life was saved after he got typhoid. The hospital is still in use, for outpatients only, and is now financed by the Jaffna Diocese, formerly part of the Church of South India. One of the three large buildings is leased by the UNHCR (United Nations High Commission for Refugees). During the recent civil war the hospital fell on bad times. The Sri Lankan army forced the Indian-trained Dr Ambalavaner and her husband to flee. From 1979-83, they were refugees in Tellippalai. Since the LTTE had their own superb medical facilities somewhere in the area under their control, perhaps in the jungle, the Manipay hospital lay unused for nearly three years. Dr Ambalavaner has come back there now but she told us how difficult it was for her to recruit doctors.

We now headed north to Kankesanturai, to see the place where Woolf had searched for the body of the missing boy for two days in 1905. Stopping for lunch at Chunnakam, I bought two *ulundu vadais* and a banana, while Lucky and Somasiri, our driver, went into a dingy shack for their necessary rice and curry. Afterwards we were disappointed to discover we could not get to Kankesanturai. It is uninhabited, under the control of the navy; the Government keeps careful watch over this section of the north coast, presumably to prevent the landing of arms from India intended for the Tamil Tigers or indeed an invasion.

Driving eastwards along the coast to Point Pedro, we came to Velvettiturai, the birthplace of the LTTE leader Prabhakaran. In this area, in 1985, the Sri Lankan Government launched an operation against Jaffna and its surroundings. The operation was going very well for the army and had even injured Prabhakaran in the leg, when India began to drop food parcels all over the Jaffna district. There were reports that the Indian army was being readied for an invasion of Jaffna. The operation against the Jaffna peninsula was therefore called off and the Sri Lankan army returned to its barracks, amid much resentment at Indian high-handedness.

Still on the way to Point Pedro, we reached Nelliadi. This is in a tobacco-growing area. In Woolf's time, tobacco was second in economic importance only to the palmyra palm, and over ten thousand acres of land were under tobacco; Woolf once mailed a Jaffna tobacco leaf to Saxon Sydney-Turner. The tobacco is coarse and strong-flavoured, better suited to the Asian market than to the European. Today much of it is used for chewing and Jaffna cheroots.

As we approached Point Pedro—a corruption of the Portuguese Puerta das Pedras—I was amazed and delighted to see far less destruction than in Jaffna town. Schoolchildren were smartly turned out in white uniforms and were cycling about. In fact everyone seemed to be on bicycles except us—as in Woolf's day. It was a charming scene with no sense of the insidious danger we had got used to in the town. However I realised that this might have been only a superficial impression.

On the narrow road to Point Pedro there was a sudden crowd, a procession. We saw a white-covered bier, garlands and solemn-looking men and women led by a small group of drummers. It was a funeral. We followed respectfully

Funeral procession on the narrow road to Point Pedro.

for a good twenty minutes until the road widened allowing us to get past. Everyone was very orderly and friendly.

At the coast, the sense of space, the blueness of the sky and the silhouettes of palmyra palms etched against the horizon were overwhelming. At Point Pedro, we saw the stone marking the spot where the Portuguese missionary Baldeus had preached more than three centuries before. Then we drove nearly four miles to Vallipuram, the site of one of the oldest Hindu temples in the Jaffna peninsula. It is set in an amazingly beautiful deserted area of palmyra-fringed dunes and conifers. The isolation made it difficult to imagine that the area was once a capital of the Jaffna region. Woolf cycled there one afternoon, partly on business and partly to escape the town. He too found the area utterly deserted except for the temple set in sand.

Back in Jaffna we felt scorched and aching. At the Old Park Restaurant, Sothi served us a wild boar curry, and we drank it with palmyra arrack made on the island of Delft—which is said to be the best—that I had bought earlier in the day. Though I like palmyra arrack, I prefer the cheaper coconut arrack made from toddy and the sap of the coconut flower in the south of Sri Lanka. Coconut arrack is sweeter and smoother than palmyra arrack, which has a coarser flavour and a slightly stronger aftertaste—which, however, is easily diluted with thirst-quenching *thambili*, or coconut water. Anyway, it was a marvellous meal, spoilt only by a plague of mosquitoes resistant to citronella oil and all other protective sprays and ointments. They attacked everyone, including Sothi, our generous host.

✳   ✳   ✳

The following morning we began island visiting, first to Kayts, then Punkudutivu and Nainativu, and finally to Delft. Our diesel-driven boat, the *Samuthiratheva*, was crewed by two elderly Jaffnese boatmen. One acted as helmsman and controlled a large blue wooden rudder at the stern, the other collected fares from the passengers. He had a clever trick with the currency notes, keeping them separated by denomination in the gaps between the fingers of his left hand, while with his right hand he tore off and issued paper tickets. Men, women and children shielded themselves against the heat of the morning. They were a passive but interesting crowd to observe during the one-hour

One of the oldest Hindu temples in Jaffna district, Vallipuram.

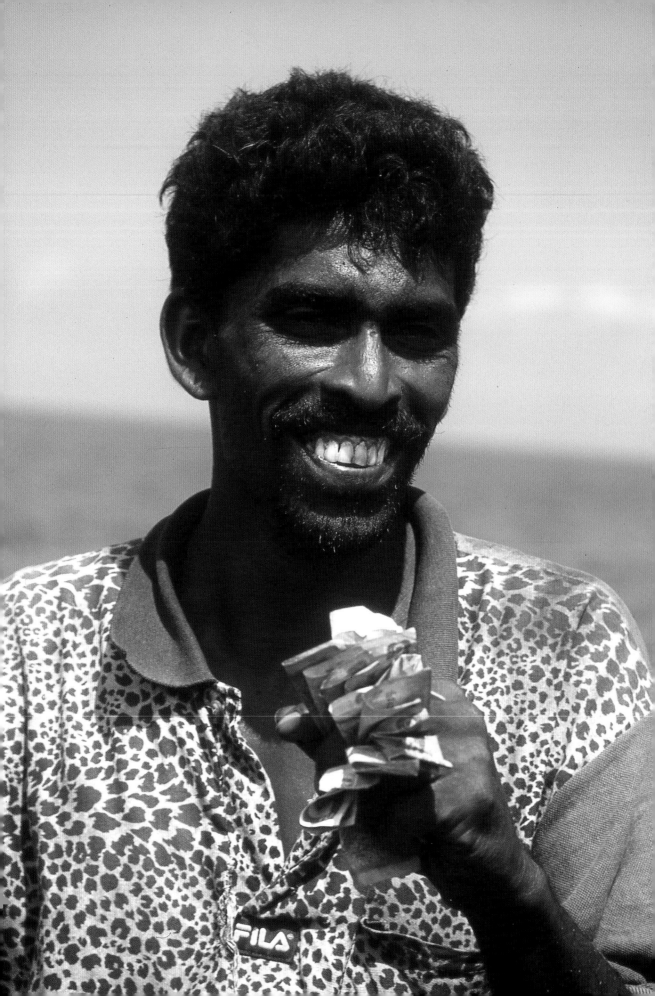

Passengers shield themselves against the heat of the morning on the boat crossing to Delft.

Opposite: Jaffnese boatman collects fares from passengers.

crossing. The sun was behind us; fishermen were out in their boats; sea birds flew gracefully overhead. The fisherman operate in what are called *dhonies*, wooden boats made in Jaffna, usually brightly coloured. Shipbuilding has always been an important craft around Jaffna, particularly on Kayts.

The old Dutch houses on Kayts have been abandoned but there is plenty of habitation. The island is flat, palmyra-fringed, dry and full of wide-open plains with abundant bird life—Brahminy kites, stilts, egrets, cormorants and terns. A lot of fishing goes on, and there are palmyra plantations and prawn farms; and of course the distilling of toddy to make palmyra arrack. There were a fair number of checkpoints and I was pleased that we had Lucky's 'charm' with us. We looked on in amazement as Lucky talked, laughed and exchanged what appeared to be intimacies with Sri Lankan army and government officials who at first looked uneasy but soon fell under Lucky's spell.

From Kayts there is a bridge to Punkudutivu and from there we took a ferry to Nainativu, the island famous for its Nagadipa temple. We joined about a hundred and fifty pilgrims in the small, shallow wooden vessel, some thirty to forty feet long, with planks for its deck and a shoe-flower offering in the bow. The pilgrims stayed below deck. The temple is said to mark the site of the Buddha's sermon on reconciliation which he preached on his second visit to

Lanka. Two *naga* kings had been fighting for the throne for several years and the Buddha settled the dispute, so the kings built the *dagoba* in his honour.

Delft was originally called Pasuthivu or Nedunthivu, which means the island of cows—hence Ilha das Vacas to the Portuguese. The present name is of course Dutch. It stretches seven miles and is inhabited by four or five thousand Tamils, half of them Hindu the other half Christian. Delft is unscathed by the civil war. It is a landscape of barren plains, populated by wild ponies introduced by the Portuguese in the seventeenth century; there are also two kinds of snake, the poisonous viper *Echis carinata* and the harmless sand boa. We travelled about there in a tri-wheeler hired after considerable negotiation; there were no other vehicles except for a solitary bus. By tri-wheeler we visited the remains of a Portuguese fort, positioned at one of the few points on the island with favourable mooring facilities, and saw a remarkable banyan tree with a canopy two hundred feet in diameter. The Quindah tower, which was once a prominent navigational landmark, loomed high on the horizon.

On our way back to Jaffna we stopped at the ferry embarkation point for Karaitivu Island to get a clear view of Fort Hammenhiel. This stands at the

Remains of the Portuguese fort, Delft.

Opposite: Fort Hammenhiel at the entrance to Jaffna lagoon.

Our driver Somasiri Liyanage under a baobab tree on Delft.

Opposite: The ruins of the old fort in Mannar still dominate the causeway and the town.

entrance to Jaffna lagoon, and is built of coral in an unusual circular shape. During the siege of Jaffna in 1658, the fort's wooden rain-water tank was smashed, forcing the thirsty Portuguese to surrender to the Dutch, who considered Hammenhiel to be the key to Jaffna. They built a brick reservoir to strengthen their vital garrison. As we looked on, women collected palmyra leaves from the lagoon in front of the fort, while five young Tamil boys fooled around in the shallow bay.

The islands off the northwest of Sri Lanka—thirteen of them in all—are the most beautiful islands I have ever seen. They seem somehow different from the rest of Sri Lanka. The Tamils there are, I am sure, fed up with war and the army checkpoints ruining their peaceful life of agriculture and fishing, and the beauty of these flat arid pieces of land. When I was on the islands, I could not help feeling that the Tamils and the Sinhalese do not have great differences and certainly do not hate each other. The war seems to be an argument not between two peoples but between the LTTE and the Sri Lankan Government and its army.

* * *

The sun was just coming up as we negotiated our first checkpoint on the way from Jaffna to Mannar, revealing crowds in the dusty streets and army recruits exercising in the dirt at the edge of the road. We were back on the A9 road out of Jaffna, heading for Elephant Pass. There were at least two hundred people queuing, and since I was the only fair-skinned person, I felt distinctly out of place as my UK passport was studied carefully. But we were allowed through soon after 7 a.m. Only ten minutes later, at Pallai, there was an LTTE checkpoint, and here our car was searched thoroughly and efficiently by a young LTTE cadre who issued it with a pass. The examination of our personal documents was much more aggressive; my passport seemed to give the LTTE more trouble on the way out of Jaffna than on the way in. Finally we were let out of the peninsula. There was one more LTTE checkpoint and then a Sri Lankan army checkpoint before we reached Vavuniya.

We had passed through this place on our way to Jaffna. Now we stopped there to see the Vavuniya *kachcheri* Woolf had visited on his return to Ceylon in 1960, a relatively modern building. Sadly, Vavuniya today is notable for its refugee camps—eleven of them, and two more on the way to Mannar. There was considerable fighting in the town during the civil war, as mentioned earlier, and some of those displaced have apparently gone south to form armed gangs still dedicated to the LTTE cause. I visited camp number six at Poonthottam, two miles outside of Vavuniya. It had a well-publicised fire in 2002 when a woman tried to light a stove with kerosene and nearly burnt down the entire camp. I saw a scene of devastation and felt a sense of hopelessness. The refugees had a blank look. Women carried sticks back and forth with an aimless air, while children ran around naked. Some of the refugee shacks were covered with UNHCR sacks.

The sun was high above us as we left Vavuniya driving eastwards towards the coast along the road to Mannar. The air became hotter and drier, and when we passed the mighty Giant's Tank some miles before Mannar, where there is a bird sanctuary, the tank was almost empty. Soon we were on the two-

The refugee camp at Poonthottam near Vavuniya displays a scene of devastation and hopelessness.

mile causeway from the mainland to Mannar Island with shallow sea water on either side.

The old fort in Mannar still dominates the causeway and the town. But, as in Jaffna, the fort has been entirely destroyed, along with the interior of the church. Two or three Mannar police officers, who I initially mistook for Sri Lankan army personnel, seemed to be living in two makeshift rooms in the fort. I tried to find the entrance to the Residency where Woolf based himself during his month in Mannar as assistant government agent in 1906, but nothing was recognisable. The *kachcheri* is in ruins.

We drove the length of the island to Talaimannar. This is where Adam's Bridge begins, the series of islands like stepping stones across the narrow strait between Sri Lanka and India. In the epic *Ramayana*, the stones are laid down by bears and monkeys for Rama and his army to enter Lanka and rescue Sita from Ravana's clutches. The bears and monkeys are assisted by squirrels which roll in the dust at either end of the bridge and then shake their coats until all the gaps between the stones are filled up to make a causeway for the army. The squirrels are tormented so badly by the monkeys that they complain to

Talaimannar was the embarkation point for the ferry to India, which has not operated since 1984.

Rama. He strokes them gently, leaving the black stripes that are still visible on their coats.

Talaimannar was the embarkation point for the ferry to India. Before my teens, in the mid-1940s, I used to take the train from Colombo through Mannar to Talaimannar, then get on the ferry to India. There I caught a steam train up into the Nilgiri Hills where I went to Breeks Memorial School. It was a thrilling time and a thrilling journey. I was accompanied by two older cousins, but they were teenagers. We three were free and irresponsible, but somehow our parents trusted that we would get to our Indian school safely.

The ferry terminal is a sorry sight at the tip of this beautiful peninsula. The ferry has not operated since 1984, and the railway line leading to the terminal has been shattered by the war; there were the usual warnings of land mines with barbed wire surrounding the most dangerous area. I had to watch constantly where I stepped while taking photographs of the Talaimannar lighthouse, which has survived the fighting. The human destruction is emphasised by the beauty of the natural setting, close to the ocean. We noticed eight baobab trees on the way to Talaimannar. I had seen only one baobab earlier, on the island of Delft. They are extraordinary trees, over a thousand years old, and thought to have been brought to Sri Lanka by Arab traders. Some even speculate that the baobabs were used by early Arabs, pre-Islam, as totems for animist worship.

The fort at Mannar was constructed by the Dutch out of the revenue from pearl fishing. Ten miles south of it is a second fortress, at Arippu, which once guarded the oyster banks around Marichchukaddi. The Dutch considered the area so unhealthy that soldiers stayed there for only four months at a time, yet still half of them succumbed to fever. The pearl fishery during the Dutch period was similar to what it was in Woolf's time, though not as systematic. A difference was that a diver was allowed to open oysters and keep any pearl he found in them before the next diver surfaced. There was the same motley crowd of dealers, merchants and criminals present under the Dutch, but there were more fatalities. The pearl fishery continued until 1925, when it was abandoned by the British, and Marichchukaddi reverted to being a mere dot on the map.

We tried to reach Arippu via the coast but the causeway was impassable. Forced to detour inland through Murunkan and then take a road back to the coast, we reached Silavatturai, a place just south of Arippu, where we were surprised to discover a Catholic community. The village, as well as the nearby village of Kondaichchi, was destroyed in the war and both villages are still heavily mined. Our journey there was through a no man's land, possibly controlled by the LTTE but definitely on a road in a state of complete disrepair. We arrived at Arippu fort in time to photograph it against a sun that was beginning to set. It stands in what is virtually a barren wilderness of thorn and scrub jungle; no wonder the poor Dutch soldiers perished in such numbers. Yet it was to Arippu, one day in 1679, that there stumbled a man who would become internationally famous for his exploits as a prisoner in Ceylon, and a source of inspiration for Daniel Defoe's classic of desert island life, *Robinson Crusoe.*

Robert Knox was an ordinary British sailor who had been arrested on the east coast of Ceylon by the soldiers of the Kandyan kingdom in 1660 and who spent 18 years in the captivity of the king. Detailed descriptions of the flora, fauna and society of the Kandyan kingdom, and of other parts of Ceylon, as well as the dramatic story of Knox's eventual escape, are contained in his book, *An Historical Relation of the Island Ceylon,* which he published in London in 1681, almost immediately after his return to England. Knox's book is the fullest available documentation of Ceylon in colonial times. In a recent book, *Knox's Words,*

Arippu fort, ten miles south of Mannar, once guarded the oyster banks at Marichchukaddi.

Richard Boyle analyses the influence of Knox on subsequent authors in Ceylon, and discusses the 26 words of Sri Lankan and regional origin that Knox introduced into the English language.

With darkness coming, it was time for us to leave. From the fort of Arippu, having travelled all the way from Kandy, Knox finally sailed home. I was now going to do his journey in reverse, from Arippu to Kandy.

With the setting sun behind us, we drove in an easterly direction, back along the dry, red, dusty road to Murunkan. We had only twelve miles to go but the road was very bad, and as darkness began to envelop us, the knowledge that this was an LTTE area took on a heavier significance. Night falls very quickly in the tropics. We had a bit of a wild ride to Murunkan and on down to Medawachchiya and Anuradhapura. Rain suddenly hammered down and the only lights I saw were oncoming lorry headlights blinding us and occasional flashes of lighting. Villages were dark shapes at the side of the road. Our driver, Somasiri, had been driving for over twelve hours since leaving Jaffna, yet he was still wide awake—without nerves and full of purpose. We stopped just once, to get some king coconuts and roadside snacks.

All thoroughly exhausted, we flopped at the Tissawewa Rest House in Anuradhapura with the remains of the palmyra arrack. Dinner was especially delicious. My God the food was good! I had fried tilapia again, *pol sambol* (grated coconut and chilli)—very hot, *mallung* (chopped green vegetables), *wambatu* (egg plant), dal and a special *jak* curry made from the fruit of the *jak* tree. This is one of the commonest hardwood trees in Sri Lanka, found nearly everywhere on the island, but it is illegal to cut it down. Dessert was *watalappam*, cashews cooked in coconut milk with jaggery (raw sugar from the *kitul* or coconut palm). Of course it was far too much, too late in the evening, but too tempting to resist. I crawled into bed before 11 p.m., satisfied by an exhilarating day.

✶ ✶ ✶

Breakfast the following morning was wonderful too, as it always is at the Tissawewa Rest House—string hoppers, *pittu* and *roti*. Today we were to travel to Polgahawela, the railway junction south of Kurunegala, where Woolf changed trains on his way from Jaffna to Kandy in 1907. No bone-crunching bullock-cart 'mail coach' for him this time! He simply travelled by train from Jaffna, via Anuradhapura, to Polgahawela and there, after killing time for an hour or two, took the railway line into the hills to Kandy. Unfortunately for me, as with his train journey from Colombo to Anuradhpura in 1905, Woolf could not recall any of his impressions of the journey except for the brief interlude at Polgahawela—a fact that he himself found curious in *Growing*.

His destination, Kandy, is of course one corner of today's "cultural triangle"—the others being Anuradhapura and Polonnaruwa—so I decided to take Woolf's silence about his journey as my cue for a brief detour to Polonnaruwa and Sigiriya in the triangle, places that I have loved visiting since I first returned to Sri Lanka. Regrettably, Woolf does not seem to have visited them during 1904–11, though he must have been aware of their historical significance. So I shall only touch on their marvels here.

Polonnaruwa is in a shimmering lakeside setting by the Parakrama Samudra, also known as the Topa Wewa, which is always busy with fishermen and bathers, pelicans and other bird life. This incredible feat of irrigation was the work of Parakramabahu I, who joined several smaller tanks together in the twelfth century, creating what is almost a sea (*samudra*). Every schoolboy in

Ceylon in my time learned that this 'sea' was thirteen times the size of Colombo harbour.

The ruins at Polonnaruwa are more compact than those at Anuradhapura and for many visitors, including me, they are aesthetically the more exciting. Perhaps most impressive is the palace of Parakramabahu where parts of the red walls still stand ten feet thick and two storeys high, marked with traces of plaster and paintings. There is an impressive courtyard and the peaceful gardens contain a royal bath flanked by gargoyles. However, the best-preserved monuments are the Buddhist temple, the Vatadage ('hall of the relic'), protected by guardian stones featuring a snake king with a cobra, dwarfs with lotus flowers and conch shells; and the giant stone Buddhas, one of them reclining, carved in beautifully grained and banded granite at the Gal Vihara ('cave of the spirits of knowledge').

Like Anuradhapura and Polonnaruwa, Sigiriya was hidden in the jungle for several centuries, having been deserted since the twelfth century, apart from a brief military occupation in the sixteenth and seventeenth centuries. As one approaches the site, there is thick jungle on either side of the road before

Like Anuradhapura and Polonnaruwa, Sigiriya was hidden in the jungle for several centuries. It is surprising that throughout his time in Ceylon Woolf made virtually no mention of the art-historical aspect of the island.

the landscape opens up into lush paddy fields with the rock of Sigiriya towering above them. On top of it are the remains of the palace built by Kassapa I in the fifth century, after he had murdered his father and fled to Sigiriya to escape his avenging brother Mogallana. In 495 AD, after 18 years on the rock, Kassapa decided upon a great battle with the army of Mogallana; he was killed and the palace was taken over by monks who remained there until 1155.

One of the most notable features of Sigiriya are its caves and rock shelters, some of which predate the palace and its gardens. Their ceilings and floors were plastered and painted. Only 21 frescoes have survived and are now almost as famous as the cave paintings of Ajanta in western India. Interpretations of them differ. Some think that the voluptuous women were ladies of the court; others, such as the scholar Ananda Coomaraswamy, consider them to be *apsaras* (celestial nymphs) as the torsos are cut off at the waist by clouds. Beneath the frescoes there is a wall coated in plaster, egg white, lime and beeswax, which gives it an entrancing mirror-like shine.

Now we were almost back on Woolf's railway route at the ancient site of Yapahuwa, not far from the railway line between Anuradhapura and Kurunegala. This fortified rock once matched the impregnable rock at Sigiriya and was a Sinhalese capital like Polonnaruwa, which was briefly taken by Tamil forces in the thirteenth century. A fine temple was built there to house the Buddha's tooth relic, which the Tamils captured in 1285, but all that remains of it is an ornate porch. However, the mixture of artistic influences at Yapahuwa, including Cambodian, is fascinating; the guardian lions even have a distinctly Chinese look.

We stopped for lunch at Kurunegala, whose history was briefly described in chapter two. Then, on to Polgahawela. The main interest here, for me, was the railway station, where Woolf arrived in August 1907, and the rest house, where he briefly passed some time alone in a long chair on the verandah waiting for his train, and where we decided to stay overnight before catching our train.

Woolf wrote magically of Polgahawela:

> What a soft liquid gentle Sinhala word this—Field of Coconuts—was when one compared it with Tamil places like Kangesanturai and Kodikanam! And the place itself, the air, the trees, the sky itself were as different from those that I had left a few hours ago as the Sinhala language from the Tamil. I had left behind me the bareness, austerity,

At Scouts' Hill, British army engineers blasted through rock to build the road to Kandy in the 1820s.

burning dryness of the sands of Jaffna and now I was bathed, embraced by the soft, warm, damp, luscious luxuriance of the tropics ... As I lay back in my chair and looked up into the sky through the great trees, I saw through the branches the brilliant glittering stars, and all round the branches and the changing leaves were hundreds of tiny little brilliant glittering stars weaving a continually moving pattern—hundreds of fireflies. My two-and-a-half years in Jaffna, the Prices, Gwen and the seaweedy sands on the shore, my bungalow on the wall of the fort—all this seemed already to have faded away into a long-forgotten dream.

After dinner I went out to the verandah and sat there in the dark, trying to go back a hundred years and imagine myself as Woolf, at least for a minute or two.

Woolf travelled to Kandy on the train at night, which was a real loss since the line is considered one of the world's most scenic mountain routes, though of course he made up for this later in travelling back and forth by train from Kandy to Colombo. We travelled in the morning, catching the train from Colombo at 7.30 a.m. I took a seat on the right-hand side of the train, said to offer the best views. I suppose I was being wildly optimistic but I was hoping to see some talipot palms in blossom. This happens only once in the palm's lifetime, which may be a hundred years or more, and I was out of luck.

At Rambukkana, the train began its slow climb and the landscape became increasingly dramatic. During Woolf's day, it was possible to look out of the window and see both the front and the rear of the train, because the curves were so sharp. In *Ceylon along the Rail Track*, Woolf's contemporary Henry Cave offers this effusive description of the views:

> At one moment, on the edge of a sheer precipice, we are gazing downwards some thousand feet below; at another we are looking upwards at a mighty crag a thousand feet above; from the curves by which we climb the mountain sides fresh views appear at every turn; far-reaching valleys edged by the soft blue ranges of distant mountains and filled with luxuriant masses of dense forest, relieved here and there by the vivid green terraces of rice fields; cascades of lovely flowering creepers, hanging in festoons from tree to tree and from crag to crag; above and below deep ravines and foaming waterfalls dashing their spray into mist as it falls into the verdurous abyss; fresh mountain peaks appearing in ever-changing grouping as we gently wind along the steep gradients.

At Allagalla, halfway up, the terrain is still precipitous, but it is covered by tea plantations. The elevation is now nearly four thousand feet. A little further along and we were at Scouts' Hill, where British army engineers blasted through rock to build the road to Kandy in the 1820s. At the time there was said to have been an old prophecy that whoever managed to penetrate the rock and make a road to Kandy would gain the kingdom as his reward. This road, and then the railway, were what enabled the British Government finally to subdue the entire island under the *Pax Britannica*.

One hour from Polgahawela, at about 8.30 a.m., the train pulled into Kandy station. Here, for about a year, Woolf would encounter colonial Ceylon at its most imperialist: a unique mixture of British pomp and circumstance and Sinhalese feudal life and ceremony.

The dramatic train journey to Kandy sometimes left passengers on the edge of a sheer precipice, gazing downwards some thousand feet below.

5

Kandy

I certainly, all through my time in Ceylon, enjoyed my position and the flattery of being the great man and the father of the people. That was why, as time went on, I became more and more ambivalent, politically schizophrenic, an anti-imperialist who enjoyed the fleshpots of imperialism, loved the subject peoples and their way of life, and knew from the inside how evil the system was beneath the surface for ordinary men and women.

LEONARD WOOLF, *Growing*

KANDY IS UNIQUE in the history of Sri Lanka for being the last part of the island to have fallen under European domination. The kingdom resisted annexation for some three hundred years after the first arrival of the Portuguese in Ceylon, only finally losing its independence in 1815 to the British, as we know. Although Ceylon's Portuguese and Dutch rulers tried on numerous occasions to subdue Kandy, each time its Sinhalese ruler successfully repulsed the invaders using guerrilla tactics. The attacking armies could not wage a victorious war in the rugged, malarial country around this city of hills, in which a lack of any good roads prevented their troops from being adequately supplied.

When the British took over the administration of Ceylon from the Dutch East India Company in 1796, they were keen to develop trading; and this meant controlling Kandy. For many years they had been sending 'embassies' to Kandy, such as that of John Pybus in 1762, but without obtaining any concessions. They had also used John D'Oyly, an expert in Kandyan affairs, to create a network of spies and forge links with those among the Kandyan aristocracy

Kandy is Sri Lanka's second largest city and was the last part of the island to fall under European domination in 1815.

Above: Sir Robert Brownrigg, governor of Ceylon.

Below: Sri Vikrama Rajasinha, the last king of Kandy.

who opposed their king, Sri Vikrama Rajasinha, a ruler with a reputation for tyranny and cruelty. Several times, his noblemen had risen against him, but Rajasinha had crushed each rebellion. He executed the conspirators, including his prime minister, which only served to increase the opposition and to foster secret negotiations with the British. When a new prime minister, Ahalepola, tried to revolt, he was forced to flee Kandy into British territory, abandoning his family to be murdered by Rajasinha. According to one account, Ahalepola's children were beheaded and their mother forced to pound their heads in a rice mortar before she herself was drowned in Kandy's Bogambara tank along with her sister.

Foolishly, Rajasinha extended his atrocities beyond his own people to include the British. Always fearful of spies, he captured a group of British merchants, had them mutilated, and sent them back to Colombo with the body parts strung around their necks. Out of the ten men, nine are said to have died on the road to Colombo, each having had his nose, right ear and right arm cut off. The British governor, Sir Robert Brownrigg, described this act as a "wanton, arbitrary, and barbarous piece of cruelty". To Brownrigg it was ample reason for war. However, the governor was subject to dictates from London, where the Government opposed aggressive action unless

Old Kandy.

British territory had been invaded.

In due course, Rajasinha's men chased a group of insurgents out of Kandyan territory. This was the excuse Brownrigg had been waiting for. He chose to view the incident as an invasion of British territory and in January 1815, assisted by the disaffected Ahalepola, he proclaimed that "war was being undertaken on behalf of the oppressed Kandyan people". It was more of an invasion than a war, since Rajasinha's troops were in collusion with the British, and it was over in 40 days. The king had fled by the time British troops arrived in his city, but he was captured and exiled to Vellore in India, where he was kept in style until his death in 1832.

The British takeover was not popular in Kandy, however. The Kandyan people had not supported any of the earlier abortive rebellions against their king, and they were not enthusiastic about changing their ruler. K. M. de Silva's

A *History of Sri Lanka* describes the fall of Kandy in 1815 as "a conspiracy hatched by the aristocracy against a ruler whose government was a threat to their interests as a social group; but the conspiracy achieved its purpose only because the British saw in it an opportunity to achieve their own objectives." Kandyans at all levels of society soon missed their indigenous monarchy. According to Lennox Mills in *Ceylon under British Rule*, "Like all Kandyans the nobles were strongly attached to the institution of monarchy, and deeply resented its disappearance. The distant court of George III was no substitute for the court of a visible monarch where they had enjoyed elaborate ceremonial, unbounded flattery, and the opportunity to display their magnificence." As Governor Brownrigg warned the Colonial Office in London some months after the takeover in 1815, the whole nation "wanted a king whom they could see, and before whom they could prostrate and obtain summary justice." They disliked the British as foreign conquerors: "they made no complaint of oppression or misrule, contenting themselves with expressing a wish that we should leave the country."

By 1817, there was the distinct possibility of a rebellion. A year later, the British power in Kandy and its provinces was severely threatened. Ahalepola was involved in the uprising, and he was seized by the British and kept in custody in Colombo. The Kandyans adopted the guerrilla tactics that had proved so successful in the past. The British responded by starving and terrorising villages suspected of harbouring guerrillas. In October 1818, with its morale in tatters and divisions among its leaders, the Kandyan rebellion collapsed.

Part of it had been masterminded by a bogus prince, whose followers used the unrest to remove the famous tooth relic of the Buddha from its temple, the Dalada Maligawa (the Temple of the Tooth), in the centre of Kandy. The British exposed the prince and recovered the tooth relic, which was a definite asset in trying to win over the Kandyans following the rebellion. They also slightly modified the structure of the civil service, which helped the process of Kandyan adjustment after 1818. The number of government agents was increased, allegedly to bring the Government closer to the people but really to remove any administrative power from the Kandyan noblemen and scotch another uprising. In addition, wherever possible, the administrative structure incorporated existing feudal and caste hierarchies and employed only Sinhalese headmen to liaise with the people. (This policy became a dogma: a Colonial Office report of 1881 stated that it was "absolutely essential . . . that

Woolf was always more interested in Sinhalese life than in the Tamils on the tea estates.

the headman ... be a pure Sinhalese of good family. A Burgher or a Jaffna Tamil ... would be utterly unable to fulfil his duties".) A unified civil service for the entire island was established in 1832, and by 1840 Kandy was fully absorbed under the British crown, as the rest of Ceylon had been after the defeat of the Dutch in 1796. In the 1820s, the building of roads began in earnest, and during the middle of the century Kandy was established as a centre of plantation agriculture. By the end of the century, the British were widely regarded as the beneficent saviours of Kandy. For example, an American writer, John Fletcher Hurst, wrote of Kandy in 1890:

> Here are tall people, the giants of this isle of dreams and history...Their spears have been very weavers' beams. The English would not be here today, with their good rule and even justice, but for the cruelty of the native king, whom the wise native chiefs asked English help to rid them of. The English were waiting. They are heroes of an opportunity. Here they stayed, and are now as firm here as the granite sides of the isle itself.

* * *

I was born in Kandy in 1933. The Ondaatjes have an old link with the city—the Ondaatje family once owned a large house there and an Ondaatje was involved in the construction of the magnificent botanical gardens outside the city at Peradeniya. However I did not return there until my father moved our family to a tea estate at Pelmadulla in the foothills. We children spent most of our time on the estate but my father made frequent trips to Kandy and occasionally we went with him. Once—this is a notorious story in the family—after a heated, alcohol-fuelled argument with my mother, my father stormed out of Kandy's Queens Hotel and threw himself in front of the principal elephant of the annual Kandy Perahera procession, bringing it to an abrupt halt. (This famous festival offers quite a spectacle, as well as being of complex sociological significance, as explained by H. L. Seniviratne. I am surprised that Woolf, in his chapter on Kandy in *Growing*, does not describe the festival, but then he ignores too, as already remarked, the glories of the "cultural triangle".)

Like my father, I always stay at the Queens Hotel when in Kandy. In his youth, and especially before that, when Woolf was in Kandy, the Queens was a grand hotel—the most popular place for those seeking a break from the heat and grind of Colombo. Today's hotel is very run down and only two floors are available to guests. Yet there is still something special about staying there. On my latest visit I was awoken at 5 a.m. by tom-tom drumming from the nearby Temple of the Tooth for the early-morning puja. Kandy is one of those towns with charm, an atmosphere that cannot quite be defined. The population is now over two hundred thousand, rather than the thirty thousand inhabitants of 1910. Yet it has a calm, with its sloping tile roofs, despite the clamour of its market and the hive of commercial activity along the road to Peradeniya. Afternoons in Kandy have a ghostly quality, while the evenings are luminous and lively, except for the dark, sleepy water of the lake that lies somewhere beyond the busy vendors in front of the Queens Hotel.

On his arrival in Kandy in 1907, Woolf stayed very near the Queens in a dark bungalow behind the Temple of the Tooth. I tried to locate the place and decided it was probably one of two extant buildings, either Marlborough House or Queens Chamber. Woolf shared the house with Tyrrell, the superintendent of police, who became Sir Francis Graeme Tyrrell, and who turned out to be "far the best stable companion" during the many months Woolf spent living with others while in Ceylon. Even so, he would have preferred to live alone; but European life in Kandy was geared to the opposite of solitude: a non-stop whirl of club, tennis matches and dinners, all of which adhered to the etiquette required by an imperialist society. The ritual was a good deal more serious in Kandy than in Jaffna because it involved not only top civil servants but also planters, army officers and visitors from Colombo, as well as their wives, sisters and daughters.

When Tyrrell went home on leave at the end of the year, Woolf's own sister Bella arrived and stayed in the bungalow with her brother until the following August when he was posted away from Kandy to Hambantota. Bella had some literary talent, and in due course wrote a number of books on Ceylon, including the first pocket guidebook to the island and two children's books, *The Twins in Ceylon* and *More about the Twins in Ceylon*, which were beautifully illustrated. In 1910, she married Robert Lock, the assistant director of the Peradeniya gardens and settled in Ceylon. Some years after his death in 1915, she married her brother's former colleague, Southorn, who went on to be colonial secretary in Hong Kong and, after being knighted, governor of the Gambia. Bella's sociability in Kandy undoubtedly aided her brother's career in Ceylon, although he regretted not having more time to himself. Of all his family, Bella was the closest to him and "until his marriage she was the person in whom he most fully confided", notes Frederic Spotts, the editor of Woolf's letters.

Bella Woolf arrived in Kandy in 1907 and shared a house with her brother until he was posted to Hambantota the following year.

* * *

As was so often the case in the heyday of empire, the focal point of British social life was the club. The Kandy Club was "a symbol and centre of British imperialism", wrote Woolf in his memoirs, in which the social elite congregated

The old Kandy Club, a symbol and centre of British imperialism.

in a 'public school' atmosphere to drink, play bridge, dine and play billiards. He remembered his first night there only too well, as he found himself once again having to adjust, after the relative isolation of Jaffna, to the need to mask his true feelings under a social carapace. He failed to bid on a hand of bridge and was humiliated by a cutting remark from his partner, a cantankerous old judge: "I suppose, Woolf, in Jaffna you don't bid diamonds unless you have thirteen of them." It was a trivial incident—and Woolf played the next hand extremely well—but somehow it must have hurt a lot since he chose to retell it more than fifty years later and to comment: "how much deeper pain goes than pleasure, and unkindness than kindness". Not long after, he told Lytton Strachey in a letter: "For five days I have walked a wondering ghost among it all. A seal of silence has fallen on my lips and I am unable to talk a word to a soul." Yet despite his feelings of social inadequacy, his protestations that he was not a naturally good mixer, Woolf remained adept at learning to be accepted as a 'good fellow'. So successful was he with his superiors that he was promoted and left Kandy after only a year.

An event that greatly helped his colonial career was his skilful handling of a visit to Kandy by the Empress Eugénie of France. The government agent was away, allowing Woolf to step into a more senior position and prove himself. He

Empress Eugénie of France.

met the empress at the station and escorted her at a painfully slow pace—she was more than eighty years old—to a carriage, which transferred her to the governor's residence, the luxurious King's Pavilion. (This had been built by the governor from 1824–31, Sir Edward Barnes—responsible for major road-building—who spent so lavishly on his own comfort that he got into trouble with the Colonial Office.) Meanwhile he carried on so appropriate a diplomatic

The Dalada Maligawa in Kandy houses the sacred tooth relic of the Buddha.

conversation with the empress's party and handled the whole arrival with such ease that he was mistaken for the government agent and invited to tea. Woolf found the etiquette of his situation rather absurd, as the empress had in fact 'retired' 37 years previously; he could not bring himself to bow and kiss her hand as required by protocol, and only shook it. He also noted in his memoirs that although she was said to have been beautiful when young, he thought her "positively ugly". Fortunately her appearance was compensated by an affable nature and an interest in history and religion. She expressed a desire to view the tooth relic of the Buddha, and this request was one that Woolf was well placed to grant.

The tooth relic has been kept in Kandy since the late sixteenth century, following its somewhat turbulent earlier history. Tradition says that it was brought to Sri Lanka from India in the fourth century AD. In 1284, Kublai Khan despatched a mission to the island to capture it, but failed. Around the 14th century, Indians from the Malabar coast recaptured it and took it back to India, but it was soon recovered by a Sinhalese king. In 1405, the Chinese admiral

Cheng-ho tried to capture it, failed, but returned five years later and seized a Sinhalese king, his queen and some nobles and took them back to China. Then in 1560, the relic was said to have been taken to Goa by the Portuguese and publicly burnt by the Catholic archbishop in the presence of the viceroy of India. But the Sinhalese rejected this claim, saying that the Portuguese had been fobbed off with a fake. Even in our own time, the tooth relic has attracted trouble, when its temple, the Dalada Maligawa, was bombed by the Tamil Tigers in 1998 and suffered considerable damage.

In Woolf's time, the shrine housing the tooth had to be guarded by both the British and the Sinhalese to ensure its safety. Moreover the British were aware of a Kandyan belief that whoever was in possession of the tooth relic was the ruler of Kandy. There were two keys required to open the shrine: one held by the guardian of the temple and the other by the government agent, of which Woolf was the custodian. It was generally opened only for royal visitors, for Burmese and other pilgrims on certain occasions, and annually for the Kandy Perahera, when the tooth relic is still paraded on the back of an elephant. Woolf, along with the Kandyan chief, the Diyawadana Nilame, opened the shrine thrice during his tenure as the representative of the government agent in 1907–08, one of the occasions being for the Perahera.

His sister Bella, in her guidebook to Ceylon, colourfully evokes the aura of the shrine when it was opened for pilgrims:

> The courtyard is crammed with worshippers of all ages, bearing offerings in their hands, leaves of young coconut, scent, flowers, fruit. As the door opens, they surge up the dark and narrow stairway to the silver and ivory doors behind which lies the tooth.
>
> The doors are opened and a flood of hot heavy scented air pours out. The golden *karandua* or outer casket of the tooth stands revealed dimly behind gilded bars. In the weird uncertain light of candles in golden candelabra the yellow-robed priests move to and fro. The tooth is enclosed in five *karanduas* and slowly and solemnly each is removed in turn; some of them are encrusted with rubies, emeralds and diamonds.
>
> At last the great moment approaches. The last *karandua* is removed— in folds of red silk lies the wondrous relic—the centre point of the faith

Overleaf: The feudalism of the Kandyans seemed purer to Woolf than the imperialism of the British.

159

of millions. It is a shock to see a tooth of discoloured ivory at least three inches long—unlike any human tooth ever known. The priest sets it in a golden lotus—the temple *korala* gives a sharp cry—the tom-toms and conches and pipes blare out—the kneeling worshippers, some with tears streaming down their faces, stretch out their hands in adoration.

On this particular occasion, with his royal visitor, the Empress Eugénie, Woolf was also accompanied by Sir Hugh Clifford, the colonial secretary and acting governor of Ceylon. Clifford happened to be in Kandy, had never seen the tooth relic and was interested to join the group. "It all passed off extremely well ... The empress was suitably impressed. I earned a good deal of unearned kudos from the colonial secretary." But Woolf was not receptive to the religious reverence surrounding the tooth relic and noted matter-of-factly in *Growing*: "If my memory is correct, it is a canine tooth, about three inches long and curved." It put him in mind of the teeth of Sinhalese devils (*yakku*), which appear in sculpture and mural paintings with projecting canine teeth curved upwards, and which form an affecting folk-religious element in Woolf's novel, *The Village in the Jungle* (see chapter seven).

Tooth relic worship apart, the year spent in Kandy was the beginning of Woolf's strong affection for the Sinhalese as people. He came to admire them both for their culture and their religion, declaring that "if one must have a religion, Buddhism seems to me superior to all other religions." He thought Buddhist ceremonies civilised and often went to the Dalada Maligawa on *poya* (full moon) days to witness the offerings of flowers and listen to the priest's readings.

The requirement that Ceylon civil servants learn both Tamil and Sinhala led Woolf to seek lessons from a Buddhist priest named Gunaratana, who became a friend. They would spend quiet evenings on the verandah at the Oriental Library, overlooking the lake, in order to discuss Buddhism. It was a welcome escape from the rigours of imperial life, as well as an insight into another religion and an opportunity to engage in the kind of intellectual discussion Woolf appreciated. Gunaratana's explanation of Buddhism as being more of a philosophy than a faith appealed to Woolf, as did the absence of the "anthropomorphic and theological nonsense which encrusts other religions." Also appealing was the way in which Buddhists liked to withdraw into solitude and contemplation. Woolf had experienced the joy of this on his brief trip to

Mannar when he was stationed in Jaffna. Consciously or subconsciously, Buddhist ideas now prepared him for the pleasures of isolation he was to experience in Hambantota, although the Buddhist idea of a formal retreat in a temple never attracted him.

Gunaratana was critical of how Buddhism was frequently taught and practised in a form that was not pure and idealistic; he disapproved of the superstition and devil worship so common in religious ceremonies in Ceylon. Woolf naturally sympathised with his view, but he was more indulgent than Gunaratana, accepting that Buddhism "recognises that different people must be given different beliefs, a different Buddhism, according to the stage of spiritual development attained by them." His view chimes with that of an expert in Buddhist philosophy, Ediriwira Sarachchandra, in his book *The Folk Drama of Ceylon*:

> The folk religion is based on a belief in supernatural beings and the efficacy of prayer and ritual. Strictly there is no place in Buddhism for such beliefs. But Buddhism had to adapt itself, from being an individualistic and monastic creed, to a religion serving the needs of an organised lay community. What it did in Ceylon, was, therefore, to allow the people to go on with their usual practices, which they found useful to them in their daily life, and to make them turn to Buddhism for guidance in moral conduct and in matters concerning man's final destiny and the after-life.

Indeed, this last sentence by Sarachchandra neatly encapsulates Woolf's interpretation of Buddhism in the final, overtly philosophical section of *The Village in the Jungle*.

Mostly, though, Buddhist priests looked after the worldly interests of their communities and of themselves, as Woolf would experience in Hambantota. Yet even under these circumstances he thought there was a gentleness and humanity visible in Buddhism, which he did not find in other religions. In *Growing*, he associates Roman Catholicism with "that horrible insistence upon sin and crucifixion"; Islam is described as "too hard, formal, and hostile to the infidel"; while Hinduism comes off worst with "the multiplicity of its florid gods, their grotesque images, the ugly exuberance of the temples, the horrible juggernaut processions with the terrible retinue of fakirs, saniyasis, and beggars"—the very aspects of Hinduism which of course Buddhism had rejected. To some extent Woolf revised this damning view of Hinduism when he revisited Ceylon in 1960 and had the symbolism explained to him by Sir Kanthaiah Vaithianathan. But he was not truly convinced:

> Like the esoteric Buddhism of my friend the priest Gunaratana, this esoteric Hinduism was a metaphysic rather than a religion. Yet it seemed to me inferior to Gunaratana's Buddhism, because it was a tiresome symbolism and therefore had never completely disentangled itself from the crude, uncivilised superstition connected with the gods and goddesses and their ceremonies.

But he felt obliged to admit that Gunaratana was "the only real Buddhist whom I met in Ceylon".

⋆   ⋆   ⋆

Most of Woolf's time in Kandy was necessarily spent in white society—or at least in a European-style setting. He worked hard at his job, telling Strachey: "I am enmeshed and immersed in it so much that sometimes I think I shall just bury myself in it and never come back again." His working day began at 6.30 a.m. with early tea on the verandah, a time when "everything in Kandy sparkles, including the air." He would sort through letters, then go to the *kachcheri* close to his bungalow (the building is now occupied by the district court of Kandy). There he worked from 7 a.m. until 12 p.m., then from 1 p.m. until at least 5 p.m.

The boundaries between work and leisure were often vanishingly small. He recalled dining with a judge of the Supreme Court and his family, and having to be on his best behaviour as he had recently been reprimanded for not attending the opening of the assizes. Worse, on this particular evening he was suffering from a strange cold which produced serious giddiness. Afraid of being thought drunk he endured the evening by forcing himself to sit bolt upright. But when he left the house in relief and had to negotiate a precipitous flight of steps, he could not avoid falling down the last few. Luckily the only witness was a rickshaw boy. From this incident, which he tells in *Growing*, we can see how important Woolf felt it was that he should keep up appearances in Kandy.

In his first few months there he hardly read a book—a remarkable abstinence for an intellectual like him—and instead immersed himself in socially approved sporting activities. In addition to tennis he played squash with the

Elephants bathing in the Mahaweli Ganga near Kandy.

superintendent of police and hockey with a Punjabi Hindu regiment. He was keenly aware of cultural differences in hockey: "they played like demons and some of them were very good, but they got frantically excited and, when they lost their tempers, dangerous." There were also Muslim teams and mixed teams, and once a year a tournament. Sometimes fights broke out mid-game. Woolf witnessed a persistent attack by a Punjabi teammate against an opposing Eurasian planter whom the Punjabi repeatedly cracked on the shins. The Eurasian finally lost his temper and there was a fight, to the evident satisfaction of the Punjabi. Woolf described this as a 'racial' incident. Maybe so, but it seems as likely that it was the result of a colonised people's regarding the hockey pitch as a place where they could vent their frustrations in a way that did not sit comfortably with the British mythology of sportsmanship. At any rate, the incident provides a sharp picture of tensions in imperial Ceylon—

whereas the following story is more revealing about Woolf as an individual.

For a few weeks around November 1907, he spent nearly every evening with a young man called Smith and two sisters, the daughters of a planter, whom Woolf called Ethel and Rachel Robinson in *Growing* (their real surname was Jowitt). Smith was very keen on Ethel and asked Woolf to accompany him on their evening rides so that he could be alone with her while Woolf stayed with Rachel, and Woolf reluctantly agreed. They rode in the unspoilt hills above Kandy, admiring the view of the great lake and the city below them, the terraced rice fields, the distant villages and the mountain peaks—all "extraordinarily romantic". In an era that regarded women as existing for leisure and pleasure after the working day, many of the most attractive drives, rides and walks had been named after the wives of the governors of Ceylon: Lady Blake's Drive, Lady Horton's Walk, Lady Longden's Drive, and so on. The governors, and Queen Victoria, naturally had the major roads of Kandy named after them.

Woolf was surprised to discover that he became very fond of the 19-year-old Rachel. In his letters to Strachey he wrote that, "it so happens that I am really in love with someone who is in love with me. It is not however pleasant because it is pretty degrading, I suppose, to be in love with practically a schoolgirl." Although this seems an exaggeration about her age, especially for 1907, the gap of eight years between them obviously mattered to Woolf.

What did he mean by saying that his feelings were "degrading"? Possibly that they were not altogether genuine or mainly physical (as witness his earlier comment from Jaffna on Gwen): in *Growing* he wrote that he was not in love with Rachel, but "liked her very much and reached the maximum of intimacy with her allowed by the extraordinary etiquette and reticiencies of the age." To Strachey he also wrote of this relationship that "sometimes I think really I am only in love with silly intrigue and controlling a situation, and sometimes merely with two big cow eyes which could never understand anything which one said and look as if they understood everything that has ever been, is or will be." While such comments have led some critics to condemn Woolf outright as a male chauvinist, it is important to place them in the context of their age, a century ago, before we can really understand him.

In *Growing*, written when he was nearly eighty, he expanded on how in his youth he was very attracted to what he called "the undiluted female mind". He distinguished it from the minds of great women such as Virginia Woolf and Jane Austen, claiming that in those days most women had such a mind, the characteristics of which were to be un-intellectual, undistinguished and un-introspective. But he believed this undiluted female mind also to be "gentler, more sensitive, more civilised" than that of men, though it was only possible to discern these qualities by listening carefully to women.

Of course Woolf knew that few women received the same education as men in the early twentieth century—even the exceptionally intelligent Virginia Stephen, whom he married, had been educated at home. Given how few such educated women there were in England, and how few of even his male colleagues in Ceylon were interested in the life of the mind, it becomes less surprising that Woolf was critical of Rachel. One of his most persistent frustrations in Ceylon was that he did not meet like-minded people with whom he could talk at an intellectual level—whether male or female. His criticisms of the English men in Ceylon were actually much sharper than his comments on the women.

Woolf lost contact with Rachel for about two years, by which time he was in charge of the Hambantota district. He had travelled into the hills again for a meeting and found himself staying very close to her father's tea estate; when her mother wrote and invited him to stay for two days, he decided to visit. His favourite sister Bella had visited the estate earlier and told him that Rachel's parents spoke so kindly of him she was sure they wanted him for a son-in-law. Once again he went riding with Rachel, revelling in the female company he had been starved of, and relishing the coolness and beauty of the hills after the aridity of Hambantota. Before dinner on his last evening, they went for a walk together on the estate. As he remembered in *Growing*:

> We had slipped into a long silence and suddenly the narrow path turned round a great rock and brought us out on to a broad ledge with a sheer drop thousands of feet down to the sea level and the low country, and with a superb, terrific view over the miles and miles of jungle to, in the dim distance, the line of the sea and the coast—and somewhere there Hambantota and my bungalow. A strange, painful feeling came over me. I felt as if somehow I had been taken up into this high mountain and was being shown all the kingdoms of the earth and was being tempted, but the temptation was not the kingdom of the earth below, but in the girl beside me.

However he remained silent, and eventually the two of them turned away and returned to the house where Rachel's parents were waiting, and he spent "a very uncomfortable evening". Early the following morning he left them on his bicycle, and coasted straight down the mountainside, "mile after mile down through the deliciously cool fresh mountain scenery", until he reached the hot, dry jungles of his beloved district.

He saw the family only once or twice more in his life, though he occasionally corresponded with Rachel even after she married. His reluctance to propose to her that evening may, at least in part, have been because of the constraints imposed on personal relationships by the civil service; a junior civil servant was moved from a posting if he became engaged. As Woolf told Strachey while in Kandy, "According to the Ceylon Govt you may copulate but you must not marry or become engaged." His sister advised him: "You'd better marry as soon as you have got into a class where the Govt. doesn't faint at matrimonial intentions." But Bella admitted that there were more significant difficulties in marrying than his job: "I can't think of any girl who would suit you in Ceylon. You need a very special girl and if you don't find her you'd better steer clear of matrimony… If you marry a weak character you'll squash her. You *must* marry someone who can hold her own with you and yet be good-tempered."

* * *

Woolf's friendship with a planter's daughter must have given him insights into the world of the tea estates which his official contacts with planters and their estate workers would not have done. Most of this contact concerned the sale of crown land for the development of the estates. He found it very dull work, but he knew that since the main crop in Kandy was tea, and tea was a national obsession at home, the work was undoubtedly important.

The extraordinary history of tea is inextricably linked with Ceylon's history as a British colony. The British obsession with the drink began when a Portuguese princess, Catherine of Braganza, married Charles II of England in 1662. Her impressive dowry included £500,000 in cash to pay off Charles's debts, rights for Britain to trade in the East, and some land on the coast of western India that would become the great port of Bombay. She also brought along a large chest of tea since she was a tea addict, and the drink soon became fashionable, its popularity spreading from the court to the middle class and thence to the rest of British society. However it was not until the mid-eighteenth century that the British demand for tea became almost insatiable:

The extraordinary history of tea is inextricably linked with Ceylon's history as a British colony.

13,082 pounds of tea were imported in 1699, nearly five million pounds in 1750. High government duties led to smuggling, and a whole system of organised crime, often vicious, developed around tea—as has happened today with illegal drugs. To address this problem, in 1784 William Pitt the Younger slashed the tea tax from 119 per cent to 12.5 per cent while massively increasing the window tax in compensation for the lost government revenue. The smuggling of tea into Britain ceased virtually overnight.

At this time, the end of the eighteenth century, British tea still came from China, but in the century to come India and Ceylon became the main source of supply. The huge success of tea in Ceylon makes it easy to forget that the original crop grown there was coffee. Civil servants, suffering from the effects of the Colebrooke report of 1832, which reduced their salaries and removed their pensions, were encouraged by the Government to invest in coffee growing to make a decent income. At the same time the calibre of civil servants dropped considerably and official duties were neglected. But by the 1850s, the increase in government revenue from the success of coffee had produced a surplus which allowed higher salaries and pensions to be reintroduced on condition that civil servants no longer actively participated in planting. In the second half of the century, much of the development of the Ceylon civil service was directly linked to the plantation economy: first that of coffee, then that of tea. Earlier, district judges had usually been civil servants with little or no legal training, which led to complaints from colonists and Burghers in the plantation areas. Their pressure led to a ruling in 1872 that all district judges must be trained barristers—but only in Colombo and Kandy, the main provinces with plantations. Even the impressive repair of Ceylon's ancient irrigation system in the late nineteenth century was in part driven by the needs of the plantation economy, for immigrant plantation workers from India needed to eat rice, which could be grown in Ceylon with the help of the ancient irrigation systems rather than having to be imported from south India.

In the 1870s, however, the coffee plantations were wiped out by a leaf disease. Tea cultivation now took over entirely. Although development was slow for a while as a result of the collapse of the coffee trade, by 1900, 384,000 acres of Ceylon were under tea—almost four times the acreage in 1885—and 150 million pounds of tea were exported, an incredible amount for an island the size of Ceylon. Some 15 per cent of this was owned by one man, Sir Thomas Lipton, and his advertising campaigns further increased the demand for tea.

Tea planting rose up the social scale accordingly and soon attracted men from 'good families'—unlike those of the first planters—who insisted on behaving like gentlemen. Evening dress would often be worn for dinner on the remotest tea estates, and planters used their profits to build the clubs which were to become such an integral part of imperial life. The society that Woolf encountered at the Kandy Club in 1907 was built almost entirely upon tea, and tea's dominance was maintained by a civil service funded by government revenues that depended so substantially on it. Between 1900 and 1911, the Ceylon civil service collected such a surplus of revenue that it was able to increase spending on activities such as road and rail construction by 85 per cent. Revenue stood at £1.2 million in 1890; by 1929, it was a staggering £8 million.

There was one major difficulty with tea cultivation in Ceylon: the refusal of the Sinhalese to labour for the British. Roy Moxham, a former tea planter in

Tamil tea planters and their kangani *outside a tea factory.*

Africa, quotes a contemporary comment on the Sinhalese in his history of
tea that "working for hire is repulsive to their national feelings, and is looked
upon as almost slavery. Then being obliged to obey orders, and to do just
what they are commanded is galling to them." The British planters had already
encountered this Sinhalese resistance to regimentation while cultivating coffee;
they overcame it by using seasonal workers from southern India, Tamils who
worked on the rice harvest at home during the rest of the year.

At first, the Tamils came in boats to the northwest of the island around
Jaffna, then walked the north road (the A9 we had travelled on) to Kandy, an
arduous 150-mile trek. Many perished from malaria or exhaustion en route:
as many as 70,000 people, according to a debate in a Ceylon newspaper in
1849. They also died within a few weeks of arrival on the coffee estates, being
unused to the altitude and cold. Clothed in nothing but a loincloth they would
brave the chilly early-morning temperatures and work from 6 a.m. until 4 p.m.
without any break, not even for a midday meal. Many died from bronchitis and
pneumonia. The health situation improved in the 1880s with the building of
estate hospitals and the switch to tea rather than coffee, but the exploitative
conditions remained.

In the 1880s, famine struck southern India and many Tamils were forced to

By 1900, there were some three hundred thousand Tamil workers on the Ceylon tea estates.

Opposite: The year he spent in Kandy was the beginning of Woolf's strong affection for the Sinhalese as people. He came to admire them for their culture and their religion.

look for full-time work on the Ceylon plantations simply in order to survive. This suited the tea planters, who needed to keep the coolies on their estates all year round because tea, unlike coffee, is not a seasonal crop. By 1900, there were some three hundred thousand Tamil workers on the tea estates, which was around seven per cent of Ceylon's total population at the time.

The planters employed a *kangani*, a kind of foreman, to recruit workers in south India and bring them back to Ceylon. The *kanganis* went first to their own villages and recruited both men and women; children were an advantage since they could be put to work on the estates from the age of five. Relatives and fellow villagers were picked for migration, and others from the same caste as the *kangani*. Most of those chosen were already field labourers. Many already owed money to the *kanganis* and had little choice but to go and work in Ceylon to repay these debts, though few succeeded in doing so, such were the high rates of interest. Wages on the estates were low and did not keep pace with rising prices, as Moxham notes in his history of tea: "The price of food-stuffs other than rice increased by 50 per cent over the last two decades of the nineteenth century, while wages remained static. Many labourers found they could only make ends meet by taking out bigger loans, which tied them further to their *kanganis*."

The *kanganis* not only recruited the coolies, they also managed them for the planters on the tea estates, accommodating them along caste and kinship lines. They were greatly feared as they had the power to punish the workers for any wrongdoing. This system of caste-organised labour was beneficial to the British in controlling the workers, so they were content to leave much of the detail of estate management to the *kanganis*. Despite this, while conditions were certainly not ideal on the Ceylon tea plantations, they were considerably better than those in Assam. Many planters treated their workers well and were admired and respected by them.

When we were children on my father's tea estate, I remember we were not allowed to go anywhere near the 'coolie lines'. They were strictly out of bounds. But I have always been fascinated by local lore, superstition, witchcraft and spells. Apart from the house servants on the estate, I knew I could get such stories only from the estate labourers. I was beaten several times for going to the coolie lines.

Even as a child, I found their accommodation shocking. It consisted of long compartmentalised cement structures, usually against a bank with a floor sloping down to a shallow ditch. I have seen as many as eight people sleeping in a simple room nine foot by twelve foot in size. Sanitary facilities were

non-existent, and cooking was done in a separate place. Babies were slung in what looked like sheets hung from the ceiling to make a sort of hammock. While the women went out to pluck tea, one (usually older) woman stayed behind to baby-sit. I always wondered where the men were. Almost invariably it was the women who plucked the tea and the men who worked in the tea factories. Despite today's trade unions on the tea estates there is massive unemployment among the men, who can hardly fail to realise that there is a better life away from the estates.

* * *

Woolf was always much more interested in Sinhalese life than in the Tamils on the tea estates. He thought the Sinhalese were the most charming people he had ever come across: "They were typically mountain people, independent, fine mannered, lively, laughing . . . isolated, unchanged and unchanging. It was extraordinary to deal with them after the dour Tamil of Jaffna living behind his *cadjan* fence under the remorseless sun in the unending plain."

His work at the *kachcheri* in Kandy brought him into close contact with Kandyan culture and customs. For example, polyandry was practised; a wife might be married to two brothers. Although the Government had not interfered with Sinhalese matrimonial laws following the absorption of Kandy as a Crown Colony, it was responsible for administering the laws and adjudicating cases. Divorces intrigued Woolf and he would deliberately let cases drag on while he listened to half a village in the courtroom, as the villagers revealed fascinating facts about their way of life. Having encouraged an atmosphere where they forgot their shyness, he even managed to hear a few stories from the women's point of view, which was almost unheard by government officials in the Ceylon of 1907. Here is a further indication that Woolf was no stereotypical male chauvinist.

It was while hearing an exacting divorce case one afternoon that a white man attempted to swindle him. Most of his mind was on the case, which involved two husbands, a wife and many villagers overwhelmed by the strangeness of the *kachcheri*, who were taking their time to tell their stories. At the same time, as was usual in the late afternoon, Woolf was being bombarded with minor requests to sign routine paperwork. He permitted Sinhalese and Tamils to interrupt him so as to avoid his clerks acting as gatekeepers in exchange for bribes. Europeans, however, were under strict orders to see him by appointment only and to explain their business beforehand. Woolf was therefore annoyed when an unpleasant-looking white man interrupted the divorce proceedings to request a marriage licence. Fraudulent paperwork was thrust under his nose which he signed unthinkingly, while preoccupied with a vital judicial point. Suddenly he realised what he had done—signed a cheque wrongly and granted the man a licence for nothing. He had him hauled back into court and forced him to pay for the licence in cash. Later he discovered that the man was a professional swindler. By then he had escaped to Malaya, but he was sent back to Colombo, arrested and jailed. There may well be an echo of this experience in Woolf's dissolute character White in his short story "Pearls and Swine".

While Woolf enjoyed much of the work in the *kachcheri*, he had the same battle with his head clerk to improve efficiency as in Jaffna. Only much later did he realise how unpopular with his office staff this had made him, when he bumped into the head clerk at Kandy railway station and invited him to share his carriage to Colombo.

> Suddenly he said to me that when I first came to the *kachcheri* and said that everything must be brought up to date and that practically all letters must be answered at once, there had very nearly been an open revolt against me. Nobody in the office, including himself, had believed the thing in the least degree possible. But everyone, including himself, agreed that, once the change had been made, the thing had proved to be feasible and everyone's work became easier.

Soon after this confession, the clerk opened the train door as it came into a station in order to buy a snack, slipped and fell between the train and the platform. In the nick of time, Woolf grabbed him around his waist and held him up until the train stopped, thereby saving his clerk's life.

* * *

Unlike in Jaffna, Woolf now had a direct and grave responsibility for the penal system, which involved him in work that was both repugnant and distressing. It was a government agent's duty to be present at the execution or flogging of a prisoner, however the government agent always left this duty to his deputy, who in this case was Woolf. In *Growing*, he wrote caustically of his experience of hangings:

> Kandy was . . . a lovely place and it never looked more lovely than in the early morning when I stood in the Bogambara Prison in front of the gallows and everyone waited for me to give the signal to the executioner for the 'drop' which would hang the man. I stood rather above the gallows, and in front of me in the fresh air and gentle sunshine just after dawn I looked across to the lovely hills surrounding the lake.

As for flogging, he thought that "the flogging of a man with a cat-o'-nine-tails is the most disgusting and barbarous thing I have ever seen—it is worse even than a hanging." The man's arms and legs were tied to an iron triangle about six foot in height. After every ten lashes, given by a prison warder in the presence of the superintendent of the prison, the man would be inspected by a medical officer to see if he was fit enough for the flaying to continue.

But judging from *Growing* the hangings appear to have been more horrific than the floggings, because they sometimes went wrong. This happened in two out of the six or seven hangings certified by Woolf in Kandy. In a letter to Strachey, he described one of the occasions, when four men were hanged:

> The first two were hanged all right but they gave one of the second too big a drop or something went wrong. The man's head was practically torn from his body and there was a great jet of blood which went up about three or four feet high, covering the gallows and priest who stands praying on the steps. The curious thing was that this man as he went to the gallows seemed to feel the rope twitching round his neck: he kept twitching his head over into the exact same position they hang in after death. Usually they are quite unmoved. One man kept on repeating two words of a Sinhalese prayer (I think) over and over again all the way to the gallows and even as he stood with the rope round his neck waiting for the drop.

Woolf was opposed to capital punishment for reasons besides its inhumanity. He thought it ineffective as a deterrent, because most of the offences that he saw punished by hanging were the result of uncontrolled passion rather than premeditation. As for the drawing of attention to such crimes in a sensational way in the 'popular' press, exaggerating their horrors, Woolf thought this more likely to encourage, rather than to deter, similar crimes.

His experiences as a magistrate and judge led him to form definite opinions on law and order. He believed in the implementation of a law, even if it was overly harsh and inappropriate to the crime, in order that the law's wrongness should be exposed and a case for change made. Woolf was someone who obeyed the rules even if he objected to them—as he makes clear in his portrayal of the judge in *The Village in the Jungle,* who sends a man to prison for stealing on the evidence available, despite his strong but unprovable suspicion that the man is innocent.

As for the prisons, he felt that in Ceylon the penal system was even more inhumane and iniquitous than the legal system. He wrote: "The prisoners were confined in cages like those in the lion house in the Regent's Park Zoo, two, three, or even four men sometimes to a cage. The buildings were horrible. The prisoners hammered coconuts into coir or walked round and round the yard holding on to a moving rope which, I imagined, was a modern version of the ancient treadmill." On his return trip to Ceylon in 1960, visiting the prison in Jaffna after half a century, he was pleased to note an improvement in both the conditions and the atmosphere.

On my visit to Kandy this time I was determined to see inside Bogambara Prison, where Woolf had given the order for hangings. My lawyer friend Lucky Senatilleke made the request to a friend of his, Sangabodhi Wijesinghe, who is

Entrance to Bogambara Prison, Kandy.

the chief medical officer of prisons in Colombo, and we were granted a great privilege: a tour of Bogambara Prison, including the gallows and 'death row'.

Having introduced ourselves to Nelson Abeywira, the superintendent of prisons at Bogambara, and his senior assistant Upali Jayasinghe, we were treated first to ginger tea and then to a thorough introduction to the enormous prison, constructed by the British in 1876. With its high walls, turrets and massive internal building containing the cells, the place was at first frightening, as we watched some two thousand prisoners wait outside the feeding centre in the courtyard, until we came to appreciate the prisoners' patience and discipline. They were dressed in loose white shorts and white tunics, except for the long-term detainees in maximum security, who wore long white sarongs. Seventy-nine prisoners had been condemned to death (awaiting appeal), and a further 17 were waiting on death row, housed in cells that lead directly to the gallows. These allow for several hangings at a time, as we know from Woolf's letter to Strachey—in 1915, after serious riots, as many as ninety executions were carried out in Bogambara—but since independence in 1948 the law has decreed that only one prisoner may be executed at a time. In actual fact, no one has been hanged in Bogambara Prison since 1975, and in Sri Lanka as a whole the last hanging took place (in Welikada Prison in Colombo) in 1976. However, the death penalty has been suspended, rather than formally abolished, and as I write this in 2004, I note that the president of Sri Lanka has announced that capital punishment will be reinstated in response to the killing of a high court judge, probably by gangsters from a drug ring. Indeed a special hangman's rope has already been purchased from Pakistan.

After some persuasion we were eventually allowed to see the gallows chamber itself. There was a wide platform with a trap door and lever, above which three ominous and substantial hooks hung downwards from a cross-beam. Ropes and nooses were fastened to the hooks. The 'drop' was precip-itous. A large door from the inner courtyard, away from the prisoners' cells, allowed officials such as Woolf and invited guests access to witness the executions.

Our whole tour lasted perhaps two hours and we became accustomed to walking amongst the prisoners, even the maximum-security prisoners, whose cells we visited. Only two of the prisoners directly confronted me with requests

Prisoners in the courtyard of Bogambara Prison, which was constructed by the British in 1876.

for help. They were immediately brushed away by the guards. For obvious reasons I was not allowed to photograph any prisoners, but I was permitted to take some photos of the busy courtyard from the third floor of the central building through a cell window. To get there we trooped up a steep, narrow, wooden staircase, worn with age, to the long dark corridors from which the cells jutted behind steel bars. The cell where I photographed was empty and designed for one, though I was told it has sometimes housed as many as twelve prisoners for lack of sufficient space in the prison. When we came down again, the assistant superintendent insisted we wash our hands and wrists thoroughly with carbolic soap as a protection against scabies, which is apparently a common hazard in all prisons in Sri Lanka.

* * *

Except for prison visits, official work kept Woolf at the *kachcheri*. But very occasionally he went out into the mountain villages to see for himself the feudal life of the villagers they had described to him in such fascinating detail during court cases in the *kachcheri*. The first time he did this he was astonished at his reception. He had ridden up 24 miles from Kandy to a village called Urugala, reaching the place after dark in a thunderstorm. Half a mile from the village a procession of headmen and villagers met him and conducted him into the village to the accompaniment of tom-toms and dancers. Then he was obliged to stand in the rain for ten minutes and receive a prostration from each member of the crowd, who touched the ground with his forehead.

Urugala is now called Medamahanuwara. I went there and was fortunate to interview a 76-year-old senior ayurvedic physician, N. B. G. Piyasena, who explained the circumstances of the name change. Urugala was once a kingdom and relics are still found there. Because of its historical significance, about forty years ago (others told me more recently than this), the chief Buddhist priest of the area summoned a meeting of the village elders and proposed that the name be changed to one that recalled the ancient kingdom. There is more history a mere mile from the village: the site of the last king of Kandy's second palace. All that remains are its foundations in the base of a rock on the hill high above Kandy. Here Sri Vikrama Rajasinha was found hiding in 1815 and captured by British forces at a place known as Raja Galla. We walked along a small winding path past his refuge to a solitary column commemorating the event. It was erected in 1908, when Woolf was in Kandy, at the behest of Lewis, the antiquarian government agent who had been Woolf's boss in Jaffna, so as to mark the exact spot where the king was captured. Apart from the column,

When Woolf was in Kandy in 1908, a solitary column was erected about a mile from the village of Urugala to mark the exact spot where Sri Vikrama Rajasinha was captured in 1815.

there is also a lone arecanut tree, a three-hundred-year-old tamarind tree and a magnificent view.

During the Kandyan kingdom, prostration, of the kind experienced by Woolf, was commonplace. It was the custom for the peasantry when greeting the landlord. It was also *de rigeur* for any person—foreign ambassadors included—who was presented to the king. The ritual was strictly observed at the Kandyan court.

It even survives today in a different form. Discussing Woolf's visit to Urugala with Raj de Silva, I learnt of a custom among younger Sinhalese to show respect for their elders by worshipping them, especially during the Sinhalese New Year when children visit parents and at weddings when the bride and groom take leave of their parents. Not so long ago a Sinhalese minister of education ordered that children of *all* faiths in Ceylon should worship their parents before leaving for school. There was an uproar, especially from the Christian churches, and the order was soon withdrawn.

In a letter to Strachey from Urugala Woolf commented grandly: "I believe it is the only way in the East for each nation to be kept as it was before Adam; the Tamil will only shake you by the hand and practically never salaams, and is about the most ill-mannered man you could meet; the real Kandyan grovels on the ground and touches your boots but has remained a gentleman."

In other words, the feudalism of the Kandyans seemed purer to Woolf at this time in his life than the imperialism of the British who had overthrown the Kandyan kingdom in 1815. Feudalism might appear to be about grovelling but according to Woolf it was actually about manliness and manners. Imperialism seemed to him a corrupting influence, as witness the effect of European influences on the Tamil population in Jaffna. It was the same view as that taken by W. T. Keble in his 1940 travel book about Ceylon, who wrote of the "sturdy Kandyan", any one of whom, "taken from the plough and washed, is fit to sit upon the throne." It was also the Enlightenment idea of the noble savage, unsullied by the palsied touch of civilisation, alive and well in Woolf's mind in the Kandyan hills.

In *Growing*, he was honest enough to admit that he enjoyed the honour of his reception. "I was up above in the feudal hierarchy, one of the super-chiefs, the princes, or the boyars, and, however much one may dislike the fuss and ceremony of social systems—and I do hate them—one cannot be impervious to the flattery of being a top dog liked by the underdogs." But he insisted that it was his growing awareness of the problems inherent in imperialism, provoked by experiences such as the one at Urugala, that ultimately was more important to his life and career. Like so many thoughtful imperialists, Woolf was starting to become profoundly ambivalent about empire.

None the less, throughout his year in Kandy he played his role as an imperialist with aplomb. He made a second favourable impression upon the acting governor, Sir Hugh Clifford. One evening, riding with Rachel along Lady Horton's Walk, he spotted Sir Hugh in a carriage with the glamorous wife of an officer in the Indian Army. This was no surprise, given Clifford's reputation as a ladies' man. Some days later, the acting governor sent for Woolf and asked him whether he could arrange a show of Kandyan dancing. Woolf promptly contacted his old friend, the Diwa Nilame, co-guardian of the key to the tooth relic, and so after dinner the following Thursday Sir Hugh, his lady friend and a few others (Woolf included), were treated to the very finest show of Kandyan culture available, given on the lawn by the Diwa Nilame's retainers, headmen, dancers, tom-tom beaters and musicians, in the light of about a hundred torch-bearers. Clifford was immensely pleased, and soon after this event he personally recommended that Woolf be appointed assistant government agent in Hambantota, a signal advance for a 27-year old with less than four years' experience in Ceylon.

So, on 27 August 1908, Woolf took the train from Kandy, heading for Hambantota. As he did so, he found himself reflecting that "the fate, the whole life even, of an insignificant civil servant can be fortuitously determined by empresses, the Buddha's tooth, lovely ladies, amorous governors, a few torches and dancers."

6

Journey to Hambantota

As dawn was breaking, I climbed by a rocky track to the top of the mountain, a coolie carrying my bag and bicycle, and then through the clouds and mist over the top and down on to a road. There I tipped the coolie, tied my bag to my bicycle, and coasted mile after mile down through the deliciously fresh mountain scenery until I reached the plain and jungles of the low country . . . At midday in the dry burning heat I came to the boundary of my district, and there waiting for me by the roadside was my horsekeeper with my horse and my dogs. I got on the horse and rode the weary miles to Wirawila and Tissamaharama . . .

LEONARD WOOLF, *Growing*

WOOLF TOOK CHARGE of Hambantota district a mere day after leaving Kandy in late August 1908. How he travelled there he did not reveal, except to say that he went by train. An examination of Ceylon's railway lines shows that he could have taken two possible routes: a circuitous line that passes through the tea plantations close to Nuwara Eliya and finishes in Bandarawela, southeast of Kandy; or the line that goes west to Colombo, then southwards along the coast to Galle and east to Matara. Either way, the final leg of his journey—from Bandarawela or from Matara on to Hambantota—must have been completed by bullock cart, since there was no railway station in Hambantota (whether in 1908 or now).

Weighing these options, and given that Woolf took only a day or so to get there, it seems more probable that he travelled to his new district via Colombo, where senior colonial officials would have had a chance to brief him about his posting en route. In Matara, which was the headquarters of an assistant government agent, he could have had a comfortable night in a government residence and onward transportation by road to Hambantota

Tea pluckers near Hatton.

arranged by colleagues for the following morning. By contrast, travel by train to Bandarawela through the hills would have been very slow, followed by a lengthy and exhausting journey by road. But having said this, I decided to entertain both possibilities. First, we would visit some of the tea country Woolf may have journeyed through by slow train towards Bandarawela, then we would drive to Colombo and from there follow the coast road.

We left the Queens Hotel in Kandy early in the morning and headed south towards Nuwara Eliya, gradually climbing up nearly five thousand feet in altitude through spectacular scenery and long narrow passes into cool, invigorating, mountain air. This hill resort, the highest city in the island, was established by the British in 1825 as a sanatorium for soldiers. In 1846, a young convalescent from malaria, Samuel Baker—later the explorer who discovered one of the great reservoirs of the Nile (Lake Albert) in East Africa and who was knighted for his discovery—made Nuwara Eliya his home for eight or nine years and tried to convert the place into an English farming village. Baker's utopian dream is not surprising. Nuwara Eliya today feels almost as if it could be in the English Lake District or in parts of Scotland. The houses above its lake (still named after Governor Gregory) are built in an English style; the Hill Club, though no longer the exclusive institution it was in colonial times, is still furnished in the colonial manner. A tie is required for dinner there (though it can be hired). The ghosts of long-dead planters and civil servants playing bridge—as Woolf did at the Kandy Club a century ago—or drinking a peg or two of whisky after a game of golf on Nuwara Eliya's challenging golf course, are not difficult for the visitor to summon at the Hill Club.

Although I have stayed there on many visits to Nuwara Eliya, this time I decided to continue on south and then west through Dimbulla and Kotagala. We passed through Hatton, a major centre of tea production, where Woolf spent three days in 1906 recovering from typhoid before he moved on to recuperate in Bandarawela. Then through Dikoya. Finally we reached Bogawantalawa.

Woolf never mentions this small place in the plantation country, however it has a curious connection with him, which I wanted to see for myself. Bogawantalawa was the last home of Julia Margaret Cameron, one of the finest nineteenth-century photographers and a great-aunt of Virginia Woolf. She was born Julia Pattle in Calcutta in 1815 and married Charles Hay Cameron, a jurist and philosopher, who worked with W. M. G. Colebrooke on his report on the civil service in 1832. In 1838, the Camerons moved to Ceylon where they lived for ten years until Charles's retirement, when they returned to England. But they remained in touch with the island, not least because they had invested money in coffee there.

Back in England, for her forty-eighth birthday in 1863, Julia Margaret Cameron was given a camera. She turned herself into the leading portrait photographer of Victorian England, whose best-known subjects were her friends Alfred Tennyson, Robert Browning, Charles Darwin and Ellen Terry. Also striking are her photographs of her niece Julia Jackson, who married Leslie Stephen and became the mother of Virginia Woolf. "Julia Jackson inherited a full measure of the Pattle beauty, as one can see in the famous photographs by her famous aunt, Mrs Cameron, herself one of the six Pattle sisters," Leonard Woolf writes in the first volume of his autobiography. Her portraits forfeited sharpness of focus and definition for penetrating expression of character

Julia Margaret Cameron was buried with her husband in St Mary's Church near Bogawantalawa.

and beauty. When Leslie Stephen published the first edition of the *Dictionary of National Biography* in 1885, Julia Margaret Cameron was the only photographer with an entry (among only 18 women out of a total of 420 entries).

Apart from taking portraits, she also photographed the tea estates. And this was because in 1875 she and her husband decided to return to live in Ceylon; in England they missed the tropical climate and the way of life, and their coffee plantations, which had been supervised by their sons and were now affected by the devastating leaf blight, needed attention. The Glencairn estate was named by Charles Hay Cameron and his wife. They both died there—she on 26 January 1879, at the age of 63, he the following year at the ripe age of 85. We visited the graveyard of St Mary's Church about a mile outside Bogawantalawa, where both Julia and Charles lie buried.

We were now just 90 miles from Colombo, but to get there we had to wind westwards—still in spectacularly beautiful country—through Norwood, Maskeliya and Kitulgala to Avissawella. This is a busy town, and historically important too: it is adjacent to the capital of the Sitawaka kings, whose name derives from the fact their capital is the legendary place in the *Ramayana*, where Sita (Rama's wife) was held captive by Ravana. The Sitawaka king, Rajasinha I, who fought the Portuguese valiantly in the sixteenth century, started work on a temple here, but it was not completed after his death and is now a fine ruin with beautifully dressed stone. A simple stone marks the site of the king's burial.

From Avissawella we travelled the last 30 miles to Colombo via Hanwella following the old road from Kandy to Colombo, which once was deliberately kept in an appalling condition by the Kandyan kings as a defence against foreign invasion of their kingdom. It remains a complicated and circuitous route, circumvented by the British when they constructed the new road from Colombo after their annexation of the Kandyan kingdom in 1815. By 1823, despite the loss of both European and Ceylonese workers to malaria and wild elephants, much of this new road was operational. It was pushed on towards Kandy in the time of Governor Barnes, and in 1832 it was completed with the building of the superb satinwood single-span bridge across the Mahaweli Ganga at Peradeniya.

*   *   *

At Colombo we turned south, in order to follow the coast road that leads to Galle, then round to Matara, then on to Hambantota—the route Woolf most probably took in August 1908. For the railway he would have travelled on takes exactly the same route as the road right beside the ocean until it terminates at Matara. Viewed as a whole the route also traverses much of the climatic diversity of the island, beginning in a wet zone and ending in a dry zone. However, in August the southwest monsoon would have been blowing strongly—Woolf might even have had to keep the train windows closed against the spray—whereas for us, travelling in March, there was no rain, simply the beauty of the southwest coast at its most resplendent.

"I saw the sun rising over the forests and hills on our right, as we made our way rapidly along a beautiful road, lined on either side by masses of coconut trees—their graceful stems and the delicate tracery of their foliage becoming every moment more distinct," wrote W. Knighton in 1854 in his *Forest Life in Ceylon* (he must have been travelling northwards on the Galle Road, not southwards like us, given the position of the sun). "Occasionally, we were near the sea, its waves breaking into foam on one side, whilst thick vegetation bounded our path on the other. Troops of naked children whom we saw playing in every village or in the neighbourhood of the cottages, treated us to a friendly cheer as we passed, or contented themselves with a quiet, silent stare, and then a short run after the vehicle."

Of course it requires rather more miles to get clear of Colombo when travelling by car today than it did a century and a half ago by bullock cart. The Galle Road is always crowded, but once you do escape Colombo's suburbs it offers the same entrancing views as in colonial times: fishermen's huts, catamarans and many kinds of old Sinhalese architecture set against a sweeping, palm-fringed ocean backdrop.

There are unique towns and fishing villages along the way. Dehiwala, only seven miles from Colombo, is perhaps the first, where over six hundred species of fish can be found, from the dramatically shaped saw fish to the dazzlingly coloured parrot fish. The fishermen here canoe out at night with only their onboard flares and the stars overhead for company. At Moratuwa, a little further down the coast, there are carpenters able to work wood using their toes as well as their fingers. A thriving industry here produces wooden tea chests, brass and silver work and coir goods. (Not coincidentally, there is also the technically minded University of Moratuwa.) Further on, at Kalutara, merchants do business at the mouth of the Kalu Ganga River in gems brought down-river from the gem mines at Ratnapura. This southwest coast has been associated

Unique towns and fishing villages dot the coast between Colombo and Galle.

with trade—both domestic and international—for centuries.

Galle, the most notable town on the coast, 72 miles from Colombo, was Ceylon's chief port from the fourteenth to the nineteenth century. It has a mile-wide harbour, natural for shipping, if it were not for the dangers of its sharp coral reefs and the southwest monsoon. After 17 steamships sank at Galle during the nineteenth century, the shipping companies threatened to stop calling at Ceylon. This, in part, accounts for the building of a safer harbour at Colombo, opened to shipping in 1875. By 1908, when Woolf probably passed through Galle, the place had already lost its pre-eminence as a port. Though it was still a major seat of Government, and the centre of the coconut industry, this pretty town set beside a bay and backed by wooded hills and lush tropical scenery was on its way to becoming the backwater it is today.

Nowadays Galle is known mostly for its history. Though its name is thought to derive from the Sinhala *gala*, meaning a corral where cattle are herded, it may also have a European root from the Latin for cockerel, *gallus*; it is said that the early Portuguese in Galle heard cockerels crowing there at dusk. What is much more definite is that Galle was where Europeans first set foot in Ceylon. A Portuguese sailor landed in 1501, traded with the king of Kotte, and departed. Then in 1505, Lorenzo D'Almeida, the son of the Portuguese viceroy of India, set sail for the Maldives on a mission to intercept Moorish spice ships that were threatening Portuguese trade, lost his way in a storm and chanced to reach Galle. The Moors were keen to protect their dominant position in Galle harbour. So they persuaded a Sinhalese prince to pose as the king for D'Almeida. This impostor helpfully granted the Portuguese permission to build a fort at Colombo, which they finally did in 1518 and used as a trading post. But they returned to Galle some decades later and built a fort there too in 1571, to which they were forced to retreat when they came under attack from the Sitawaka king, Rajasinha I. They added fortifications to Galle harbour including a wall and three bastions complete with watchtowers.

Relatively little is known of the Portuguese period in Galle because its records were burnt by the Dutch, who attacked the fort in 1640. More than three thousand Dutch battled against not even three hundred Portuguese, hastily dispatched from Colombo. The fort was defended by Captain Lourenço Ferrera de Brito for 18 days until finally the Dutch broke in. De Brito was badly wounded, but saved from death by his wife who apparently threw herself over his body, pleading that the Dutch kill her and spare her husband whom she loved so fiercely that she was never parted from him, even in battle. Both the captain and his wife were spared and as news of her courage spread, the Dutch general ordered that no Portuguese be killed, only that their houses be ransacked. De Brito recovered from his wounds and he and his wife were sent to Batavia as honoured prisoners-of-war.

The Dutch fort, built in 1663 and strengthened considerably in the late 1720s, is Galle's most famous building, and the reason why the area is a World Heritage site. It shows the formidable nature of the Dutch presence in Ceylon more than anywhere else in Sri Lanka. Besides covering a staggering 89 acres and still being in good repair after more than three hundred years, the fort's colossal ramparts encompass Dutch churches, houses and museums, and a unique sewage system, very advanced for its time, in which the high tide acted as a flush and the ebb tide removed the debris. The design and extent of this system did not become known to the British Government until 1922, when bubonic plague made it necessary to venture into the sewers to destroy diseased rats.

Entrance to the Dutch fort, Galle, which was built in 1663 and strengthened considerably in the late 1720s. The arms of the Dutch East India Company are visible.

Like so many visitors to Galle, I enjoy walking on the ramparts and gazing out to sea. Galle is yet another place in Sri Lanka to which I feel my family is connected. In 1773, P. P. J. Quint Ondaatje left Ceylon from Galle, bound for the Netherlands and an education suitable for a future Ceylonese clergyman. Quint was the same age as I was when I left Ceylon in 1947—but unlike me he never returned. Instead, as mentioned earlier, he used his education at the University of Utrecht to become the leader of the Patriot Party and an important figure in Dutch history. The Ondaatjes have another connection with Galle, too. In the 1950s, my sister Gillian lived in the pilot's bungalow in the Dutch fort while her husband was on duty as a naval pilot.

Soon after leaving Galle, our car reached Mirissa, a small fishing village with a peaceful rocky beach and harbour sculpted by the ocean from the red cliffs that rise from the eastern side of the Weligama Bay off the road from Galle to

The Star Fort at Matara was built by Governor van Eck and bears his coat of arms as well as the symbol of the Dutch East India Company.

Matara. I stayed the night in a house perched high on the cliffs. It has a structure like a simple pavilion, but built on a stepped plinth with rooms underneath that look straight out on a spell-binding view of the bay, where once, as in Galle, the merchant sailing ships of the Portuguese would anchor in order to trade with the Sinhalese. The owner of the house is Pradip Jayawardene, who is married to my sister's daughter, and its architect was the late Geoffrey Bawa.

Backtracking briefly the following morning, we stopped for tea at the rest house in Weligama. I could not resist this, so I could take yet another look at one of my favourite ocean views—of the island of Taprobane.

Taprobane was the ancient Greek and Roman name for Ceylon, but this modern Taprobane is an island once owned by Count de Mauny, a somewhat *louche* Frenchman who claimed that he had inherited his title from his grandmother, though many thought it bogus. (Pablo Neruda, who knew de Mauny in Ceylon, called him "a phony French nobleman" who was "a famous snob".) In 1898, when he was in his early thirties, de Mauny married Lady Mary Byng, daughter of the earl of Strafford, and they settled in a chateau in the Loire Valley in France and produced a son and a daughter. But then a scandal erupted in which the count was charged with making sexual advances to the young Oliver Brett, son of the influential Viscount Esher, who had been sent to the chateau to learn French. De Mauny's marriage failed. After a spell in England, in 1912 he visited Ceylon at the invitation of Sir Thomas Lipton, the tea magnate, and soon after this he moved there permanently. He was formally bankrupt, but he was probably paid to go away by his wife.

It was around 1927-28 that de Mauny fell in love with Taprobane. His lusciously written book, *The Gardens of Taprobane*, published in 1937, describes his first charmed encounter:

> Shall I ever forget that morning of September, now nine years ago, when, quite by chance, I first saw Weligama Bay, and in the centre of its arc the red granite rock, covered with palms and jungle scrub, rising

Pradip Jayawardene's house, designed by the late Geoffrey Bawa, is perched high on the cliffs overlooking Weligama Bay.

from the Indian Ocean: an emerald in a setting of pink coral?

I swam across the narrow strait, scrambled over rocks and briars, and reached the top of the rock. The view from this plateau was admirable: below me was the bay outspreading its long arms towards the ocean, until they were lost in the haze of the far distance; the coral reef, sparkling with diamonds of the spray; the sea, turquoise-blue, streaked with amethyst-purple. Beyond, far beyond, the bare horizon; there was nothing between me and the South Pole.

However there were plentiful numbers of cobras in this island paradise—it had been used by the locals as a cobra dump—and these reptiles the count was forced to remove rather than kill, as snakes are not normally killed in Sri Lanka. Then he built a remarkable house, octagonal in shape with a broad terrace entirely surrounding it: a building in full harmony with its surrounding tropical gardens and the sea surrounding the gardens; and a testament to de Mauny's imagination and skill as a landscape artist. He lived in this glorious creation for more than ten years, inviting as his guests various aristocrats, mostly of a

Count de Mauny built a unique octagonal house on Taprobane Island in the 1920s.

genuine variety, and other famous personalities, and holding brilliant parties.

After he died in 1941—of a heart attack while he was in Jaffna (where he is buried)—his island was auctioned and was not so loved by its owners. During this time, in the mid-1940s, my family rented it and there we spent my most idyllic holidays while growing up. I cannot remember any time in my childhood I was happier than when we were on Taprobane—swimming in the surf while watching out for the undertow, and trudging across to the Weligama rest house for string hoppers and prawn curry. The northwest room in the octagonal house where I slept looked out over the endless blue of the Indian Ocean. I am not in the least surprised that the house later became a regular haunt of writers, notably Paul Bowles, who owned the island for a while in the 1950s and wrote a novel there. Today it is owned by the Sri Lankan expatriate and London barrister Desmond de Silva, and is leased to Geoffrey Dobbs, an enigmatic businessman from Hong Kong who has restored the house to its original condition. Taprobane is a wonderfully romantic place, which, like many old colonials, I still refer to as Count de Mauny Island.

Weligama Rest House has another nearby attraction, the rock-cut statue of Kusta Rajah, a figure with an unusual headdress with a Buddha image set in the middle of it. Some say the statue is a memorial to a king who introduced the coconut tree to Ceylon. But there is a competing legend. The raja is said to have suffered from a skin disease named *kusta*, possibly leprosy, and he went to the temple at Weligama to ask for a cure. If his wish were granted, he prayed, he would carve a statue into the rock.

We now drove on to Matara, 98 miles from Colombo, and the end of the railway line, where Woolf must have disembarked. Matara too, like Galle, was heavily influenced by the Dutch, with two forts and a church. In many ways it has been the more influential of the two towns, as it was always the centre of commerce on the south coast, controlling the trade in cinnamon, gems and elephants. It is an attractive place with pleasant avenues of flowering trees, a beautiful river, fertile land, and an abundance of food and varieties of fish.

Matara was also the only major fortified European settlement in Ceylon to fall to the Sinhalese. In 1760, the peasants there revolted against Dutch land ownership laws and taxes and their own appalling poverty. They forged an alliance with Kandy, occupied the town and forced the Dutch to flee. It took the

Fishermen haul nets on the coast near Matara.

Dutch a year to recapture the place and led to a war with the king of Kandy that lasted until 1766.

The principal fort at Matara is star-shaped and made of stone and coral, with the arms of the Dutch Governor van Eck and bears his coat of arms as well as the symbol of the Dutch East India Company still above the main gate. In Woolf's time—during which he would regularly visit Matara from Hambantota on government business—the fort contained a *kachcheri* and other government buildings, and was utilised by the British in a manner similar to the fort at Jaffna. We went inside the fort and found it picturesque and park-like, with shady trees giving relief from the searing late-morning sun.

From Matara it is only a short distance to Dondra (also known as Devundera, 'God's city'). At Dondra Head, there stands an octagonal-towered lighthouse, 176 feet tall, completed in 1889 for Queen Victoria's birthday. When W. T. Keble, author of *Ceylon Beaten Track*, visited Dondra in the 1930s, the lighthouse keeper told Keble he was not lonely. "There are plenty of people about here, and a good many visitors come, and we can see the ships sometimes going east-ward towards Singapore. But it's lonely down there . . . They say there's not a piece of land between this and the South Pole. The open sea stretches all the way." Dondra holds a spectacular religious festival every July or August, similar to the Kandy Perahera. It is possibly the most notable example in Sri Lanka of Hinduism's visible influence in later Buddhist tradition.

By midday we were in Woolf territory proper. Tangalla is the first major town in the Hambantota district. Beyond Tangalla, humidity vanishes. The vegetation is no longer lush, it becomes scrub jungle. For the travel writer Harry Williams, in his book *Ceylon: Pearl of the East*, Tangalla was considered in the late 1940s to be "the last outpost of civilisation, for the jungle begins immediately beyond the citronella plantations for which the town is noted."

Tangalla Prison features in a sad episode in Woolf's novel *The Village in the Jungle* (as we shall see in chapter eight), so I was keen to see it. Originally it was yet another Dutch fort, but was converted into a prison by the British in the 1840s. Its plans show that the prison walls were cut deeply into the fort's bastions and the main accommodation was built in two blocks along the east and west sides with little space between. The fort's coral exterior has now been cemented over. Woolf used to inspect the prison, but there was no possibility of our doing so, given the heavy security.

All in all Woolf spent a great deal of time in Tangalla on administrative

Beyond Tangalla humidity vanishes. The vegetation is no longer lush, it becomes scrub jungle.

matters. Apart from the prison, there were irrigation works, schools, a hospital, opium shops and bazaars to inspect. In 1909, after a visit to the hospital, Woolf recorded an official suggestion that a separate *parangi* ward should be built. This crippling disease, also known as yaws, destroys the skin, bones and joints, and can deform the legs, nose, palate and upper jaw. Woolf encountered the effects of *parangi* constantly while examining local people seeking exemption from road building, as we shall see in the next chapter on Hambantota.

The opium rent caused particular problems in Tangalla. The opium poppy had been introduced to the area in 1821 by an assistant government agent, and the British had subsequently encouraged its growth. The Government charged the inhabitants of Tangalla a tax for growing opium. The revenue was then used for the provision of sanitation, water supply, lighting and education. But at the end of 1908, there was an official move to stop this tax and discourage opium production. In April 1910, Woolf noted that "the town of Tangalla [will lose] 59 per cent of its revenue by the abolition of the opium rent . . . It is a question whether the health of the population will not suffer as much in this way as

Tangalla fort was converted into a prison by the British in the 1840s.

by the moderate consumption of opium which before prevailed." Nevertheless, in 1910, the Government began its efforts to restrict opium consumption, leaving Woolf to make complicated arrangements to ensure its availability to addicts.

We did not stay at the Tangalla Rest House, because we wanted to press on to Hambantota. But I remembered a scintillating passage in *Growing* where Woolf describes sitting alone on the verandah of the rest house at night, and feeling his own (and his colleagues') cosmic insignificance:

> If I had to show anyone what God can do in the way of tropical nights, I think I should take him to the rest house verandah at Tangalla. The small, insignificant building lies by itself in a small bay fringed with rocks and coconut palms. The ocean laps against the verandah. The evening air is warm and still and gentle. An enormous sky meets an enormous sea. The stars blaze in the sky and blaze in the sea. Every now and then—it seems almost at one's feet—a long, snake-like, black head rises out of the stars in the sea, remains for a moment motionless

above the water looking at the stars in the sky, and then silently slides back into the sea. It seems incredibly mysterious, this black head emerging from the water to gaze at the stars in the sky, even though you know it to be only a turtle coming up to the surface to breathe. There is no sound in this melodrama of a tropical night except a faint lapping of the sea, and now and again a shivery stir of palm leaves. The sky, the sea, the stars, the turtles, the bay, the palms were so lusciously magnificent at Tangalla Rest House that Nature seemed to tremble on the verge—I don't think she ever actually fell over the verge—of vulgarity.

Even if I were capable of it, I could not hope to have relived Woolf's experience by staying the night in the Tangalla Rest House. Alas, its whole physical relationship to the sea has changed since those days. Today nothing can be seen from its verandah except a periphery wall, over which there is a distant view of the sea across a man-made breakwater and a busy fishing harbour.

But the rest house at Hambantota, 148 miles from Colombo, offers ample compensation. Its setting was, and still is, a delight. Like the *kachcheri* and Woolf's own bungalow at Hambantota, the rest house stands on a sea cliff near a Martello tower, overlooking the sweep of the bay. I stay there every time I come to Hambantota, as I did as a child playing on the beach below the rest house more than half a century ago. Once more, I settled down there for the night and was lulled to sleep by the thudding sound of the surf.

7

Hambantota

All the year round, day and night, if you looked down that long two-mile line of sea and sand, you would see, unless it was very rough, continually at regular intervals a wave, not very high but unbroken two miles long, lift itself up very slowly, wearily, poise itself for a moment in sudden complete silence, and then fall with a great thud upon the sand. That moment of complete silence followed by the great thud, the thunder of the wave upon the shore, became part of the rhythm of my life. It was the last thing I heard as I fell asleep at night, the first thing I heard when I woke in the morning—the moment of silence, the heavy thud; the moment of silence, the heavy thud—the rhythm of the sea, the rhythm of Hambantota.

LEONARD WOOLF, Growing

EACH MORNING THAT he spent in Hambantota during his two-and-a-half year posting there, Woolf took his early tea on the large Dutch verandah of his bungalow. Looking out over the ocean, he would see a long line of about forty flamingoes fly over the water along the two-mile stretch of coast from west to east, and make a right-angled turn as they passed his house towards the great coastal lagoons. When they were flying over the sea, the birds gleamed black and white, but when each bird wheeled left high over the house its colour suddenly changed in the tropical dawn light—from black and white to brilliant flashes of pink.

Hambantota, with its beautiful bay, has long been known as a safe anchorage; the Greek navigators of Alexander the Great were aware of it, as was the ancient cartographer Ptolemy, who marked it on his map of Taprobane under the name Dionysii. Today's name probably derives from *sampan-tota*,

Fishing boats in the Hambantota harbour.

Hambantota's name probably derives from sampan-tota *meaning 'harbour of the sampans'.*

meaning 'harbour of the sampans'. Malays, sailing in their sampans westwards across the ocean from Southeast Asia, came to southeastern Ceylon in search of elephants; some of them settled there, and now, as a result of further Malay immigration, Hambantota has the largest proportion of Malay Muslims in Sri Lanka. In 2004, they were among the unfortunate people who fell victim to the terrible tsunami which followed the same path across the ocean from Sumatra as their ancestors in their sampans. When the monster waves struck Hambantota on 26 December, the bay turned from being a favourite safe anchorage into a living death trap.

Hambantota district, which Woolf took charge of as assistant government agent on 28 August 1908, was then a region of about a thousand square miles with a population of about one hundred thousand, consisting of Sinhalese,

Tamils, Moors and Malays. About a hundred miles in length, the district's coastline curved from a point on the south coast nine miles before Tangalla, past Hambantota and Kirinda to the area around Yala, which was even then a game sanctuary, before finally reaching, after some miles of absolutely desolate shoreline, its eastern boundary at Kumana, which is now a bird sanctuary. The district's widest extension inland, all of which was flat, was never more than 30 miles. On the map, one can see two large bumps in its western part, the more westerly of which points towards the town of Ratnapura in the far distance, while the other one points towards Nuwara Eliya in the mountains. The rest of the district, eastwards from Tissamaharama (the area inland from Kirinda) up to Kumana, is narrower than this, forming a coastal strip about ten miles in width.

Administratively, the district was divided into three. An area mostly within the westernmost bump was known as Giruwa Pattu West; next to this, in the centre of the district, came Giruwa Pattu East; and in the east lay Magam Pattu, which included Hambantota. The first two divisions had reasonable rainfall, relatively little jungle, and were quite populous, with some irrigation and prosperous villages living off rice, grain and coconuts. Magam Pattu, by contrast, was impoverished and almost entirely covered with jungle, apart from the tanks irrigating the area around Tissamaharama (the area of the ancient Rohana kingdom). "Yet", writes Woolf, "it was Magam Pattu and the eastern part of the district which really won my heart and which I still see when I hear the word Hambantota: the sea perpetually thundering on the long shore, the enormous empty lagoons, behind the lagoons the enormous stretch of jungle, and behind the jungle far away in the north the long purple line of the great mountains"—the mountains around Kandy from which he had looked down towards the far-off ocean while walking with Rachel Robinson.

The coastal lagoons in Magam Pattu were used as salt-producing pans, known locally as *lewayas*. Salt was a profitable monopoly of the Government, for which the assistant government agent was responsible. He also oversaw the game sanctuary, an area of 130 square miles. And north of Tissamaharama, just outside the boundary of Magam Pattu, was the holy place of Kataragama, where he was expected to manage the pilgrims during religious festivals, who congregated at Kataragama from all over Ceylon and beyond, as the pearl fishermen had in Marichchukaddi. The rest of Magam Pattu, apart from Hambantota and Tissamaharama, consisted of small jungle-clad villages. It is

The assistant government agent's bungalow in Hambantota where Woolf stayed during his two-and-a-half year posting there.

these villages that would provide Woolf with the setting and drama of his novel, *The Village in the Jungle*.

In *Growing*, he writes: "It is difficult to know exactly why I found the jungle so fascinating. It is a cruel and dangerous place, and, being a cowardly person, I was always afraid of it. Yet I could not keep away from it." Twice he got lost there, and once had to spend a whole night entirely alone, during which he was forced to wake at half-hourly intervals to feed a fire so as to keep wild animals at bay. Hence the vividness of this description:

> As the night goes on the silence of the jungle grows deeper and deeper, but every now and again it is broken by a soft, sibilant shiver of all the leaves of all the trees for miles round one. This colossal whisper dies away as suddenly as it floats up out of the trees—complete silence to be broken again by strange snufflings and shufflings of some invisible creature nearby, the rattling of a porcupine's quills, the sudden snarl far off of a thwarted leopard, the bell-like call of a deer, or the tortured howling of jackals.

He tried to explain his fascination as follows:

I liked the complete solitude and silence and every now and again the noises which break the jungle's silence and which, as one learns its ways, tell one of the comings and the goings around one. For a few moments one had succeeded in getting oneself out of the world of one's fellow men—which I always do with a sigh of relief—into a world of great beauty, ugliness, and danger. The beauty was extraordinary and you never knew behind what tree or bush or rock you might suddenly see it. You slink slowly round a rock in thick jungle and there in a small opening are five or six dazzling peacocks . . . Another time on a game track I turned a corner and there in the fork of a tree twelve feet from the ground hanging over the branch was the body of a full-grown stag, and on the body lay a leopard eating it. We stared at each other for a moment, and then the leopard just poured himself off the tree as if he were made of elastic or even some miraculous fluid, and disappeared into the jungle.

Jungle images, sounds and emotions took possession of Woolf in the course of moving around the villages of Magam Pattu by horse, by bicycle or on foot during his regular circuits or while on special calls. Circuits were intended for inspecting roads, irrigation works and schools, for regulating the use of slash-and-burn clearing of the jungle to cultivate dry crops (a process known as *chena* cultivation), for keeping an eye on hunting and poaching in the game sanctuary, for settling disputes under the shade of huge tamarind trees, and for carrying out judicial work in the regular courts. A circuit generally lasted about ten days, during which period Woolf relished being out of touch. So utterly cut off was he on circuit that if England, or even Colombo, had been taken over by the Germans, he thought he would not have heard about it. He slept in old Buddhist temples, tents and dirty irrigation bungalows. Conditions were hot and uncomfortable, food and water bad, and he was often ill; on one visit, while inspecting a water channel, he was obliged to wade through paddy fields on horseback in pouring rain while vomiting at regular intervals. Yet, from Wiraketiya, a charming village beside a tank, Woolf was capable of writing to Lytton Strachey contentedly, "One could grow into a peaceful old man in a week here among the coconut palms and the enormous trees."

Special calls involved on-the-spot visits to investigate an incident such as a murder, negotiations with wily contractors for the transport of salt from the

Woolf with the Hambantota kachcheri *staff and Father Cooreman, 1908.*

lewayas, the very occasional settling of communal and inter-religious clashes, the taking of the district census, and of course the supervision of the pilgrims going to Kataragama. Woolf was a very busy civil servant indeed, both by necessity and by inclination. He wrote to Strachey: "I work, God, how I work. I have reduced it to a method and exalted it to a mania". Strachey responded, only half ironically, by dubbing his friend "Lord of ten million blacks".

Certainly Europeans were few and far between in the district. Hambantota itself could boast only a Belgian priest, Father Cooreman, and a woman from the Isle of Man who had married a Sinhalese engineer believing him to be an Indian prince. Twenty-six miles away, in Tangalla, resided a judge (Southorn, Woolf's former colleague in Jaffna) and a superintendent of police. Two irrigation engineers were stationed a similar distance away, one of them deep in the jungle. There was also a Boer named Henry Engelbrecht, a ex-prisoner from the Boer War who had stayed on in Ceylon and become the ranger of the game sanctuary (of whom more later). Apart from receiving the odd visitors, Woolf's social life as assistant government agent consisted of a monthly meeting with Southorn.

His "mania" for work may have been partly the result of his isolation. But he was also, he said, "completely immersed . . . in the life of the people. The more remote that life was from my own, the more absorbed I became in it and the more I enjoyed it." This led to a widening gap between Woolf and Strachey— sometimes they did not communicate for weeks or even months at a time. "After two or three years I ceased to write to Lytton once a week, partly because I buried myself in my work and partly because I buried my past." Woolf purposely hardened his heart against his old intellectual life in England and his regret at losing it, while, at the same time, his commitment strengthened to his life in Hambantota, in which whole weeks might pass when he spoke only in Sinhala. "In the last half of my time in Hambantota I had, I think, an extraordinarily wide and intense knowledge of the country and the people. If a man came into the *kachcheri* or the court, more often than not I could tell from his looks which village he came from."

In addition to his autobiography *Growing*, Woolf's time in Hambantota is recorded in his *Diaries in Ceylon, 1908–1911: Records of a Colonial Administrator*. Since 1808, all civil servants in his position had been required to keep a diary recording a detailed description of their daily work. Unlike the vast majority of such diaries, which are of interest only to professional historians, Woolf's were published in 1962 after his final visit to Ceylon, as mentioned earlier. They are a most valuable factual complement to his literary work, *The Village in the Jungle*. Because of Woolf's fascination with the people of the district, the diaries are far more than a mere dry record of the discharge of his official duties and responsibilities. For example, the entry for 29 April 1910, at a moment when Halley's comet was blazing in the sky above Hambantota district, records the following event:

> In evening rode Hatagala [in West Giruwa Pattu] 14 miles where I camped. A large crowd of petitioners &c. kept me until 7.30. The people informed me that they don't like the comet: the present is an evil age for the people, they say: among the misfortunes come upon them, according to the Velvidane [headman] of Netolpitiya, are (1) the road tax, (2) the V.C. tax, (3) the irrigation rate, (4) the taxes on carts and guns, (5) the restriction of *chenas*, (6) a strict assistant government agent. He invites me to take as my model Mr Murray [a previous assistant government agent] who allowed *chenas* freely and when he left the district wept among weeping headmen.

The Hambantota district relied heavily on slash-and-burn *chena* cultivation, but its effect was to impoverish the soil, quickly forcing the cultivator to find a new plot of land to clear for crops. The Government in Woolf's day tried to control the use of *chenas* by issuing permits only to deserving people, but this system was not a success. Woolf was aware how desperately the people depended on *chena* cultivation, and that some areas of the district were so dry it would have been fatal to ban *chena* cultivation. But he tried to implement a *chena*-based system of long-term benefit to the district. At Tissamaharama he gave land over to *chena* cultivation on condition that a portion of the crop be paid to the Government, with the promise that the following year the Government would return part of this payment if the land was still under cultivation. The idea was to settle the cultivators on their own land.

Nevertheless, Woolf knew that his reputation with the people for strictness was deserved, as it had been in Jaffna. He had fallen in love with the district, the people and the way of life—but he was still determined to apply the law impartially. Much later he admitted in *Growing*:

> I worked all day from the moment I got up in the morning until the moment I went to bed at night, for I rarely thought of anything else except the district and the people . . . There was no sentimentality about this; I did not idealise or romanticise the people of the country; I just liked them aesthetically and humanely and socially, but I was ruthless—too ruthless . . . —both to them and to myself.

In education, for example, he believed that lack of schooling accounted for "the colossal laziness of the people", and so he opened new schools in order to "sweep all . . . children between the ages of 6 and 12 into school each day where they could learn something other than obscenity, ill manners and the torturing of animals, which at present are the three things which make up the education of most of the children in Hambantota." He inspected the existing schools and offered definite advice. He found some to be excellent, such as the schools at Bundala and Walasmulla, others to be woefully deficient. At Katuwana, the children were unhealthy, their spleens swollen by malaria; Woolf impressed upon the teacher the importance of administering quinine. In Hambantota, he opened a new Tamil school funded from the Government's opium revenue. On his last official day as assistant government agent, in May 1911, he made a point of visiting this school along with the Sinhalese school run by Father

Cooreman. The last entry in his official diary before his handover to his successor notes of the Tamil school: "There are signs of some knowledge being driven into the heads of the youth of Hambantota." And of the Sinhalese school: "The numbers have gone up very well since we began to enforce attendance."

An amusing instance of his 'ruthless concern' for the district occurred one afternoon in Warapitiya while Woolf was selling plots of land to villagers. An old man rushed through the crowd and fell at his feet. Only one side of his face was shaved and he earnestly complained that the barber had refused to shave the other side unless he was paid 50 cents (the correct price was five cents). Woolf sent for the barber, who had the look of a rogue, made an enquiry and decided that he should complete the shave for free, but if he cut his customer then he himself should forfeit 50 cents. Several hundred villagers now witnessed the satisfactory shave under a nearby coconut tree. Woolf enjoyed judging this case because, he said, he and the villagers shared the joke. "Even in a remote village I felt that I could make a joke which would be appreciated." He claimed this to be true of European-Sinhalese relations in general, but not true in most Asiatic countries, and one of the unspoken causes of imperial racial friction.

Woolf also used sensitivity when dealing with matters of caste. One day, while he was on circuit in a remote area, he was approached by some *berawaya* (tom-tom caste) women—which was an unusual event, since most women avoided contact with government officials. Their caste meant they were allowed to wind only a strip of cloth over their breasts and under their arms, which meant they could not remain decent while pounding rice. They pleaded to be allowed to wear 'jackets', i.e. blouses. Woolf told them it was not for him to decide what Sinhalese women should wear, but he agreed to speak to the village headman. As a result the headman suggested that the women should wear jackets provided they did not put their arms in the sleeves. "I told the women they had better do this and they were quite satisfied; I felt sure, that after another 50 years, the *berawaya* women's arms would be in the sleeves."

In general, however, there is no doubt that Woolf was unpopular because he was severe. He regularly imposed fines which people struggled to pay. He did not hesitate to fine people for gambling. He received hate mail, which he thought came from the family of a builder whom he had punished for doing work that did not meet regulations. He was even in bad odour with his superior, the government agent, because he appealed against the latter's decisions taken without consulting his subordinate. In retrospect Woolf granted that he was "arrogant and offensive, and he [the government agent] had a good deal to complain of against me." His ruthlessness—combined with a mania for efficiency, which raised salt production remarkably by cutting out theft and mismanagement, and enabled him to return his census form ahead of all other districts—made Hambantota under Woolf the best-administered district in the island. But, he conceded in *Growing*, he tended to forget that efficiency is a means to an end, "not an end in itself".

Disease was an area where Woolf made little impact, notwithstanding his concern, ruthlessness and efficiency. Pleading for more medical facilities on behalf of his district, he pointed out in his diaries addressed to his superiors in Colombo that the most recent figure for the death rate in the Hambantota district among the Sinhalese population was 64.1 and in 1906, 50.7, while for Ceylon as a whole the death rate during the same years was 29.0 and 34.6 respectively. The district's biggest problem was malaria, as it still is. Most of those admitted to the hospital in Hambantota were debilitated by malaria. Only in one place, among the women of Unakuruwa, was malaria absent among the population, Woolf was intrigued to note. The reason appeared to be the women's occupation: diving for coral stones, which they sold for building purposes. (When the women appealed to Woolf for help after their stones were seized by the Forest Department as forest produce, he wrote to the assistant conservator of forests pointing out that the sea could hardly be regarded as part of the forest, and the stones were returned.)

Malaria even influenced a homicide case judged by Woolf. There was an argument between a man and a woman kept by him when she failed to pound paddy and prepare his dinner. He beat her and kicked her, to which he confessed. But Woolf did not convict the man of murder because the doctor concluded that the woman had suffered from such an enlarged spleen only a slight blow would have been sufficient to rupture it and cause her death.

Woolf wrote privately about this case to Strachey. He told him how he had been called to the scene of the killing to inspect the wounds:

> Most women naked when alive are extraordinarily ugly, but dead they
> are repulsive and the most repulsive thing is the way the toes seem to
> stick up so straight and stark and start to dominate the room. But the
> most abominable thing was the smell. One gets accustomed to the
> smell of corruption of dead things here where the cattle are always
> dying of thirst and starvation and lie on the roadsides decaying: but I

had no idea before that the smell of a decomposing human being is so infinitely fouler than anything else.

Perhaps Woolf was attempting to make light of his disturbing experience or even trying to involve Strachey by appealing to his homosexuality. But his letter went on to discuss a deeper issue. He had been reading their mutual friend E. M. Forster's new novel *A Room with a View* at the time of the murder, and by a strange coincidence the previous year he had read Forster's first novel *Where Angels Fear to Tread*, while witnessing the gruesome hangings in Kandy. He now criticised Forster and *A Room with a View* for being "muddled" with "pseudo-mystery": "He still seems to think that death is real and sightseeing unreal; I think I shall have to write to him and explain once more that it doesn't exist, that after all the smell of cheese is as real as the smell of a corpse." Throughout his life, the rational Woolf would have little truck with religion or belief in life after death.

A devastating outbreak of rinderpest among the cattle of the district in 1909 was a source of great frustration for Woolf, and provoked particular resentment of his methods. He wrote: "I have never worked so hard or as despairingly as I did during those twelve months trying to stop the spread of the disease and save some of the people's cattle." Rinderpest was very infectious with a high mortality rate. The only way of dealing with it was to isolate and shoot infected bullocks, a near-impossible task in a culture where cattle were allowed to wander freely and there were no fences. Cattle and buffaloes were people's most valued possessions, needed for paddy production and transportation. Infected cattle spread the disease to wild buffaloes, and their carcasses polluted waterholes. Woolf once spent over twelve hours bicycling fourteen miles, then riding a further 20 miles to inspect and shoot diseased cattle in remote areas. He also fined headmen for allowing cattle to stray. The work was hard and depressing, and the results difficult to assess. The disease would appear to be under control, only to flare up again of a sudden.

It was the only time in my three years in the Hambantota district, in my seven years in Ceylon, that I heard that note of communal hostility against myself or the Government from villagers . . . I knew that the villagers did not believe what I said to them; to them I was part of the white man's machine, which they did not understand. I stood to them in the relation of God to his victims: I was issuing from on high orders to the village which seemed to them arbitrary and resulted in the shooting of their cows.

Rinderpest was so severe that Woolf foresaw a failure of the paddy crop and terrible food shortages. Given the dearth of buffaloes, the only solution was to find an alternative method for muddying the fields in preparation for sowing paddy seed. Woolf demonstrated great resourcefulness by introducing American and British ploughs. He knew there would be prejudice against this new method because the villagers tended to disregard new ideas at the first sign of trouble, preferring to stick to traditional methods. So he ensured that the man sent by the Ceylon Agricultural Society to demonstrate the ploughs was knowledgeable and able to resolve difficulties. His foresight paid off: after the ploughs were demonstrated Woolf received applications for many more ploughs than he had anticipated. In the worst-hit area around Tissamaharama, he was so committed to persuading the people that he himself gave ploughing demonstrations. He won over the carters of Hambantota, once they saw the plough being used, and became quite fascinated by the challenge of teaching two bulls and himself to plough. The success of the ploughs averted a famine in the district. But once the rinderpest outbreak was over, Woolf found that the villagers reverted to their original methods of cultivation.

For all his commitment, did Woolf really feel that the condition of the villages could be improved? Doubts about the whole imperial enterprise had been creeping up on him. Contrasting the hopelessness and lack of conviction he felt while trying to alleviate poverty paternalistically in the hovels of London's East End after his return to England from Ceylon in 1911, he remarked in his autobiography that in those days, "In the Ceylon jungle village there was still a place or excuse for government paternalism. Life and the people there were still simple and primitive enough to make a simple and primitive relationship between ruler and ruled possible. Even so I had resigned from the Ceylon civil service."

In 2004, almost a century after Woolf came to Hambantota, one of his successors, Gamini Punchihewa, who worked in the district for twelve years first as an assistant lands officer and then as a lands officer, expressed his own doubts in the *Ceylon Daily News*. Speaking of one of the villages in the jungle known to Woolf, Punchihewa noted that as recently as 1992 it had been struck by famine. "Even to this day if rains do not come during the proper season, the

Rinderpest and the consequent dearth of buffaloes caused Woolf to find alternative methods for muddying the fields in preparation for sowing paddy seed.

tanks go dry and the people are subjected to great hardship by way of procuring food for their meagre living. And this whole area is still infected with the scourge of malaria." Ajith Samaranayake, editor-in-chief of the English newspapers of the government-owned Lake House Group, was even more categorical in the *Sunday Observer*:

> In spite of almost six decades of political independence, the proclamation of the Republic and brave statements from politicians that Sri Lanka lives in the village and that the farmers are the backbone of the nation, little has changed from the days of Leonard Woolf's novel *The Village in the Jungle* and its grim picture of life in a southern Sri Lankan village in colonial times.
>
> The average peasant is caught in the grip of the same inertia and the same sense of hopelessness as Woolf's protagonists. It is true that since Woolf's time, the jungles have been cleared and colonisation schemes set in place, infectious diseases have been eliminated, the headmen system replaced and other such reformist measures have been undertaken. But at bottom, the lot of the peasantry has hardly changed.

*   *   *

Even for a progressive assistant government agent like Woolf, increasing the welfare of the peasants in Hambantota district had to go hand in hand with making a profit for the imperial government. And Woolf welcomed this fact: he knew that the money raised from government monopolies and the various official taxes was needed to pay for the administration of his district. The most important source of revenue was salt, and thus a major part of Woolf's official diaries is concerned with its production. He proved to be an able businessman willing to drive a hard bargain; indeed he was sure that his training in the salt industry in Ceylon was later of significant help to him in administering his fledgling publishing business, the Hogarth Press, back in London.

The "enormous empty lagoons" of Hambantota, known as *lewayas*, must often have come to Woolf's mind, too, while advising the Labour Party on imperial and international questions during the 1920s and 30s. Especially in 1930, when Mahatma Gandhi organised his historic salt march to Dandi on the Arabian Sea. Having extracted untaxed salt from the sea, in violation of the Indian Government's monopoly, tens of thousands of Indian villagers and city-dwellers were sent to jail; the whole of India was aroused; Gandhi was arrested; and the entire world became aware of his campaign for self-government. But when Woolf was enthusiastically working the *lewayas* in Hambantota two decades earlier, he was still an innocent imperialist.

Around Hambantota salt formed naturally by evaporation of sea water from the lagoons, producing layers between half and ten inches thick. It was said to be exceptionally pure, and so these sparkling shores had long been a valuable resource to the Sinhalese. In 1791, for instance, the Dutch rulers of Ceylon attempted to withhold salt from the king of Kandy, hoping that he would exchange salt for precious cinnamon. By 1834, salt in Hambantota had become a British Government monopoly and the *lewayas* were carefully guarded against intruders. A by-product was the growth of wildlife in the district. A visitor in 1880 reported that, "Great mobs of snowy pelicans and groups of delicately rosy flamingos stand reflected in the still waters, and many crocodiles bask on the shores."

Woolf was responsible for the collection, transport, storage and sale of the salt. The principal salt towns were Bundala, Kirinda and Palatupana, all to the east of Hambantota. Bundala was the most productive *lewaya*, despite the salt formations occasionally being destroyed by rainfall. Woolf's experience in

Woolf was responsible for the collection, transport, storage and sale of salt from the lewayas.

Jaffna, and at the pearl fishery near Mannar, immediately came in useful and helped to establish his reputation for ruthlessness and efficiency. Not long after his arrival in August 1908, a group of contractors in charge of removing salt from the *lewayas* demanded a higher rate. At first, Woolf circumvented them by hiring other workers, but he knew that this was only a temporary solution. So he entered into negotiations with the head contractor who repeatedly refused to take less money. Then, cunningly, Woolf suggested to the contractor that they take an early evening stroll through Hambantota, together with the salt superintendent, to discuss the matter further. The contractor leapt at the chance to be seen in public with two such important officials and eagerly agreed. They set off, and after a while Woolf asked the contractor if he would accept a lower price to remove the salt. Despite showing signs of wilting in the heat, the man stubbornly shook his head. So Woolf told him: "I am going to walk on to Tissa which, if we go at this pace, we shall reach about two in the morning, for we have another 18 miles to go. I am very fond of walking and I think the salt superintendent is too. But I don't want you to come on if you would rather not." Knowing he was beaten, the man at last agreed to Woolf's terms. The salt contractors had discovered his strength and never troubled him again.

It is no exaggeration to say that Woolf revolutionised salt collection in

Hambantota. The collectors had previously been paid by vouchers, a system that was unreliable and open to corruption. Instead, Woolf ensured that collectors were paid on the spot for their labour which increased the amount for them. After collection at the *lewaya*, salt was weighed, checked, and then transported to a storage centre. A certain amount of wastage was allowed during transportation by bullock cart, but Woolf suspected a scam whereby incorrect weights for each bag of salt were recorded at either end and the difference skimmed off. By paying unannounced visits to the *lewayas* and to the stores, he proved his suspicions and ordered that the salt checkers be suspended for six months. They pleaded their innocence and asked him to check the weight of all bags—which he agreed to do, on condition that if these were found to be inaccurate, he would suspend the checkers for an additional six months. Having thoroughly investigated and proved his case, he proceeded to suspend the workers for a year. In *Growing*, he regretted this punishment: "Looking back it seems to me that there was unnecessary severity and relentlessness in this decision." But his policies unquestionably produced results: in 1910 there was a record collection of salt, far exceeding the previous record of 1893.

Among the government taxes Woolf had to supervise was the road tax. Each man between the ages of 18 and 55 had either to give six days' labour per year to road building or to pay a small sum of money in lieu. Needless to say, the road tax was extremely unwelcome, especially in remote areas without roads, and it was Woolf's unpleasant duty to impose the requirement on men who were physically unfit, or to fine them or sentence them to imprisonment as defaulters.

Kirama was one such remote area, 41 miles from Hambantota towards the west, at the foot of the hills. It took Woolf five days to get there along roads barely passable for a horse. In a letter to Saxon Sydney-Turner, he described Kirama as "a delightful place surrounded by forest, scarcely touched by civilisation. It is quite cool as I watch the mist come rolling down the hills across the tree tops." But his own illness and the nature of his job in Kirama took away almost all of his pleasure in the setting, as he describes in horrific language:

> At every place I stop, crowds of [tax] defaulters are brought up to me by the headmen for trial and sentence. They bring down to me wild savages from the hills, spectacles incredible to anyone who has not seen them. Naked except for a foul rag round their loins, limbs

which are mere bones, stomachs distended with enormously enlarged spleens, their features eaten away by and their skin covered with sores from one of the most loathsome of existing diseases called *parangi*, or else wild apelike creatures with masses of tangled hair falling over their shoulders, their black bodies covered with white scales of *parangi* scab, hobbling along on legs enormous with elephantitis.

Since the Government controlled game hunting, Woolf was also responsible for issuing licences to sportsmen. Big game shooting was already an organised business, with Colombo-based specialist firms providing the sportsmen with equipment and all other necessary requirements for their treks. Once, Woolf saw a prince, a duke and a count setting off to hunt in the jungle with a cartload of prostitutes.

Sometimes he personally accompanied visiting aristocrats on their expeditions. In 1909, a telegram from Colombo informed him of Baron Axel von Blixen's visit and ordered him to make the party as comfortable as possible. Blixen was delayed, so Count Frijs and his party went on ahead, leaving Woolf to bring along Blixen several days later. When the baron arrived, Woolf found him to be "extremely nervous, and, holding my hand in his two hands, besought me not to leave him alone in the jungle". Blixen turned out to be a terrible shot, missing a crocodile by nearly fifty feet. But somehow, Woolf wryly noted, the baron's luck seems to have improved at Palatupana and he shot several deer and a bear. Perhaps in this case the company in Colombo had provided an experienced shot, as was the custom, who was trained to fire at the same moment as the client. At any rate, Woolf made such a favourable impression on Blixen that when the baron returned to Europe he called upon Woolf's aunt in order to praise her nephew in Ceylon.

To begin with, Woolf found hunting exciting and spent some of the sweepstake money he had won in Kandy on guns. But the longer he spent in Hambantota the more repelled he became by killing for sport and the more his respect diminished for the sportsmen and their Colombo organisers. Eventually he shot only 'for the pot', to relieve his habitual diet of stringy curried chicken with wild deer, jungle fowl, peafowl, teal, pigeon, snipe and golden plover. Another reason for his lack of enthusiasm was perhaps, as he admitted, that although he was a good tracker he was a poor shot.

On one hunting trip, at least, he shot amazingly well. He had gone out in the jungle with an inexperienced superintendent of police and the ranger of the game sanctuary, the stiff-necked Boer Engelbrecht. In an act of fearless stupidity, Engelbrecht persuaded the other two to follow a wounded leopard up to the entrance to a cave. Engelbrecht then insisted on trying to prod the wounded animal with a long sapling and managed to force it out of the cave, whereupon Woolf, by a complete fluke, shot it dead with a bullet through the heart as the animal charged.

✳   ✳   ✳

Henry Engelbrecht was an interesting and controversial character, to put it mildly, who has always intrigued me. Born in the Orange Free State in South Africa, he had been interned in Ceylon after the Boer War, along with other Boers, some of whom died there; there is even a Boer cemetery in the hill country town of Diyatalawa. For Boer prisoners wishing to be repatriated, the British Government insisted that they swear an oath of allegiance to the king "and his successors". This Engelbrecht refused to do on the grounds—logical enough—that although he could vouch for King Edward VII he could not do the same for his successors. The Ceylon Government attempted to persuade him to change his mind by sending him to live in a disused prison, but he refused to comply and simply lived in squalor. So in 1906 he was appointed ranger of the game sanctuary at Yala to alleviate his poverty. Woolf thought Engelbrecht obstinate, stupid and cold blooded: "He behaved to the Sinhalese as the Boers behave to the Negroes in Africa and, not unnaturally, he was hated in Hambantota."

Woolf thought Henry Engelbrecht, the first ranger of the game sanctuary, obstinate, stupid and cold blooded.

Engelbrecht was the subject of a paternity case adjudicated by Woolf in his capacity as a police magistrate as well as assistant government agent. On the appointed day, half of the male population of Hambantota gathered in and around the courtroom to see a beautiful Sinhalese woman show Woolf her white baby. There was evidence that she had been living with Engelbrecht in the old prison. Woolf knew what was in the heads of the witnesses against the Boer: "He is a white man, this swine. The A. G. A. doesn't really know what he's like; he goes out in the jungle and shoots with him. What will the A. G. A. do?" Woolf found in favour of the Sinhalese woman and made a maintenance order against Engelbrecht. After his judgement was delivered he noted "a distinct drop in tension, a kind of soundless sigh of relief as they filed out of the court." But Engelbrecht was hated so much that the judgement was not enough for the locals: the woman's brothers cut the heads off his buffaloes, leaving them on either side of his doorway; another time they clubbed to death his bear cub, a harmless creature that he had rescued from the jungle and reared from birth.

On an earlier visit to Hambantota— while researching my book *The Man-eater of Punanai*—I saw Engelbrecht's grave in the town's Catholic cemetery. He died on 25 March 1928. I also met an old man, Baba Singho, now dead, a retired tracker who was rumoured to be the illegitimate grandson of Engelbrecht but who aggressively denied it, despite being remarkably fair skinned. Most probably he did not want to be associated with someone who had once been feared and despised locally. Instead of talking about Engelbrecht, Baba Singho enthralled me with tales of jungle happenings and superstitions in the old days; he had a reputation as a 'devil

Persuaded by Engelbrecht to follow a wounded leopard to a cave, Woolf, by a complete fluke, shot it dead when the animal charged.

dancer' with the power to cure people with strange maladies.

This time around, while visiting Palatupana, one of the salt towns, I encountered "Sudu Ama", Engelbrecht's 80-year-old granddaughter, and in Debarawewa, fourteen miles away, I met his 56-year-old grandson, Gam Hewage Siripala. He was frank and affable and took us to his house where he showed me a photograph of his father—the very same child who had been produced in court before Woolf. His grandmother, the Sinhalese woman who had lived with Engelbrecht, was a fisherwoman from Hambantota of the *karawa* caste, who had a remarkable eight children by Engelbrecht. His father's name was Wilbert (one of Engelbrecht's own names, which he seems to have dropped at some point in his life); and he had an elder brother called Harry. Wilbert seems to have adopted the surname Siripala—in preference to Engelbrecht. Today people apparently visit the Siripala family quite regularly for stories about Engelbrecht, and also about Woolf. A village elder, eighty-year-old Assarapulli Gamage Nandias, was happy to discuss with me the famous paternity case. It seemed fresh to him even after the lapse of almost a hundred years.

I sometimes think the game sanctuary at Yala, where Engelbrecht and Woolf once watched animals as part of their official duties, is my favourite place in the whole of Sri Lanka. Woolf liked to camp out there at the waterholes. A special feature of the sanctuary is its position in one of the driest parts of the island, where it is usual for there to be no rain between May and September. As the land desiccates, desperate deer fall victim to jackals and leopards at the dried-up waterholes; the only animals able to remember the location of water in the dry season from year to year are the elephants.

In 1910, Woolf wrote a long article on Yala for the *Times of Ceylon Annual*, entitled simply "Sanctuary". He tells of how the game sanctuary came into being in 1899, and describes how it was absolutely

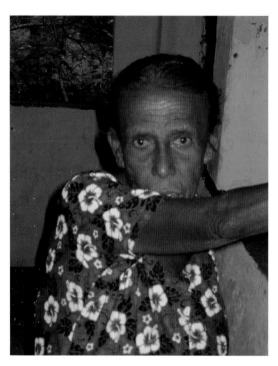

A. W. "Sudu Ama" Lilynona, Engelbrecht's 80-year-old granddaughter.

uninhabited, "except by the government game watchers, and, from time to time, by some person who is 'wanted' and who seeks in its jungles a refuge from the 'hue and cry'." The sanctuary's isolation meant that the traveller had to bring his provisions with him—food and tents—and of course arrange his own transportation. Game wardens such as himself spent so much time in the sanctuary that they got to know animals individually. One old bullock was quite aggressive and would try to attack any human he saw, once following his pony for nearly a mile. A particular buffalo was blind and the other buffaloes liked to torment her by pushing her into an area she did not know, where she would crash into trees and fall over. "Buffaloes seem to have a very low sense of humour," Woolf commented. There were distinct individuals to be seen among every species. While some elephants were placid, for instance, others would amuse themselves by charging the game wardens, though without malicious intent. Always, though, nature remained red in tooth and claw. Once, Woolf saw two bull elephants fighting, repeatedly smashing their foreheads together with a terrifying sound. He also came across an immense crocodile filling the jungle with a strange roaring noise; he shot it, and discovered that it had choked on a tortoise with an unbreakable shell. He was especially attracted to leopards (as we know from his Jaffna days). Their beauty and habits were compelling to him: the way, for example, leopards deliberately 'click' their teeth to make a sound that so terrifies the monkeys in the trees above that one of them inevitably falls down in panic and becomes the leopard's prey.

After Woolf's time, in 1938, Yala became a national park. Today it is divided into two sections but only the western part is open to visitors. The park is divided into five blocks, the first of which contains the highest density of leopards.

I am thrilled by Yala partly because I connect it with happy memories from my early years. When I was still a boy my father took me on a trip around Ceylon for a fortnight by car. The year was 1946 and I was twelve. It was probably the highlight of my life until then, and it was certainly the last thing my father and I did together, just before we were separated for ever.

It was at Yala that I saw my first leopard. Although there were leopards in the hills near our tea estates, I had never actually seen one. My brief glimpse excited me terribly and whetted my appetite for more, and when we returned to our bungalow for dinner I was full of questions for the trackers: how dangerous are leopards, what are their habits, do they eat people? Though I forgot most of what I was told, learning it again only much later, I never forgot the story of the man-eater of Punanai. Over the course of a year or two in the early 1920s, an exceptionally dangerous and audacious leopard killed and devoured at least twenty human beings in the region of Punanai, in Batticaloa district, terrorising this small village. Villagers vanished from their mud huts in the night. Coolies were taken as they worked on the railway lines. Messengers walking the stretch of road to Batticaloa were ambushed and eaten. The panic persisted until an English tea planter and sportsman, Captain Shelton Agar, at last shot the man-eater in 1924. The story gripped me so much that it made me want to return to Sri Lanka and write *The Man-eater of Punanai*.

Returning to Yala this time, we dropped our things at the bungalow overlooking Banduwewa and wasted no time in going on our first game drive with Sujeewa, our tracker. It was a dull, overcast morning but we soon confronted a herd of belligerent elephants blocking the road. Sujeewa dispersed them with aggressive language, his own particular mixed Sinhala-Malayalam mantra. On our return we had an excellent meal: rice and curry, of course, and for dessert the delicious local buffalo curd with *kitul* palm treacle. As always, it was very good to be back in Yala.

✷   ✷   ✷

The pilgrimage to Kataragama provided one of the most remarkable experiences in Woolf's time at Hambantota. There are three festivals each year at Kataragama but the most significant—and the one Woolf oversaw in July 1910—is the Esala Perahera at the beginning of the new moon in June or July, which concludes with a water-cutting ceremony on the morning of the full-moon day. For two weeks the village of Kataragama becomes an entire town; for the rest of the year it is inhabited by only twelve priests.

Many pilgrims came all the way from India, travelling via Galle and Matara to Hambantota district. From Hambantota onwards, there was no food or shelter for them, some of whom were sick with diseases that included smallpox and cholera. To control the numbers the Government issued tickets, but the demand far outstripped the supply: at Tissamaharama 300 people applied for 75 tickets. Woolf based himself at Kataragama itself, where he stayed for fourteen days, and estimated that there were between three and four thousand pilgrims. It was an endurance test for him too, with relentless heat, sandstorms and eye flies by day, and at night plagues of mosquitoes. As he drily recorded

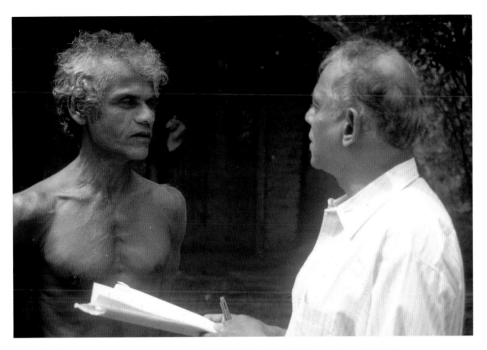

Raj de Silva questions Gam Hewage Siripala, Engelbrecht's grandson, in Debarawewa.

in his *Diaries*, "I hope the Kataragama god sees to it that the supervisor of the pilgrims acquires some little merit from this pilgrimage."

Woolf explained the Kataragama legend in *Growing*. The Kataragama *deviyo* (god), Kandeswami, used to have his temple on top of the Kataragama hill but decided one day he would like to cross the river and live in Kataragama. He requested some passing Tamils to carry him across, but they were on their way to collect salt at Palatupana and said they would carry him across on their way back. Then some Sinhalese passed and helped the god immediately. This is supposedly why the Kataragama temple priests are Sinhalese rather than Tamil. In support of the legend, Woolf was amazed at how people of low caste, even *dhobis* (washermen), were allowed into the temples—something that would have been inconceivable in a Hindu temple in Jaffna.

The significance of Kataragama predates its use as a Buddhist shrine perhaps as early as the fifth century BC. It was a place of worship for the Veddas, Sri Lanka's indigenous people, who called the Kataragama god Kanda Yakka, meaning 'spirit of the mountain'. The place is today holy for Veddas, Buddhists, Hindus and Muslims. The pioneer anthropologist of folk religion in Ceylon, Paul Wirz, notes in his guide to Kataragama: "One could actually say that all religions are represented in Kataragama and that all are getting on well with each other. All ritual differences seem to be resolved out here; all are reconciled with each other and even the feeling of caste is completely forgotten." Even so, there is some rivalry between Buddhists and Hindus to claim the Kataragama deity as their own. As for Muslims, although they are a minority at Kataragama, their presence has been influential. In the days of Portuguese rule over Ceylon, so many Muslim *bawas* made the pilgrimage to Kataragama via Jaffna that the authorities suspected a Kandyan revolt and closed the route.

Apart from his initial meetings with the district medical officer and priests, Woolf actually had very little to do while at Kataragama. So one day he climbed the nearby hill, which took four hours. He also went walking in the surrounding jungle and discovered places where poached meat was dried, away from the eyes of the game sanctuary watchers. Amazing to record, Woolf was the only government official at Kataragama with no staff or police to back him up. So secure was the Government in its imperialist confidence that it correctly assumed the presence of a single white civil servant sufficient to prevent trouble.

In Woolf's day, pilgrims made the arduous journey to Kataragama on foot.

Today many people drive to Kataragama, but in Woolf's day the pilgrims made the arduous journey on foot, earning merit from their suffering. The penances, however, have changed little since he was there. Silver needles are pushed through the cheeks and tongue, silver arrows into the chest, arms and back; there are shoes made of nails and iron hooks embedded into the skin of the back. Sometimes strings are attached to the hooks and the penitent is either led on the string or pulls a small wagon behind him containing two dolls, one representing the deity, the other his beloved.

During the penances, sacred texts are recited, purifying camphor is burned and holy water is sprinkled—all to the accompaniment of furious drumming. Wirz saw one penitent hanging from eight hooks within a scaffold mounted on a cart which was wheeled from temple to temple. The man spoke and gave blessings to people for two hours but fainted when let down from the scaffold; he was revived with fanning and 'holy water'. Wirz believed him to be in a trance. "Everybody who stays in Kataragama during this time is in fact as a man in a state of intoxication. In this state things are often done that cost them their lives. Every year it so happens that someone or another carries the tortures to extremes and dies. It also happens every year that a man who has worked himself up into such a pitch of ecstasy suddenly cuts his throat."

The other famous ritual in Kataragama is the fire-walking ceremony. A believer will walk or dance across coals at a temperature of more than thirteen hundred degrees Fahrenheit, hot enough to melt aluminium. Some walk over the coals several times, in the belief that enduring the heat for longer will bring increased spiritual benefit. Most of the fire walkers do not even have a blister. There are various theories about this, such as that the villagers' feet are hardened from years without shoes or that perspiration from their feet protects them. But for the fire walker the phenomenon is a miracle explained by nothing other than his faith.

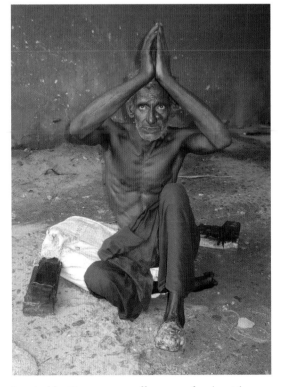

Inevitably, Kataragama offers cures for the sick. Woolf recalled only one really bad sleepless night in Ceylon, and this was when he was kept awake in Kataragama by the crying of a child outside his bungalow. It turned out that the child was blind and its parents were pinching and pricking it all night to make the child cry so that the god would hear their entreaties. The following day Woolf took the child to a doctor to see if anything could be done, but the blindness was incurable. He wrote: "It

Inevitably, Kataragama offers cures for the sick.

was these kind of strange, alien psychological encounters which fascinated me—the mixture of pathos and absurdity, of love and cruelty, in such horrible and grotesque incidents."

In the last week of the 1910 festival, it rained heavily, exposing the pilgrims to pneumonia and malaria. Woolf suggested to the government agent that in future more accommodation be provided for the pilgrims. When he returned to Ceylon in 1960, he was pleased to see more accommodation in place, but he was saddened by Kataragama's commercialism. He thought the improvement in facilities had encouraged a certain corruption of purpose. The Kataragama of old, he said, was "an authentic, spontaneous explosion of the hopes and aspirations of ordinary men and women who lived hard and bewildered lives", but its equivalent in 1960 was more like exploitation. Rupees were demanded along with the offerings of flowers and fruit. Nevertheless, when I visited Kataragama in 1990, I found myself surprisingly moved by the devotees' religious feeling. I could not help dashing a coconut onto a concrete slab near the temple exit. It split cleanly down the middle, supposedly indicating that my wish would be granted.

This is not to say that Woolf idealised the Kataragama of 1910. He found many things there evil and repellent, in particular its superstition. As a devotee of Voltaire, he always deplored superstition in Ceylon. He gave an interesting example of this in Hambantota. He was walking at night with a village headman in the days of Halley's comet. "The stars blazed with a brilliance which they have only on a clear, still, black night in the southern hemisphere. And at our feet the comet and the stars blazed, reflected in the smooth, velvety black sea." He spoke of the comet to the headman, who had been educated in English and was Europeanised, and was also, thought Woolf, an intelligent man. He therefore treated him "as I would . . . a white man". However, he was depressed to discover that the man explained the comet by astrology; it contained a prediction of when a girl would start to menstruate. Such an experience—combined with many others, for example, the villagers' resentment of his scientific attempts to control rinderpest—led Woolf to muse on his frustrations at trying to resolve the problems of Hambantota "as a moral tale about imperialism—the absurdity of a people of one civilisation and mode of life trying to impose its rule upon an entirely different civilisation and mode of life."

But still he was fascinated, as *The Village in the Jungle* so graphically

The pilgrimage to Kataragama provided one of the most remarkable experiences in Woolf's time in Hambantota. However, apart from his initial meetings with the district medical officer and priests, he had actually very little to do while at the festival.

demonstrates, by the ancient jungle beliefs on display in Kataragama and indeed everywhere in Ceylon, most of which can be traced back to the Veddas or to pre-Buddhist folk religion. These include countless omens: that dogs and cats howl at night if they see a *yakka* (usually an evil spirit) nearby; and that the cry of an owl is a sign of an imminent death. A *yakka* (plural *yakku*) can enter a person and make him or her ill or bring other troubles. *Yakku* haunt different places—large old trees, mountain caves, even village streets—but their power is such that no direct contact with them is necessary. Some are thought to devour flesh and blood so that a person cannot eat and wastes away. Woolf once met a man who claimed to be suffering from *yak leda*, devil sickness. He had gone to look at a well one night and ran into what he thought was a devil (though it turned out to have been an old woman).

An elaborate system existed for dealing with *yakku*. First, there had to be a diagnosis from a soothsayer, a clairvoyant and an astrologer. A favourable day was chosen for the exorcism by consulting the patient's horoscope and astrology was used to equate certain planets with parts of the body. The patient and his family then collected lemons, palm leaves and fruit, and made the receptacles needed to offer gifts to a *yakka*. The removal of the illness itself was the job of the devil charmer or exorcist, and the priest who mediated between the devils and mankind. Exorcists, usually known as *edura*, were of low caste, whereas the medicine men were of a higher caste. Each had a different role so that no rivalry existed between them. *Yakku* were summoned when the *edura* recited a mantra and offered gifts at certain times of the day, using very detailed and precise ceremonies. Two or three *eduras* were usually needed (each one, of course, being separately paid by the patient!). They performed the role of '*yakku* actors' and the more money a patient gave, the more *yakku* actors there were. At least one drummer was also required. Gifts were offered to *yakku* at specified times throughout the night.

Eduras could be consulted on other matters apart from sickness. The *kodivina edura* was appropriate when a person wished to inflict damage on another. Usually a wax effigy was made of the intended victim, pins inserted in various places, then it was buried in the victim's garden. Some of these spells were said to cause illness or death, others to bring bad luck into a house or to induce insanity. *Yantras*, mystical geometric designs, could be worn as amulets for protection, and mantras could be uttered at special times of the day to summon or ward off *yakku*. Wirz, writing in 1954 in *Exorcism and the Art of Healing in Ceylon*, commented:

> it almost seems as if a Sinhalese is unable to undertake anything with-out securing success or protecting himself from failure by preventive magic. His whole doing and thinking are ruled by the conception that everywhere forces are at work, and that all kinds of superior beings are uninterruptedly influencing his ways and doing, his thoughts and aspirations, so that he must always be armed, or at least, on his guard lest he falls victim to these powers and forces.

Though today most Sinhalese content themselves with consulting astrologers and astrological charts, rather than protecting themselves against evil spirits and casting spells on others using elaborate ceremonies, the influence of certain rites remains. One such is known as the 'ritual of the leopard's pot', in which all the misfortunes of an individual are put in a pot and destroyed. This can also be used for putting a curse on someone or something. The pot itself is subjected to traditional rituals: the potter takes precautions when making the pot by purifying it himself, drying it in the sun and not firing it. It stands six or seven feet tall with twelve spouts moulded into cobra and leopard heads and one large leopard-headed spout at the front. It is consecrated three times during the night when demons are thought to be active—dusk, midnight and early dawn—to the accompaniment of the beating of drums and dancing. Each householder wears a cloth on his or her head then puts the cloth in the pot with the other ingredients. The demon is asked to listen to the command of the beautiful god and banish pestilence, disease and misfortune. This ritual is still known in the low country near Hambantota.

With regard to the major religions in Woolf's district—Buddhism, Hinduism and Islam—their adherents in Woolf's district lived for the most part peaceably together, though he was always expecting friction. During his time he faced only two significant religiously inspired incidents. Just before he left the district, a riot broke out between Buddhists and Muslims in Hambantota. Woolf was called in and found that Buddhists and Muslims had been fighting each other with sticks and stones in front of a mosque. Most of the fighting was over and he was inundated with a variety of conflicting stories. Realising the difficulty of holding an impartial inquiry in such heated circumstances, Woolf noticed some witnesses from out of town and immediately took their statements. Although they included both Buddhists and Muslims, they had not had time to conspire amongst themselves. Thus the truth came out. A Buddhist procession had beaten tom-toms while passing the mosque. The Muslims had tried to stop this and a fight had broken out. All religious processions required a permit from the Government, and no procession was permitted to beat tom-toms when passing the place of worship of another religion. So it was apparent that the Buddhists were in the wrong, but then so were the Muslims for using violence against them. When the religious leaders of both groups approached Woolf the following day wishing to settle the case amicably, so as to avoid bad feeling, he fined both sides—the Buddhists for using tom-toms without a licence and the Muslims for disturbing a religious procession.

The second religious incident concerned only the Muslims. A new *hakim* of the Hambantota mosque was to be appointed, and there was a dispute between rival factions. Woolf was loath to become involved. Then a curious Englishman who was a Muslim convert, Hadji Salam Robertson, arrived at Woolf's office requesting permission to lecture in Hambantota. He had been an officer in the Leicestershire Regiment but was now a travelling preacher spreading the word of Mohammed. Woolf cleverly asked Robertson to raise the issue of the dispute in his lecture. As a result the faction leaders came to Woolf seeking a resolution, but since none could be found two rival *hakims* were appointed. Yet Woolf knew that "These were sophisticated disputes among sophisticated people, and they were dangerous because they might easily have led to large-scale violence." He therefore summoned the leaders himself and said he would hold them personally responsible for any trouble. Three days later, they resolved the dispute.

*　　*　　*

Despite his love of solitude, of the jungle and of the people of Hambantota, by the end of 1910 Woolf was keen to proceed on a year's home leave that was due to him. His return to England was delayed by the need to administer the district census at the beginning of 1911, and he stayed an additional five months. In the end he left Ceylon for England on 24 May 1911.

Although his correspondence with Strachey had diminished while in Hambantota, a recurring theme in it had been the idea of Woolf's marrying Virginia Stephen. In February 1909, he had written: "The most wonderful of all would have been to marry Virginia . . . Do you think Virginia would have me?" Strachey urged him to marry Virginia, after his own proposal to her had been turned down, as she was not in love with him. In September, Woolf told him:

> Of course I know that the one thing to do would be to marry Virginia. I am only frightened that when I come back in Dec. 1910 I may. For though when one had and everything was completed and consummated, life would probably be supreme; the horrible preliminary complications, the ghastly complications too of virginity and marriage altogether appall me. Really if it weren't for that and for the question of money I actually would telegraph.

Woolf's anxiety about virginity and marriage seems to have prevented him from acting for some time—he joked to Strachey that rather than telegraphing his intention to marry Virginia, he would wait and marry a widow or an ex-prostitute.

He arrived back in London undecided about his future—whether to return to Ceylon or to stay in England and marry. Back in his family house in Colinette Road, Putney, after being away for more than six years, he felt somewhat depressed: "After the unending jungle, the great lagoons, the enormous sea pounding on the shore below my bungalow, the large open windowless rooms in Hambantota, I felt the walls of the Putney dining-room pressing in upon me, the low ceiling pressing down on me, the past and twenty years closing in on me."

Ceylon stayed very much in his mind as he started work on *The Village in the Jungle*. But at the same time he was falling in love with Virginia Stephen. He gradually came to realise that even if she would not marry him, he would not return to Ceylon and a career in the Ceylon civil service. The only way that he could imagine returning there, he fantasised, would be if he could spend the remainder of his days administering the Hambantota district—a somewhat improbable option for a capable civil servant. This work was what he liked, he claimed, not the European side of the job, "the white sahib side of it, the kind of second-rate (as it appeared to me) pomp and circumstance which surrounded one in Kandy and Colombo." He now knew he did not want to become a successful imperialist. While the Ceylon civil service might give him power, it could never give him enough freedom.

In February 1912, still unsure about Virginia's reaction to his marriage proposal, Woolf wrote to the Colonial

Leonard Woolf married Virginia Stephen on 10 August 1912.

Office requesting that his leave be extended for four months. As he refused to state why he needed the extra time, he knew that his request was almost bound to be denied. "I did not feel that I could explain", Woolf recalls in *Growing*, "that I had come to dislike imperialism, that I did not want to become a governor, that I wanted to marry Virginia Stephen, and that, if I didn't marry her, I would like to continue to be a Ceylon civil servant provided that they would appoint me permanently assistant government agent Hambantota."

On 7 May 1912, his resignation from the Ceylon civil service was formally accepted. He married Virginia Stephen a few months later, on 10 August. In November, *The Village in the Jungle* was accepted for publication. Woolf would not return to Ceylon for half a century, by then as a visitor to an independent country.

8

The Literary Woolf

> The jungle and the people who lived in the Sinhalese jungle villages
> fascinated, almost obsessed me in Ceylon. They continued to obsess me
> in London, in Putney or Bloomsbury, and in Cambridge. *The Village in*
> *the Jungle* was a novel in which I tried somehow or other vicariously
> to live their lives. It was also, in some curious way, the symbol of the
> anti-imperialism which had been growing upon me more and more in
> my last years in Ceylon ... The more I wrote *The Village in the Jungle*, the
> more distasteful became the prospect of success in Colombo.
>
> LEONARD WOOLF, *Beginning Again*

WITH THE PUBLICATION of *The Village in the Jungle* in 1913, when he was 32, Leonard Woolf became a professional writer. He would go on writing to within a few months of his death at the age of 88 in 1969, publishing his books himself under his increasingly famous Hogarth Press imprint. If we set aside Woolf's substantial political and historical writings and his extensive journalism, his literary output consists of two early novels, first *The Village in the Jungle*, then *The Wise Virgins*; three short stories under the umbrella title *Stories of the East*; a play about the impending catastrophe in Europe in the late 1930s, *The Hotel*; his five-volume autobiography published in the 1960s under the titles *Sowing, Growing, Beginning Again, Downhill All the Way* and *The Journey Not the Arrival Matters*; and his letters, edited by Frederic Spotts and published in 1989.

Of all these literary works, the ones that directly concern Ceylon are *The Village in the Jungle, Stories of the East*, the second volume of the autobiography (*Growing*), and some of the letters, especially those written to Lytton Strachey, chiefly in the period 1904–11. Since the previous chapters of this book have already discussed and quoted from the short stories, *Growing* and the letters

Woolf in Hambantota, around 1908.

at various points, the primary focus of this chapter will be *The Village in the Jungle*, although at the end we shall look, too, at the critical response to *Stories of the East*, as well as touch on the rest of Woolf's literary career.

Woolf started writing *The Village in the Jungle* in October 1911, three or four months after returning to England from Ceylon, and he continued to work at the novel for a year. His friend E. M. Forster encouraged him to publish with his own publisher Edward Arnold, and in November 1912, after the book was accepted by Arnold, Woolf wrote to the publisher thanking him and asking him to mark some passages in the manuscript that the publisher's reader had objected to, with a view to making revisions before publication. He added that he would be pleased to give Arnold first refusal on his next book. In Woolf's collected letters his editor Spotts notes that, "In a condescending reply, Arnold predicted poor sales and deprecated [Woolf's] wish to keep the copyright, dismissing the notion that foreign publishers would have any interest in the book." In the event, *The Village in the Jungle* would be translated into Sinhala, French and German, and its sales in its first year of publication would require two reprints. Arnold changed his tune—as so often happens with publishers—and now told Woolf that he heard "nothing but enthusiastic praise from everyone who has read it", and requested another book from him. There was a further reprint of the novel in 1925, and by 1929 it had sold 2,149 copies and earned its author £63—figures that Woolf himself, ever the publisher, noted scrupulously in his autobiography. While they may not sound impressive, this was a respectable sale for a literary novel in its time—especially a first novel without any European central characters—and indeed the sales were rather more than for Virginia Woolf's first novel over the same period.

The Village in the Jungle was dedicated to 'V. W.' with the comment:

> I've given you all the little, that I've to give;
> You've given me all, that for me is all there is;
> So now I just give back what you have given—
> If there is anything to give in this.

For her part, Virginia Woolf wrote to Lytton Strachey that "Our great event has been that Arnold has taken Leonard's novel with great praise. Of course he makes it a condition that certain passages are to go out—which we don't yet know. It's triumphant to have made a complete outsider believe in one's figments." But she does not appear to have been very interested in *The Village in*

Virginia Woolf thought her husband's second novel, The Wise Virgins, *better than his first,* The Village in the Jungle.

the Jungle as literature herself, either at the time of its publication or in later life. According to Bella Woolf, Virginia thought Leonard's second novel, *The Wise Virgins,* better than his first.

Her indifference is not at all surprising. *The Village in the Jungle* differs from the vast majority of novels with a colonial setting written in the late nineteenth

When Woolf's closest friend Lytton Strachey read The Village in the Jungle, *he detested it.*

and early twentieth centuries in that, although its author was a white westerner, its main characters were all non-whites, and peasants to boot. Even Forster's *A Passage to India*, published a decade later, would avoid drawing its Indian characters from the lower strata of society. When Woolf's closest friend Lytton Strachey read the novel, he detested it, and wrote to Saxon Sydney-Turner: "I was disappointed to see that it was about nothing but blacks—whom really I don't much care for." The Bloomsbury group may have been radicals in Edwardian English society, but they were not radical enough to take seriously a viewpoint utterly removed from their own intellectual and aesthetic world—even through the literary filter of one of their own number.

Woolf's novel is emphatically not about what the East means to white people; it does not fantasise about the jungle and the people who live there from a European perspective. It is not a fictional equivalent of Bella Woolf's guidebook, *How to See Ceylon*. Instead it shows a remarkable, deep empathy for the hard lives of poor Sinhalese jungle dwellers and their psychology. Though it undoubtedly is anti-imperialist, *The Village in the Jungle* is not *merely* anti-imperialist but a more complex work that has earned a place in English literature—admittedly a minor place—long after the passing of the imperial milieu that produced it.

The very first sentence takes us straight into the setting of the book: "The village was called Beddagama, which means the village in the jungle." Where did Woolf get this name from, and was there an original village on which he based the story?

In considering these questions, there can be no doubt at all that Woolf's personal experiences of the Hambantota district are explicitly recalled in *The Village in the Jungle*. An article in the *Ceylon Daily News* written by Basil Mendis in 1950 observed that some entries in Woolf's *Diaries in Ceylon* closely resemble passages from *The Village in the Jungle*, even though it is certain that Woolf had no access to his official diaries at the time of writing the novel in London. For example, the novel describes how for ten months of the year the area around Beddagama is so dry that even the pigs die of thirst and only the elephants remember where there is water. Woolf's diary entry for 28 January 1909 records: "The great want in this sanctuary is water in the dry season . . . it is only the elephants who remember where the rivers lie and who make off at once to the water: the other animals, the buffalo and deer, have forgotten the rivers, they smell the water in the wind . . . Some of them die of thirst and exhaustion before they wander to the rivers."

None the less, Woolf himself declared firmly (in the *Ceylon Observer* in 1960): "*The Village in the Jungle* is not based on any single village in Ceylon. It is really a composite picture of a number of villages north of Magam Paituwa [Pattu] in the Hambantota district." But even if we accept his statement at face value—and I must admit I am reluctant to, given that Woolf was a lifelong stickler for factual and historical accuracy—this leaves open the question of how he chose the name Beddagama.

Here a curious situation exists. There is no village called Beddagama in Hambantota district, nor was there a village with this name in Woolf's time; but there was and is a village called Baddegama some twenty miles from Galle—spelt only slightly differently from Woolf's fictitious village but located well outside Hambantota district. And this village has a strong, if unproven, connection with Woolf.

In the archives of Trinity College, Cambridge—Woolf's college—are the papers of the Mayor family. These record, in fascinating detail, how in 1817 Robert Mayor and his wife Elizabeth Bickersteth went out to Ceylon with the Church Missionary Society. They spent their early years in Galle and then moved to Baddegama, where they built a stone church that was consecrated (after due precautions had been taken against ants and termites) in March 1824. Two sons were born to the couple in Galle and a third, John Eyton Bickersteth, in Baddegama. He became professor of Latin at Cambridge in 1872 and was president of St John's College from 1902–10. His son Robert John Grote Mayor (known as Robin), the grandson of the missionary in Ceylon, was an Apostle at Cambridge at around the same time as Woolf; the two of them shared "talking and walking" tours in Cornwall and Devon. In his autobiography Woolf states how he enormously enjoyed these get-togethers inspired and arranged by the philosopher G. E. Moore, because the group was such a close-knit one. Did he and 'Robin' Mayor discuss Ceylon and Baddegama on one of these tours? It seems virtually certain that they would have done.

There is a village called Baddegama, some twenty miles from Galle, which has a strong, if unproven, connection with Woolf.

As for whether there was one particular village in Hambantota district that formed the basis for Woolf's Beddagama, I kept asking the question as we journeyed from village to village in the area. Eventually, my persistence paid off. But the story of how I may have found the 'real' Beddagama must wait until the Epilogue; here I shall deal only with Woolf's fictional village.

*   *   *

Beddagama, the novel tells us, "was in, and of, the jungle". The jungle is presented in the book as feared and "evil", as it encroaches upon the village's ten mud huts. Their inhabitants are "very near to the animals that live in the jungle around them"—and none more so than Silindu, the novel's main character, a hunter in the jungle with an old gun, who has the face of the grey monkeys in the trees and sleeps with one eye open. When Silindu's wife gives birth to twin girls he rushes into their hut and beats her for producing female offspring. The village's headman Babehami, who is a relative of Silindu's wife, runs to the hut with other villagers and pulls Silindu off his wife. This incident marks the beginning of a hostility between Silindu and Babehami.

Silindu's wife dies two days later. His sister moves into his hut to raise the twin girls, Punchi Menika and Hinnihami. Silindu ignores his children until they are three, then suddenly begins to notice them, taking the girls hunting in the jungle and treating them like sons, to the distaste of other villagers. The girls are beautiful, not marked by disease and dirt like the other villagers, and they are

Fetching water from the tank of a village in the jungle.

closer to each other, to their father and to the jungle than to the rest of the village. The other villagers regard the family as outsiders, even as outcasts.

A rare period of happiness and contentment arrives when Babun, the headman's brother-in-law, falls in love with Punchi Menika. She reciprocates, and the two live as husband and wife, despite the angry protests of the headman, who has no regard for Silindu. For a while, the marriage of Babun and Punchi Menika makes Silindu's family more acceptable to the rest of the village. Babun is a good worker and the family enjoys productive harvests and the unfamiliar sensation of having enough to eat.

The peace is shattered when the eye of the village *vederala* (its doctor and dealer in spells), Punchirala, falls on Hinnihami and he desires to marry her. He is a bitter, one-eyed, *parangi*-ridden man with a mauled face—the result of a past encounter with a wild bear. Hinnihami and her father Silindu reject the marriage proposal and so Punchirala places a curse on Silindu, and he sickens. In the hope of exorcising this spell, Silindu and his family make a pilgrimage to Beragama (a fictionalised Kataragama) and make prayers to the god, but Silindu remains ill. By 'coincidence', while still at Beragama, the family encounter Punchirala, the *vederala* from their village, who suggests that they ask a holy man at Beragama to advise on a cure for Silindu. His advice, unsurprisingly, is that Hinnihami must give herself to Punchirala. Reluctantly, for the sake of her father, she does so on the return journey from Beragama to Beddagama, and Silindu recovers. But back in Beddagama, Hinnihami's resistance remains strong and unbroken. Refusing to live with the *vederala*, she threatens to harm him physically or through her own evil powers, and in terror he leaves her alone.

Some months later, Hinnihami gives birth to a child, a result of her time with Punchirala. She simultaneously nurses a baby fawn Silindu has rescued from the jungle, to the disapproval of the villagers, who realise that although Hinnihami loves her child, her love for her fawn is deeper. A short time after this, the village suffers drought, disease and hunger. The villagers regard Hinnihami's fawn as the bringer of their bad luck and stone it to death. Hinnihami expires soon afterwards in grief.

The villagers live in constant debt to the headman, Babehami, who administers the *chena* licences that permit them to cultivate crops. The *chenas* are insufficient, so Babehami loans them rice and money. In addition, the villagers borrow from a moneylender, Fernando, who lives in the town but now takes up residence in the village, so as to collect his debts. With the connivance of the headman, Fernando tries to seduce Punchi Menika, but she refuses to go to him and betray Babun, the husband whom she deeply loves. Fernando's pride is affronted and he schemes with Babehami (who is still furious with Babun for marrying Punchi Menika) to frame Babun and Silindu for theft. The scheme is successful, and Babun and Silindu are charged and taken to court in the town, where they are tried by a British magistrate. Babun is sentenced to six months in Tangalla prison; Silindu is let off, as there is insufficient evidence against him and the magistrate thinks he is not right in the head. Punchi Menika is left defenceless against the headman and moneylender in Beddagama.

The injustice galvanises Silindu into action at last. He feels like a buffalo being hunted—not by evil in the jungle but by the human evil in Babehami and Fernando. Goaded to fury, he takes up his old gun and blasts both of his persecutors to death, then walks through the jungle to the town and gives himself up, rather than becoming a fugitive in the jungle subject to the 'hue and cry' of the law. His case is transferred to a higher court, and Silindu is sentenced to hang for the double murder; but the highest authorities reprieve him from the noose and his sentence is commuted to 20 years' imprisonment. Prison becomes a refuge for him, and there he eventually dies.

Far away in Beddagama, unknown to Silindu, the village disintegrates after the murders, as families move away and die off. Babun never returns; he apparently wastes away in Tangalla prison like a caged animal—though Punchi Menika can learn nothing of his fate, despite making the long and weary journey to the prison to enquire. In the end, the sole inhabitant of Beddagama is the prematurely aged Punchi Menika, barely existing on jungle food in the ruin of her hut. Listless and feverish, she is finally claimed by death, as a great boar "glided like a shadow towards her into the hut."

✳   ✳   ✳

The encroachment of the jungle on the village and the solitary annihilation of Punchi Menika epitomise Woolf's own fear of the jungle, which we encountered in the previous chapter. He loved animals, especially the unique beauty of wild animals, but he understood in his guts that:

> the jungle and jungle life are also horribly ugly and cruel. When I left Ceylon, and wrote *The Village in the Jungle*, that was what obsessed my memory and my imagination and is, in a sense, the theme of the book. The more you are in the jungle, particularly if you are alone, the more one tends to feel it personified, something or someone hostile, dangerous. One always has to be on one's guard against it or against— one never quite knows what.

The mysterious "evil" of the jungle, of which the novel repeatedly speaks, is therefore its power to ravage and destroy all life, including human life, at a moment's notice. (Despite writing decades after Darwin, Woolf is quite willing in this novel—perhaps rather too willing for the taste of a modern reader—to make a moral judgement on nature.) The jungle cannot wait for Punchi Menika to die a natural death. As she sees it, the shadow that glides menacingly towards her at her end is not a wild animal but Appochchi, the "devil from the bush". Yet ultimately the novel does convince us that an evil really does stalk the jungle in Beddagama. It is this evil that is really responsible for Punchi Menika's miserable manner of death—the evil in human hearts, rather than that in any animal or jungle devil.

Woolf's novel is convincing in its portrayal of life in the Sinhalese jungles not so much for its philosophy but because he was so emotionally involved with both the people and the jungle. As we have come to understand, he knew at first hand the villagers' harsh environment: hot, dry, windy above the trees yet still on the ground, and full of thorny vegetation; an area that looks as if it is dying but in fact is full of life. The lack of water and the need to find water in order to survive make Beddagama and its surroundings into a threatening place: "a strange world, a world of bare and brutal facts, of superstition, of grotesque imagination; a world of trees and the perpetual twilight of their shade; a world of hunger and fear and devils, where a man was helpless before the unseen and unintelligible powers surrounding him." The existence of these powers explains to the villagers why they suffer from drought, malnutrition, malaria, *parangi* and early death—all the pestilences that Woolf saw and tried to alleviate in his work as assistant government agent in Hambantota.

The closeness of the villagers to wild animals is a recurrent theme of the novel: "They look at you with the melancholy and patient stupidity of the buffalo in their eyes or the cunning of the jackal." Even more explicitly:

> People who live in towns can hardly realise how persistent and violent are the desires of those who live in villages like Beddagama. In many ways, and in this beyond all others, they are very near to the animals; in fact, in this they are more brutal and uncontrolled than the brutes; that, while the animals have their seasons, man alone is perpetually dominated by his desires.

Silindu is more like a brute than the rest of the village because he frequently hunts in the jungle, which he both loves and greatly fears. He is not easily angered, but if roused "then suddenly he would rise and search out his enemy and fall on him like a wild beast". The British magistrate who commits Silindu for trial for murder views all jungle people as animals, who simply want to be left to themselves and only attack if provoked: "They won't touch you if you leave them alone." When Silindu rejects Punchirala's offer of marriage to Hinnihami, he does so by telling the *vederala* that Hinnihami is "of the jungle, wild, not fit for your house".

Desire and passion—above and beyond the elemental urge to survive—lie very close to the surface in the novel, and often break loose. Silindu desires to be left alone to hunt but is tormented by the anger and greed of the headman and moneylender. The headman never forgets his rage at Babun for marrying Punchi Menika and desires revenge. Hinnihami rejects Punchirala's touch with a shudder of her body and a fire in her eyes that kindles the *vederala*'s desire for her. In a fine introduction to *The Village in the Jungle* written in 1981, the literary academic E. F. C. Ludowyk sees desire as a key driver of the novel, whether it is the love of Punchi Menika and Babun or the lust of Punchirala and Fernando for Silindu's daughters.

Unsurprisingly, economic hardship has a significant part to play in provoking the suspicions, fears, superstitions and desires for revenge of the villagers. Silindu tells his daughters that the hunger caused by drought is because the jungle devils are angry. But during the time of plenty after Babun and Punchi Menika's marriage, there is much less talk of such devils. A belief in evil spirits, charms and spells is a natural way for peasants to make sense of a harsh environment—though as Ludowyk remarks, devils are well known throughout Ceylon, not only in its jungles, and are "too commonplace to be associated with 'evil'", as Woolf assumes. Still Woolf was right in his understanding of the great power such a person as Punchirala could have wielded over a Sinhalese rural community a century ago. A *vederala* like him, as the village 'doctor', was both respected and feared, especially in bad times. Hence Woolf gives Punchirala a certain stature and cunning: when Silindu's sister asks him for help in curing her brother, Punchirala suggests that she take him to the government hospital, for, he says, he can do nothing as "only a poor *vederala*". But the sister is convinced—and Punchirala anticipates her reaction—that a hospital is no place to cure a man possessed by a devil. Although Woolf himself hated superstition, he understood it well enough to make Silindu's sickness and its treatment at Beragama compellingly credible. He knew that in his district the people's fears and superstitions were self-fulfilling prophecies. Silindu is sick because he believes in the *vederala*'s powers; Hinnihami, though she is as superstitious as her father, suffers no ill effects when she resists the *vederala*, because she does not believe in his particular powers.

Superstition and religion are intertwined in *The Village in the Jungle*. The pilgrimage to Beragama is full of hope for Silindu's family because they believe that the god at the holy site is close to the devils whom they know in their jungle. Their faith, though it may be called Buddhist in government statistics, has little to do with Buddhist philosophy, as we discussed in chapter five. But near the end of the novel, as Silindu is led away to a distant place for his trial, Woolf introduces Buddhism in a more recognisable form. Silindu meets a beggar along the way. The man is thought by people around him to be slightly mad, but he impresses Silindu. He tells him of the Lord Buddha's injunction not to kill and explains the path to freedom from desire and enlightenment. He says that not only is there no rest or peace for the hunted, there is also none for the hunter. He recommends a life of begging for everyone in order to avoid sin. The people around him disagree, but Silindu—who is both hunted and hunter—is overawed and throws himself at the beggar's feet. It is a moment of epiphany for him, in which he at long last begins to understand his own torment and to imagine the possibility of being at peace with himself.

Silindu is therefore happy to be imprisoned, not only because of the regular food he receives but because he thereby escapes from his life as a hunter. Before shooting the headman and moneylender he confesses that he is afraid of everything—the jungle, the devils, the darkness, but, above all, the feeling of being hunted. The evil of the jungle and the evil of men have become inextricably linked for Silindu, and he desperately needs to escape from both: "in the jungle there would be no rest. It was just in order to escape the terror— the feeling of the hunted animal, the feeling that someone was always after him meaning evil—that he had killed the Arachchi [the headman] and the Mudalali [the moneylender]."

*   *   *

The way in which *The Village in the Jungle* depicts the characters' relationships with the Government is bound to be of special interest, given the career and experiences of its author.

At first, Silindu and Babun try to resolve their difficulties with the village headman Babehami and the moneylender Fernando by seeking assistance through official channels from the assistant government agent in coastal Kamburupitiya. It takes Babun three days to walk there from Beddagama, only to discover that the official is away on circuit for ten days. A friendly Moor in town (who knows and dislikes Fernando) helps the illiterate Babun to draft a petition, telling him that the assistant government agent would help him if he knew about it; but Babun's petition is suppressed by the clerks in the *kachcheri,* who require bribes before passing petitions on to their boss. While Babun takes time over his pointless written request and walks back to Beddagama, the headman and the moneylender hatch their conspiracy against him and Silindu in the village. This entire episode in the novel is transparently based on Woolf's knowledge of his subordinates and the alliances and antipathies between various local notables in Hambantota and the villages. Recall, for instance, Woolf's conversation in the train to Colombo with his head clerk from Kandy and his stand-off with the salt contractors in Hambantota.

The trial of Babun and Silindu for theft from the headman's house is where Woolf cleverly reveals the inadequacies of the British legal system as imposed on a quite different culture. According to Prabhath de Silva, who served as a magistrate in Hambantota district in the 1990s and who has examined Woolf's time as a judge in Ceylon and its influence on his writings, "These scenes in the novel reflect Woolf's profound understanding of the litigants, witnesses and native officials, which he had gained through his interaction with them within the colonial judicial and administrative system . . . His technical knowledge of criminal procedure is well displayed at various stages of the trial".

De Silva considers that Woolf dealt with real trials in three mental stages. First, he weighed up the available facts intellectually. Then, he used his intuition and looked for telltale signs and gestures among the witnesses. Lastly, he tried to be completely impartial and avoid judging the case by appearances. De Silva recounts a typical lawyer's anecdote about Woolf in action in Ceylon. Once, in open court, Woolf admonished an over-loud lawyer by telling him not to bark like a dog. The lawyer replied that he could not help himself, as there was a wolf on the bench. His repartee had a serious point, since Woolf was known to be quite obstinate as a judge.

In *The Village in the Jungle,* the courtroom, with its bench, dais, dock and witness box, is portrayed as an alien and intimidating setting for most of those who appear in it. The proceedings are in English, which is of course incomprehensible to Babun and Silindu (though not to the wily headman Babehami), except when the judge and prosecutor examine the witnesses using a Sinhalese interpreter, which further confuses Babun and Silindu. At one point, the judge says something to the interpreter, who then asks the defendants for their names in an angry and threatening voice. Such a tone derived from a feudal attitude, explains de Silva, characteristic of a native official addressing a supposed inferior. At another point, by contrast, the judge's tone is angry because he distrusts the prosecution witnesses, while the interpreter's tone is soothing. The overall effect is that Babun and Silindu do not understand what is happening to them. "This was 'a case' and they were 'the accused', that was all they knew."

In addition, Woolf describes the view through the open windows of the courtroom of the bay, fishermen and their boats, and the endless jungle in the distance clouded by grey dust storms. Reading the whole trial scene and then the courtroom descriptions in *Growing*, it is difficult not to equate Kamburupitiya with Hambantota and the British judge with Woolf himself.

In the novel, after a persistent attempt to get at the truth, the judge himself admits that the system is flawed. In his summing up he states that he is sure there is more to the case than has come out but that he is bound to consider the facts before him, even though the complainant (the headman) "impressed me most unfavourably". Ludowyk here sees Woolf as questioning, "What is man and how should he be governed? The judge is as much the prisoner of the processes of law as are Silindu and Babun in their cage at the courthouse."

The next encounter with the law follows Silindu's murder of his persecutors in Beddagama. He walks to Kamburupitiya and wearily confesses his act to the same British magistrate who had tried him for theft and released him only a few days previously. Silindu is vaguely encouraged, as this time the white man speaks to him in Sinhala and because he is aware from seeing a gun in the white man's house that he too is a hunter and understands the jungle.

The white magistrate is portrayed as a sympathetic character who questions the government's notions of justice, as Woolf did. He looks beyond the obvious facts of the case—the murder confession by Silindu—and tells his native assistant, the Ratemahatmaya, that Silindu's confession is "Damned curious. I thought he wasn't right in the head when I saw him in court before. Well, I'm glad *I* shan't have to hang him."

"You think he will be hanged, sir?"

"He'll be sentenced at any rate. Premeditation, on his own showing—clearly.

And a good enough motive for murder. A very simple case, so they'll think it. You think so, too?"

The assistant takes the bait: "It seems to be a simple case, sir."

"I see you would make a very good judge, Ratemahatmaya. I don't mind telling you—unofficially of course—that I'm a very bad one. It does not seem at all a simple case to me. *I* shouldn't like to hang Silindu of Beddagama for killing your rascally headman. Now then, Ratemahatmaya, here you are; a Sinhalese gentleman; lived your whole life here, among these people. Let's have your opinion of that chap there. He's a human being, isn't he? What sort of a man is he? How did he come suddenly to murder two people?"

"It's difficult, sir, for me to understand them; about as difficult as for you, sir. They are very different from us. They are very ignorant. They become angry suddenly, and then, they kill like—like—animals, like the leopard, sir."

"Savages, you mean. Well, I don't know. I rather doubt it. You don't help the psychologist much, Ratemahatmaya . . ."

The naive Silindu wants the white magistrate to try him, but murder is outside his jurisdiction. However he does take Silindu back to Beddagama for an inquiry, and after this Silindu is taken away to the prison in the old Dutch fort at Tangalla to await trial. Again he understands nothing of the procedure, nor the point of any of the questions directed at him. While awaiting his execution he is happy. However,

> Four days before the day fixed for the execution, the jailer came to Silindu's cell accompanied by a Sinhalese gentleman dressed very beautifully in European clothes and a light grey sun-helmet. Silindu was told to get up and come forward to the window of the cell. The Sinhalese gentleman then took a document out of his pocket and began reading it aloud in a high pompous voice. It informed Silindu that the sentence of death passed on him had been commuted to one of 20 years' rigorous imprisonment.

No explanation for this official decision is given to Silindu.

Considering the above scenes with officialdom, especially the courtroom scene, a case could easily be made for *The Village in the Jungle* as an effective critique of imperialism. But Prabath de Silva chooses to interpret them differently. For him, as a lawyer in Sri Lanka, the legal scenes reveal rather the weaknesses of the colonised, especially the way in which "obsolescent native intermediaries could interfere with the smooth functioning of the colonial judicial and administrative system." De Silva adds: "The colonial judicial system provided much more advanced safeguard for the interests of the people than the arbitrary methods of justice prevalent under native kings." With a judge such as Woolf, it seems that the system did work fairly well, but there were other British judges who were less knowledgeable and imaginative than Woolf. We should also remember Woolf's own verdict on himself as a judge in Ceylon: that he was not prepared to spend his life doing justice to people who thought that his justice was injustice.

✲ ✲ ✲

Since its publication in 1913, *The Village in the Jungle* has not received the level of critical attention in England that it deserves, but this is not true in Sri Lanka. In the country that the novel depicts, there has been much discussion of it; and Woolf's handwritten manuscript was donated to the University of Peradeniya in 1974 by Trekkie Parsons, the executor of Woolf's estate, who accompanied Woolf to Ceylon in 1960 and became the owner of his literary work after his death in 1969.

Let us first consider the response to the novel primarily as a work of literature. A leading Sri Lankan literary scholar, Yasmine Gooneratne, has studied Woolf's manuscript and identified many significant alterations made prior to publication. In the original version, when Babun first makes love to Punchi Menika in the jungle, she cries, "with joy and desire mingled with the fear and the pain": "It hurts me so." In the published version, Woolf substituted for these four words the familiar Sinhala exclamation: "Aiyo! aiyo!" Gooneratne calls this "a positive improvement, permitting the Sinhala exclamation to carry . . . the haunting message of her voluntary and conflicting emotions." In another example, Woolf substitutes *vesi* for "whore". Taken together, Gooneratne concludes, "the changes made have a profound effect on the tone of the narrative as a whole, establishing the author's attitude to his subject in these key passages as being sympathetic and serious, rather than condescending or coldly analytical." In her view, Woolf's novel undoubtedly transcends the limitations of the colonial situation that produced it. She agrees with the English novelist Alec Waugh (and indeed Pablo Neruda, quoted earlier on the novel), who believed that no western novelist, such as Kipling, Maugham or Forster, had successfully created an Asian character—until a Malay student advised him to read Woolf's novel. Waugh did so and wrote to Woolf in the 1960s: "You have done what I did not think was possible for a Westerner to do—get inside the mind and heart of the Far East. It is a unique achievement."

In 1980, the English Association of Sri Lanka commemorated Woolf's birth centenary by commissioning some academic essays on his novel. In this publication, Nihal Fernando considers *The Village in the Jungle* to be unique in its examination of the problems faced by dry-zone peasants in Sri Lanka. Of the final disappearance of Beddagama as a village, Fernando writes:

> The village is destroyed by a number of factors working together. A hostile environment, the shortcomings of an inefficient colonial administrative system, the activities of urban civilisation and the destructive evil in some of its inhabitants, are the chief causes of its downfall. The novel is, in an important sense, an articulation of Woolf's conviction of the futility of attempting to maintain agricultural communities in the arid zones of Sri Lanka.

In this respect, Fernando rates Woolf above the efforts of indigenous writers: "Though Woolf was an Englishman his sympathy for and imaginative insight into the lives of the simple villagers was such that he was able to realise in his art a level of realism which is totally lacking in the works of local authors who attempt to deal with similar subjects and experiences." Ranjith Goonewardene agrees. Woolf's characters are alive for Goonewardene, unlike the characters in Conrad's *Heart of Darkness* and Forster's *A Passage to India*, which Goonewardene considers to be somewhat lifeless metaphors.

None of the western novelists we have just mentioned shared Woolf's rare dedication to the foreign people he was describing, his knowledge of their languages, and his experience of living among them in relative isolation from colonial white society. All these factors combined in his novel to make it authentic. But these strengths in a civil servant could be regarded as a handicap in a serious novelist, hindering him from liberating his imagination from his own experiences and emotional involvement with the people he is writing about. Quentin Bell, Virginia Woolf's nephew, said as much in his affectionate introduction to Woolf's autobiography, written after Leonard Woolf's death. According to Bell, "In *The Village in the Jungle* Leonard comes so close to direct reporting of that which he has seen that we are continually held, delighted and horrified by what he has to say. It need not, I feel, have been a work of fiction

Quentin Bell wrote an affectionate introduction to Woolf's autobiography discussing The Village in the Jungle.

and would have been better if he had not imposed a fictional form on it." But Bell's is a minority view. While it is true that no major novelist has embraced Woolf's novel as a great novel, almost everyone who has read it agrees that it is of real and continuing interest, from very many points of view: historical, political, sociological, economic and, not least, literary.

In the context of other literary books on Ceylon, *The Village in the Jungle* is often compared with John Still's *The Jungle Tide*, a collection of factual descriptions of Still's jungle experiences, published in 1930. Like Woolf, Still was born in 1880 and was also English, but spent a much longer period in Ceylon, from 1897–1927. In a newspaper article, M. B. Mathmaluwe praises Still and criticises Woolf:

no two personalities could have been more different in outlook and temperament . . . The two books are worlds apart in theme and approach to the jungle. The chief quality that emerges from every line of Still's writing is his abundant humanism, his understanding and empathy for both man and beast, whereas in the entire gamut of Woolf's writings what one sees is his dehumanised and almost robot-like approach to wildlife and other human beings.

Specifically, Mathmaluwe dislikes Woolf's depiction of the jungle as an evil place. He claims that villagers who live in the jungle do not think like this. "Still has not made a silly fetish of his fear of the jungle, as Woolf has done." But the comparison of the two writers seems seriously misguided, since *The Village in the Jungle* is fiction and *The Jungle Tide* is non-fiction. For dramatic purposes, it was necessary for Woolf to depict the jungle as sinister, threatening and evil. Woolf's own factual account of Ceylon, *Growing*, contains many positive, and even lyrical descriptions of the jungle, in particular his love of the wildlife in the Hambantota region, which was unquestionably his favourite region of Ceylon, notwithstanding how he wrote of it in his novel. It is also the case, as remarked by D. V. Hapuarachchi, that "Woolf uses the jungle very effectively as a 'reflector' of Silindu's mind, a method which is very useful to a novelist interested in exhibiting psychological conditions as a means to character portrayal." But I concede, with Ludowyk and others, that Mathmaluwe does have a point about Woolf's overdoing the "evil" of the jungle.

In 1935, Edward Arnold (the publisher of Woolf's novel) published *Grass for My Feet* by J. Vijayatunga. Set in a village near Galle, its characters are more sophisticated and westernised than Woolf's peasants, and its atmosphere is sunny and nostalgic. *Grass for My Feet* has been heaped with praise for years in Sri Lanka. In the *Sunday Observer* in 2003, Karel Roberts Ratnaweera called it "one of the best books on life in rural Ceylon of the time." He compared the Buddhist new year celebrations of today with Vijayatunga's evocation of new year customs. The novel's accurate representations of specific facets of Ceylonese life probably accounts for its enduring popularity in Sri Lanka. In other respects, Viyayatunga's novel has been criticised for its sentimentality. A criticism, I need hardly add, which cannot be levelled against Woolf's novel.

Turning now to the less specifically literary response to *The Village in the Jungle*, it is not surprising, given its colonial subject matter, to find that the novel has been both widely praised and widely attacked by those reading it from a political, sociological or feminist angle.

A particularly harsh critic is Irene Coates, the author of *Who's Afraid of Leonard Woolf?* She assumes that Silindu and his family are actually Vedda tribals, and this is why they are social outcasts. This leads her to suggest that the novel should have been written from the point of view of Punchi Menika and Hinnihami, as the Veddas have matrilineal social customs. Not only is Coates mistaken in her assumption, her suggestion would obviously mean the total collapse of the novel's structure, since Silindu is the central character.

Coates further interprets the characters of Punchi Menika and Hinnihami as "two dominant sisters who can be broadly recognised as Vanessa and Virginia [Woolf]". But she offers very little evidence to support this claim. Hinnihami's early death from a broken heart after the slaughter of her fawn is somehow linked by Coates to Virginia Woolf's mental illness. She accuses Leonard Woolf of having "no hesitation about killing the young Virginia-figure, who is described as 'mad' . . . Thus Leonard consigns his Virginia-figure to madness and an early death in his book, which never actually recovers from her loss, while the litany of misfortune and death continues." Yet it is obvious to any unprejudiced reader that the narrative actually gains in pace after the death of Hinnihami with the arrival of the moneylender, and that the trial scenes sustain the pace. And Hinnihami is hardly the only 'mad' character in the novel; far more attention is given to Silindu's parlous state of mind.

Moreover, the writing of *The Village in the Jungle* in 1911–12 predates any detailed knowledge Leonard may have had about Virginia Woolf's illness. In *Beginning Again*, Woolf writes:

> During the time that I lived in the same house as Virginia in Brunswick Square, and particularly in the months before we married, I became for the first time aware of the menace of nervous or mental breakdown under which she always lived. I had no experience at all of nervous or mental illness and it was some time before I realised the nature and meaning of it in Virginia.

We cannot be certain whether or not Leonard Woolf was still writing *The Village in the Jungle* in 1912 when he became aware of Virginia's illness, but it is doubtful he would have known enough about it to have incorporated it into his novel. To suggest that he would deliberately represent Virginia as a character in his novel who is mad and must be killed off, when he was about to marry her, also seems far-fetched.

As for Woolf's attitude to imperialism in the novel, we have cited Fernando's high praise of its sympathy for the peasants. Ludowyk agrees: "though villages like Beddagama may no longer exist, [Woolf] shows a classic level of under-standing of the human situation to be met with in shanty towns, ghettoes, labour and refugee camps, and other places where the rejects of society are concentrated." But others disagree. Rajiva Wijesinha thinks the novel is patron-ising and objects to the way in which all the native officials and headmen are shown as corrupt or incompetent like Babehami, with no criticism offered of the British officials; and he criticises the omission of a strong sense of commu-nity that he says exists in real jungle villages. Wijesinha therefore dismisses the idea that the novel is anti-imperialist, as claimed by Woolf himself.

Arguably, however, there is a strong sense of community in Beddagama—it is just that Silindu and his family are, for various reasons, outside of it. Goonewardene has noted how the other villagers, by marking Silindu's family as outsiders, are able to redirect their communal anger and hatred at them. The villagers are all of the *goiya* caste, which means they are cultivators of rice. So is Silindu, but because he takes Punchi Menika and Hinnihami into the jungle, the others label him, intending it as an insult, a *vedda*, in other words a jungle dweller like the original inhabitants of the island. "Gradually the hut of the *veddas*, as they were nicknamed, seemed to other villagers to fall under a cloud."

Wijesinha's other claim—about anti-imperialism—is probably harder to refute. Another critic of Woolf, Jeanne Thwaites, writing in the *Lanka Guardian* in 1996, remarked:

> A writer who is either a member of a colonised people, or is a coloniser, may not consciously be aware of how his writing is affected by the group he is born into. Even when it is his intention to identify with the other group, (the colonised with the colonisers, or the coloniser with those colonised), he cannot help but fall back into some stereotypical role-playing of the over- or underdog.

Despite Woolf's misgivings about imperialism, there is no escaping the fact that he had been a very successful imperialist.

✳   ✳   ✳

His return to independent Ceylon in person in 1960 regenerated interest in *The Village in the Jungle*, and many newspaper articles discussed its merits. Mervyn de Silva, a well-known journalist, declared: "Woolf's picture of the village community was a total one, a portrait of both the physical and the inner life of the peasant, his beliefs, his ways of thinking and feeling. For a foreigner, this is indeed an extraordinary achievement." De Silva complimented Woolf's sensitivity to the rhythms of rural speech—such as the refrain, "What can I do? What can I do?"—in capturing the fatalism of the Sinhalese peasant. Above all, he was impressed that Woolf's novel "was able to distinguish Buddhism the orthodox doctrine from its actual character as it existed in the popular consciousness."

Since then, *The Village in the Jungle* has enjoyed a high profile in Sri Lanka, both among intellectuals and among the general public, partly as a result of its being adapted for the cinema in 1980. The film was directed in Sinhala, not

English, by Lester James Peries, the leading Sri Lankan film-maker, and was entitled *Baddegama* (the spelling of the real village near Galle, curiously enough). In 1981, *Baddegama* was selected as one of 20 films (out of 421 submissions) to be shown at the Directors' Fortnight in the Cannes film festival.

Peries's adaptation, unlike the novel, introduced a small role for Woolf himself. This was played by Arthur C. Clarke, who wrote about the experience of pretending to be Woolf just before the film was shown at Cannes. Although Clarke had no acting experience, he had a long connection with Sri Lanka, having lived there since the 1960s and used Hambantota as a base for diving. The film opens with Clarke (as Woolf) arriving by bullock cart in the colonial garb of an assistant government agent, complete with sola topee, at the near-deserted village of Baddegama, carrying a set of census forms. Clarke saw this as an opportunity for some delightful and authentic dialogue with the district official appointed to meet him:

> Woolf: This rinderpest business is terrible. But the villagers won't take any precautions—they blame it all on Halley's comet.
> District official: Another evil they blame on the comet, sir, is a very strict government agent.

The film of *The Village in the Jungle* therefore manages to incorporate Woolf and his actual experiences into his own fictional creation.

Clarke's main scene, as the judge who sentences Babun, is a wonderful re-enactment of how Woolf himself once sat at the exact same dais, gazing out on the bay at Hambantota while considering court cases. Nothing in the real courtroom had altered since Woolf's time, save for the royal coat of arms behind the judge, which had been replaced by the emblem of the Republic of Sri Lanka. Clarke thoroughly enjoyed his role and Lester James Peries insisted he receive the union rate for his work. Clarke donated his fee, by presenting the cheque to the prime minister, into a fund for indigent actors. He quipped: "I hope no one accuses me of trying to safeguard my own future."

Peries received some criticism for distorting Woolf's novel, but pointed out the changes necessary in adapting any novel for film. If the novel had been transferred slavishly to the screen, Peries estimated that his film would have been seven-and-a-half hours long. The film does indeed differ from Woolf's novel in certain respects. But on the whole it was well received in Sri Lanka. Its chief importance perhaps lies in its very existence; in the fact that an English

Ernest Macintyre adapted The Village in the Jungle *in 1994 and presented it as a play in Australia.*

writer has given to Sri Lankans a story in Sinhala which they consider to be part of their own culture. (In 1994, it was adapted again by another Sri Lankan, Ernest Macintyre, who presented it as a play in Australia, where he now lives.)

✷   ✷   ✷

The Village in the Jungle is certainly the most important of Woolf's fictional writings on Ceylon, but we should not forget his three short stories, "A Tale Told by Moonlight", "The Two Brahmans" and "Pearls and Swine", which were summarised in chapters two, three and four respectively. Woolf wrote them some time after his return from Ceylon but they were not published by the Hogarth Press until 1921, when they appeared as *Stories of the East*. They were then republished in 1962 as an appendix to Woolf's *Diaries in Ceylon* (where their title was changed, for some unknown reason, to the slightly different *Stories from the East*).

Although they sold poorly at the time, and have been largely overlooked by literary critics since, all three stories are of interest—especially in understanding their author's mind. As Mervyn de Silva notes in his introduction to *Diaries of Ceylon*, the stories are clearly the work of "an intelligence of fine quality, morally aware, humane and inquisitive but, most of all, disturbed by the impact of the East, and uneasy before its strange, exacting demands on understanding."

Jeanne Thwaites (who criticised *A Village in the Jungle* for failing to transcend its author's imperialist mindset) is also critical of "A Tale Told by Moonlight". In a separate article in the *Lanka Guardian* in 1995, she drew attention to an undoubted truth: that attractive, uneducated Sinhalese and Tamil girls were often chosen as concubines by English planters. However racial segregation meant that these women could not mix socially with white people, nor were their mixed-race children accepted by their own caste-bound families; and in many cases the planters themselves looked down on the women as inferiors. The somewhat similar relationship in Woolf's story—the affair between the expatriate Reynolds and the prostitute Celestinahami—involves, says Thwaites, the primary narrator (Woolf himself?), hearing the story from a second Englishman (Jessop), who tells it about a third Englishman (Reynolds). "I see this as Woolf's ploy to avoid blame for the story's content—a device he also uses in his other racist stories on Ceylon."

Anindyo Roy views the story very differently, and, I think, much more perceptively. Roy takes up its constant references to the "real". Reality and truth were ideas much discussed by Woolf and his contemporaries in Cambridge under the influence of G. E. Moore. "Implicit in this questioning about the 'real' is also a dramatisation of a trauma, a trauma that I argue had its source in Woolf's personal experiences in Ceylon and that subsequently acquired an intensely political dimension." Roy thinks that Woolf's horror at the hangings in Kandy exposed to him the chasm between the fantasy and the reality of imperialism. Thus Jessop, the second narrator, struggles with the impossibility of communicating the 'real' to his English listeners, who have not shared his romantic and brutal experiences in the East and who regard his tale as "sentimental". Roy writes: "In a sense, that impossibility has to do with Woolf's own efforts to translate a personal experience into one of shared meaning."

The way in which love is debated in the story is similar to the way the Bloomsbury group discussed it, observes Roy. Each member of the group in the story is expected to speak in a clear, unambiguous way about love. Jessop's inability to do this may have been Woolf's own comment on an inadequacy in the Bloomsbury group's approach to love. Jessop's friend Reynolds is initially drawn to the prostitute because her eyes seem to offer the possibility of knowing the 'real'. But when he buys Celestinahami out of the brothel, he betrays this possibility by showing "the power of the white man to insert the woman into a system of colonial exchange as a way to hold on to its own fantasy." Jessop's difficulty in communicating these issues to his English audience means that they consider Celestinahami's subsequent suicide dressed in European clothes to be a tragic consequence of love. But in Roy's view, Woolf makes the death "a symbolic act of defiance against the entire colonial civil and legal apparatus fashioned in order to secure the privilege of the white man." Far from accusing Woolf of racism, like Thwaites, Roy claims that "A Tale Told by Moonlight" is a story that "articulates a troubling vision about the fundamental impossibility of holding on to a truly emancipatory politics while continuing to defend the standard liberal position on empire."

Roy's separate essay on "Pearls and Swine" draws attention to how Woolf uses the group of Englishmen in the hotel's smoking room to bring different political perspectives on imperialism into the discussion. The character known as White appears at first to be a self-confident imperialist but in fact he is pathologically self-deluded. "Mr White serves both as an extreme image of colonial delusion as well as the culminating figure in this narrative trauma through which Woolf repeats his own 'madness' expressed in his letters to Strachey." Here Roy is referring to Woolf's letter to Strachey from the pearl fishery: "Depression is becoming, I believe, a mania with me, it sweeps upon and over me every eight or ten days, deeper each time." Another character, Robson, is apparently the voice of reason and progress, but "Robson's views . . . reflect an ethos of scientific management that had provided the economic and political basis for imperialism in the new century, and which was to find support from capitalist industrial interests operating in far corners of the globe, who all claimed to be intimately familiar with local affairs." In other words, in this story Woolf recognises and dramatises the contradiction between the fact that the basis of imperialism is economic, while its apologists claim for it a moral basis.

One other reaction to *Stories of the East* is worth quoting, as amusingly recounted by Woolf in the fourth volume of his autobiography, *Downhill All the Way*. In 1921, Hamilton Fyfe declared in the *Daily Mail* that "Pearls and Swine" deserved to "rank with the great stories of the world". This was picked up by the American literary agent Henry Holt, who wrote to Woolf offering to place the story in America for him. Woolf sent Holt a copy of the book, but "When he read the story, it was obviously a bit of a shock to him, being a good deal too plain spoken for the two hundred pound bracket in the United States of

America. He wanted me to tone it down a bit—he called this euphemistically "a few artistic alterations'". Woolf refused, saying that he could not bear to rewrite anything from long ago and suggested Holt deal with the matter himself. Holt sought the opinion of another American literary agent, Ann Watkins, and she, said Woolf, "also thought the story a masterpiece, but was also obviously horrified by it and the idea of offering it to the American market." Watkins reckoned that perhaps only two magazines would touch the story: "You see, we here in the States are still provincial enough to want the sugar-coated pill; we don't like facts, we don't like to have to face them." This was quite astute—and echoed Woolf's own ambivalence in trying to present the 'real' in his stories.

Yet Watkins and Holt were still keen to represent Woolf in America. Holt pursued him relentlessly, writing letters that promised commercial success if Woolf would only tailor his style to the American market. He even turned up unexpectedly at Woolf's house in Sussex and tried to persuade him in person with the promise of a potential income of £3,000 a year. But Woolf said he did not want to write stories and anyway could not think of suitable plots. So Holt sent him a plot to make into a story. When Woolf ignored this plea, the matter was finally dropped. Woolf had too much integrity to alter his stories for money; he was also already very busy with the publishing of serious litera- ture by authors such T. S. Eliot through his Hogarth Press; and perhaps he was also put off by his wife's growing stature as a fiction writer.

His move from fiction to political and historical writing in his mid-thirties is often explained as the natural response of a man married to a literary genius. But it had begun a considerable time before Virginia Woolf's literary success, with his second novel *The Wise Virgins*, published in 1914, a year before Virginia's first novel appeared. This second novel deeply offended Woolf's family, most of whom considered it an attack on them. His sister Bella was strongly against publication, and his mother Marie wrote to him: "If you publish the book as it stands, I feel there will be a serious break between us." Woolf's own circle— Vanessa Bell, E. M. Forster, Lytton Strachey *et al*—were divided as to whether he should publish. The upset and strain connected with *The Wise Virgins* exas- perated him so much that he told Strachey, when sending him the manuscript for his candid opinion: "I am so sick of the whole affair, that I shall be relieved if you don't condemn it, but probably just as relieved if you do . . . I shall never write another book after these damned Virgins." When the novel did finally appear, after Woolf had made some changes, the public response was largely negative and it did not sell, though its prospects were not helped by the outbreak of a world war in the year of publication.

Seen from today, the future trend of Woolf's writing—away from fiction and into politics—was already evident in *The Wise Virgins*, and requires no further explanation. The novelist Helen Dunmore put it well when she said of that novel in a recent interview:

> It's such an angry, passionate, nakedly candid account of a courtship between two people who seem as if they ought not to be together at all. And it exposes Edwardian middle-class social values; the anti-Semitism, the constricted lives enforced on women, the abuse of millions of lives through domestic service. You can tell from this book that Leonard Woolf isn't going to be a novelist for long. He's going to immerse himself in politics and social reform, and the long, complex marriage whose beginning is dramatised in *The Wise Virgins*.

9

Ceylon Revisited

Imperialism and colonialism are today very dirty words, particularly east of Suez. I hoped, if I revisited Ceylon, to be able to go to the places where I had worked as a government servant and see something of how, now that Ceylon was a sovereign independent state, their administration compared with ours. But to do this I would need to have some help from the Sinhalese and Tamil administrators of today, and I feared that I might find them, not unnaturally, contemptuous if not hostile. Would they not say, or at any rate think: 'Fifty years ago you were here ruling us, an insolent, bloody-minded racialist and imperialist. Thank God we have now got rid of you and really we don't want to be reminded of how you lorded it over us and exploited us in the bad old days.' . . . My fears were entirely unnecessary.

LEONARD WOOLF, *The Journey Not the Arrival Matters*

ALTHOUGH WOOLF DID not actually visit Ceylon again until 1960, he remained preoccupied with imperialism and the politics of the island for the rest of his life, both as an activist and as a writer. "My seven years as a civil servant in Ceylon had made me very much a political animal, and I have remained such ever since," he wrote in *Growing*.

The International and Imperial Committee of the Labour Party, with Woolf as its secretary, was set up during the Great War, and when it later split in two Woolf continued as the secretary of both committees for 25 years. During this significant period of change in empire, Woolf's contacts with Labour politicians placed him in a quite influential position. His book *Empire and Commerce in Africa*, written in 1918 for the Fabian Society, was followed by three essays confirming and detailing his anti-imperialist views: "Mandates and

Woolf in Ceylon, 1960, reading his official diaries from Hambantota.

empire" (1920), "Economic imperialism" (1921) and, the longest of the three essays, *Imperialism and Civilization* (1928). As Woolf defined the basic problem in "Mandates and empire", it was that an imperialist system gave "to some particular Power the right to govern despotically and exploit economically millions of people who neither desired nor understood the governmental and economic system imposed upon them."

Woolf located the arguments in his essays against the existing systems of imperial government within the practical context of the League of Nations and its mandates, and proposed how certain articles in the league's covenant could be used to help colonised countries. For example, article 22 stressed that instead of individual European powers administering colonies in their own way for their own gain, the objective should be "the well-being and development of" the inhabitants. European countries should therefore lose their sovereign power over their colonies and become agents of the League of Nations. He also detailed how land might be returned to the people of Africa and their education improved so that they could govern themselves. Obviously, his hands-on experience of development problems in the Hambantota district in 1908-11 was a crucial influence on him in making these recommendations, as was his genuine affection for the people he had once tried to 'develop'.

As early as 1912, after his honeymoon with Virginia, while employed as the secretary of the famous post-impressionist art exhibition organised by Roger Fry, for which he had to deal with purchase enquiries, Woolf had experienced the reaction of most visitors to the exhibition when confronted with the paintings of Picasso, Matisse and Bonnard—either outrage or laughter. It made him think, he wrote frankly, "how much nicer were the Tamil or Sinhalese villagers who crowded the verandah of my Ceylon *kachcheri* than these smug, well-dressed, ill-mannered, well-to-do Londoners."

He was beginning to develop a non-doctrinaire and very individualistic socialist conscience, partly as a result of his experiences in Ceylon, which made him ask generally of an idea or policy—not, "Is it socialist?", but rather, "Is it civilised?" (in the words of his obituary in the *New Statesman*, written by William Robson). In 1912, Woolf believed he was only halfway towards active socialism, but then his first political experience in England pushed him firmly to the left of the Labour Party. A cousin of Virginia's was involved in charitable work in the East End of London, and Leonard was briefly drawn in; he was appalled by the poverty he saw, as mentioned in an earlier chapter. But having refused in the end to play the role of a benevolent father to Sinhalese villagers, he decided he would not try to do so in London either. Instead he would make it his priority to study and understand the social systems of England from which he had been cut off in Ceylon. However, he noted in his autobiography, "I began to look at the politics and economics of London and Britain—and very soon Europe—in the way in which I had looked at those of the Hambantota district and Ceylon."

Ceylon came home to roost and affected Woolf's life in a rather more direct manner in 1916. He had been excluded from military service in the war due to a long-standing tremor in his hand and his need to care for his wife. Therefore he was available for consultation when two Sinhalese political leaders came to London and asked him to draft an appeal to the British Government. On 28 May 1915, rioting had broken out in Kandy and lasted two days before spreading to Colombo where it became extremely violent and lasted for six or seven days, until 5 June, with the smashing and looting of Muslim shops. The riots had arisen after the Ceylon Government failed to subdue a religious disagreement between Buddhists and Muslims over the route of a Buddhist religious procession past a mosque—just the kind of dispute that Woolf had managed to defuse in his last months in Hambantota. Many people, including Woolf, considered the real cause of the riots to be economic wrangles between Buddhists and Muslims, but the Government in Colombo took a different view. It imposed martial law on 2 June throughout the island, not just in Colombo and Kandy, and did not repeal the law for three months, despite the fact that order had long since been restored.

About fifty people had been killed in the riots. Now, under martial law, many Sinhalese were shot, hundreds were arrested without trial, and some were sentenced to hang (in prisons such as Bogambara in Kandy) or to long prison sentences on charges of 'treason'. There was a general rule of terror as women were held hostage by the authorities until their men surrendered and the houses of prominent Sinhalese were searched, while at the bottom end of the social scale, there were stories of Sinhalese workers being deliberately sent to Tamil areas where they could not get work. Financial penalties were imposed on the Sinhalese population, forcing them to pay compensation for riot damage, whether they had been involved in the rioting or not. The reason given by the Government for all these ruthless measures was that the riots were seditious in intent, an attempt to undermine the colonial administration.

Two Sinhalese, Don Baron Jayatilaka and Edmund Walter Perera, were determined to prove otherwise and to seek redress. Jayatilaka was an Oxford-educated barrister who had returned to Ceylon to head a leading Buddhist school in Kandy, and who was active in the temperance movement. He had himself been arrested on 21 June, allegedly for making seditious speeches and writing inflammatory articles; he was ordered to be shot, held for six weeks, but finally freed. Perera was a Colombo-based advocate and a Christian, with an interest in Sinhalese history and politics. Together they felt they had the expertise to petition the British Government in London.

Perera arrived in England on 20 July 1915, with a mission to press the British Government into holding an independent enquiry into the riots. On board ship he carried an important document in his shoe. Later, in a speech in Colombo in 1919, he recalled how worrying a journey it was from Ceylon to England: "Every day on board was a day of anxiety, for I did not know what was happening in Ceylon, whether my friends had not already been marched out of their cells, placed against the wall and shot as had been done to others."

His first letter to Whitehall in August 1915 elicited only the response that his claims were at variance with official reports and contained vague rumours and allegations. Undeterred, he continued to campaign. In October he cited the treaty of 1796, under which the British took over the government of Ceylon from the Dutch, which stated that the island's inhabitants were allowed to follow their occupations and enjoy liberty, and on this basis he maintained that martial law was "oppressive and unconstitutional".

After he left Ceylon, Woolf remained preoccupied with the politics of the island for the rest of his life.

Jayatilaka joined Perera in London in January 1916. The two men now sent the Government a detailed statement about the riots and the injustice of martial law. "These stern measures, illegal and unconstitutional, were taken under the belief of a conspiracy against the Government which never existed, and in support of which no evidence whatsoever was discovered." It was soon after making this statement that Jayatilaka and Perera made contact with Woolf.

As always, Woolf approached the matter from a rational perspective, carefully sifting the evidence before deciding that the Sinhalese case was entirely correct: "83 persons were condemned to death and 60 sentenced to life imprisonment. There is no doubt that many of these people were completely innocent of the offences with which they were charged." He worked with the Sinhalese representatives for over a year in order to rouse the press, progressive institutions and the House of Commons. For example, he advised speakers from the Anti-Slavery and Aborigines Protection Society to draw attention in their speeches to the loss of Ceylonese confidence in the good faith of the British Government. The *Manchester Guardian* was notably sympathetic and commented that justice in the colonies had been sidelined by England's preoccupation with war. Woolf also suggested a general amnesty for those imprisoned. In the meantime, the Colonial Office, obviously rattled, recalled the governor, Sir Robert Chalmers, and appointed a new one, Sir John Anderson, who declared that the military in Ceylon had handled the riots with methods suited to the Wild West by stampeding his popular predecessor into declaring martial law. (There was considerable Sinhalese sympathy for Chalmers, who had just lost two sons killed in action in France; he was also a student of Pali and Buddhism and a firm advocate of higher education for Ceylonese students.) At last, in January 1918, the under-secretary of state for the colonies grudgingly received a deputation from Woolf and others, but no official notice was taken of their views and their request for an inquiry was refused. "Who killed imperialism? I, said the imperialist, with my imperialism," wrote Woolf in his autobiography with, as he put it, "a certain amount of cynical pleasure". Nevertheless, the British Government began to recognise the need for change in the administration of Ceylon.

During this period Woolf naturally got to know the two Sinhalese representatives quite well, and described Jayatilaka as "an exceptionally nice person" (while keeping quiet about Perera). They would dine at his house, where Mrs Jayatilaka would sing Sinhalese songs even more beautifully than Woolf had heard them sung in Ceylon. His own wife Virginia was rather less enamoured by the visitors. In her diary for 16 October 1917, there is the following, precisely devastating entry:

> We came back to find Perera, wearing his slip and diamond initial in his tie as usual. In fact, the poor little mahogany coloured wretch has no variety of subjects. The character of the governor, and the sins of

the Colonial Office, these are his topics; always the same stories, the same point of view, the same likeness to a caged monkey, suave on the surface, inscrutable beyond. He made me uncomfortable by producing an envelope of lace—'a souvenir from Ceylon Mrs Woolf'—more correctly a bribe, but there was no choice but to take it.

The derogatory comments, on both Perera and Jayatilaka, continue in later entries. Leonard "is now menaced with a gold watch, owing to the success of the Ceylon business"; and, "Home to find the two darkies here." No wonder Virginia Woolf was indifferent to *The Village in the Jungle*! But then she had been doubtful about marrying Leonard because of his Jewishness, considering him "so foreign". Many of her friends, such as Lytton Strachey, would have shared her mild racial antipathy, while holding progressive views about English society (and deploring anti-Semitism of the contemporary Nazi variety). But his wife's attitude must nevertheless have been painful for Leonard to live with, especially her complete inability to empathise with his profound affection for Sinhalese people. So much so, it would seem, that this was one subject about which Woolf felt unable to write frankly about in his autobiography, preferring to take his feelings about it to the grave.

The distress and the suspicion of the colonial power created by the suppression of the 1915 riots had far-reaching effects in galvanising Ceylonese nationalism. Under the leadership of Sir Ponnambalam Arunachalam and Sir James Peiris, the people of Ceylon were determined to achieve self-government to make such high-handed repression impossible ever again. The first political expression of this sentiment was the Reform League, which soon evolved into the Ceylon National Congress, formed in 1919. It attracted wide support initially, particularly from the Young Lanka League, but its impact was less than expected as a result of its conservative stance.

Jayatilaka (who in due course was given a knighthood) played a leading role in the reform movement of the 1920s and became minister of home affairs in the pre-independence State Council. He retired from politics in 1942 and was succeeded by D. S. Senanayake, who became the first prime minister of independent Ceylon in 1948. Perera, too, influenced Ceylon's history by devising the future flag of Sri Lanka. On his trip to England in 1916, he discovered, in the Royal Military Hospital in Chelsea, the royal standard of the last king of Kandy, which had been captured by the British in 1815. The lion was incorporated into the flag, earning Perera the nickname 'Lion of Kotte', in reference to the ancient capital near Colombo of the Sinhalese kings during most of the fifteenth and sixteenth centuries.

Woolf remained active in lobbying the British government. William Clarance, a commentator on Sri Lankan politics, notes that in 1926, "Woolf took up the cause of responsible government in Ceylon when in another advisory committee memorandum, addressed to the Trades Union Congress and the Labour Party, he cited Ceylon specifically as a country where the measure of self-government demanded by the inhabitants should be granted immediately." In 1927, the Donoughmore Commission investigated why the 1924 Ceylon constitution had been unsuccessful and recommended constitutional changes necessary for eventual self-rule. The commission has been described by the historian C. R. de Silva as a blend of caution and courage:

> They stopped short of recommending full responsible government and instead, proposed a system of sharing power with seven [Ceylonese] councillors and three public servants forming a board of ministers. On the other hand, they decisively rejected communal representation and recommended a vast extension of the suffrage; all men over 21 years of age and all women over 30 were to have the right to vote.

However the resultant constitution, inaugurated in 1931, was still under the ultimate control of the British governor of Ceylon. Perera therefore left the Ceylon National Congress, as he thought the reforms had not gone far enough.

In the 1940s, Woolf continued to write influential political articles in favour of self-government for the colonies. He drew attention to Ceylon's ancient civilisation and its intelligent and educated people. They had already shown, he said, that they were capable of full self-government, just as the Indians had. Referring to the struggle for Indian independence, granted in 1947, the year before Ceylon's, Woolf was scathing in his autobiography:

> During the 1914 war the British Government had declared that it would cooperate with the Indians in order to establish self-government in India. The White Paper, the Round Table Conference, and the India Act of 1935 were the steps by which British conservative and imperialist patriots sought honourably to dishonour this promise. What they gave with one hand—niggardly reforms—they took away with the other—

the massacre at Amritsar, the Rowlatt ordinances, the cat-and-mouse imprisonments and releases of Gandhi and Congress leaders. The vicious circle of repression and sedition, sedition and repression—the implacable legal violence of an alien government and the murderous, illegal violence of native terrorists—established itself . . . Any politically self-conscious Indian could only conclude that once more the tragedy of freedom would have to be acted out in India—the alien rulers would release their hold on the subject people only if forced to do so by bloody violence.

Of course, no one can be sure of any What Might Have Been in history. But I have no doubt that if British Governments had been prepared in India to grant in 1900 what they had refused in 1900 but granted in 1920; or to grant in 1920 what they had refused in 1920 but granted in 1940; or to grant in 1940 what they refused in 1940 but granted in 1947—then nine-tenths of the misery, hatred, and violence, the imprisonings and terrorism, the murders, floggings, shootings, assassinations, even the racial massacres would have been avoided; the transference of power might well have been accomplished peacefully, even possibly without partition.

∗   ∗   ∗

On his return visit to Ceylon in February 1960, aged 79, Woolf—with his travelling companion Trekkie Parsons—was able to see the vast changes that had taken place since 1911. The display of self-government reminded him, he wrote in his autobiography, of how the imperial Government failed "to associate the people of the country with the government of the country; this applied particularly to the upper regions of power, prestige, and government." However he could not fail to notice that self-government had led to serious political instability.

S. W. R. D. Bandaranaike's Sri Lanka Freedom Party had taken control in 1956. It was a largely socialist party and also a strongly Sinhalese nationalist one. Capitalising on the 2,500-year anniversary of the death of the Buddha, Bandaranaike announced that Sinhala was to be the country's official language. Both Tamil and English were considered by the party to be cultural imports, provoking much anger among non-Sinhalese. In 1959, Bandaranaike was assassinated, though not for reasons to do with his language policy: he

Woolf, Trekkie Parsons and representatives from the Ceylon Government, visit Anuradhapura, 1960.

was killed by a Buddhist monk in connection with the business affairs of another highly placed monk whom the prime minister was not willing to favour. The post of prime minister passed to W. Dahanayake, on whose shoulders it therefore fell to welcome Woolf. A month or so after the visit, in March 1960, Dahanayake's government was unable to hold a coalition together and was defeated.

Woolf had his own misgivings about his return. For one thing, not long before he planned to go, there had been Sinhalese-Tamil riots, and he did not want to visit if he could not see certain areas of the island. The Ceylon high commissioner's office in London assured him the danger was over and he was free to travel throughout the island. In the event he saw very little physical evidence of the communal conflict. But much more important was his trepidation at the reception that he feared would be given to a former imperialist. Here his worries were also unfounded and he received a positive, friendly and helpful welcome from almost everyone he met—in fact he was treated as a VIP, and rather guiltily admitted to enjoying it. He attributed this, no doubt correctly, to three factors: his involvement in the appeal against the 1915 riots, the existence of his broadly sympathetic official diaries, and *The Village in the Jungle*, which was available in Sinhala and had been widely read. Woolf felt that his novel "won me the reputation among many Sinhalese and Tamils of not only loving the country and sympathising with the people, but also of understanding them."

During the visit, a newspaper quoted a speech in 1919 by Perera (who had died in 1953) acclaiming Woolf: "His active interest in the welfare of Ceylon never abated nor was his faith in the justice of our cause shaken by official misrepresentation." In 1961, Woolf made the 'riot letters' (his own correspondence on the appeal) available to Shelton C. Fernando, who published them in the *Ceylon Historical Journal*. The high commissioner in London wrote to Woolf thanking him, and noted that without Woolf's assistance Perera and Jayatilaka would probably not have achieved as much as they did.

Prime Minister Dahanayake met Woolf on his visit and publicly instructed Fernando, who was the permanent secretary in the ministry of home affairs, to arrange for the publication of *Diaries in Ceylon*. The manuscript of the diaries was presented to Woolf by Fernando at the Galle Face Hotel in Colombo at the beginning of his visit, to allow him to refresh his memory before revisiting Hambantota. Then he went to Hambantota on a five-day tour in which the people had arranged welcome receptions. He went to villages in the district similar to that in *The Village in the Jungle*; much of the jungle had disappeared by 1960, however. He also visited Tissamaharama, Kataragama, Kandy, Nuwara Eliya, Bandarawela, Polonnaruwa, Anuradhapura, Vavuniya, Mannar and Jaffna, while reading the manuscript of his diaries and refreshing his memory of Sinhala. Interviewed for the *Ceylon Observer*, he admitted to hunting in the jungle, but said the jungle was not kind to its people, who had little to eat—to them, he maintained, the jungle was a frightening place.

In Anuradhapura, he at long last spent time looking at the numerous historic sites with their magnificent architecture. He thought the Samadhi Buddha statue one of the most wonderful sights he had ever laid eyes on but expressed concern that it needed protection from the sun and rain. He also revealed

Woolf discusses the publication of his diaries with journalists in Colombo, 1960.

that his sister Bella's wedding had taken place at the Residency. In Jaffna he felt the place had not changed much since his time and was told that the people there were very conservative. Even in 1960, Jaffna had a character distinct from other towns.

An interviewer in Hambantota wrote of how softly Woolf spoke, as he remarked on the prosperity of Hambantota compared with 1911, with its new schools and plentiful paddy fields. In an article for the *New Statesman* written not long after his return, he said he was opposed to the industrialisation of Ceylon and thought it should continue to promote agricultural production, as the people living on the land seemed far happier than those in the cities.

One thing that was unchanged was the courtroom, where Woolf was puzzled to discover the proceedings still being conducted in English with an interpreter for Sinhala-speakers. Commenting later he also noted how many of the civil servants he met were keen to praise the older administration, despite the benefits of self-rule. Many of them accused politicians of betraying civil servants in exchange for votes. In the *New Statesman*, Woolf mentioned listening to one Sinhalese politician "screaming in a monotonous frenzy which carried me straight back to the days before the war when one turned on the wireless and heard Hitler screaming through the microphone at the frenzied Nazis."

By his own admission, Woolf's return visit to Ceylon was a sentimental and nostalgic journey, that reminded him of his youth. He wrote in his autobiography: "Ceylon and youth! Youth and the sun and the sand and the palmyra palms of Jaffna; youth and the lovely friendly Kandyan villages and villagers up in the mountains; youth and the vast lone and level plain of the low country in Hambantota, the unending jungle which tempered in me the love of silence and loneliness." At the end of the visit he said: "You don't know how happy I am. I have fulfilled my ambition. I have seen my village in the jungle." These positive comments were not merely for the benefit of the press in Ceylon. Speaking at the Ceylon Tea Centre in London a few months later, he called his visit "the best three weeks I have spent anywhere". And he spoke of his continuing belief in self-government, which dated from when he was a civil servant. "I did not know I was an imperialist but I gradually learnt it and that was one of the reasons I resigned."

There was at least one sour note, though, of the kind that Woolf had originally feared before coming to Ceylon. It involved a former subordinate of Woolf in Hambantota. Two years after his visit, after *Growing* had been published, an article appeared in the *Ceylon Observer* written by E. R. Wijesinhe. Now an old man in his late eighties, Wijesinhe had been a local government officer—a *mudaliyar*—in charge of headmen in East Giruwa Pattu in the Hambantota district, when Woolf was the assistant government agent. He had some old bones to pick with him.

In 1960, during Woolf's visit, he went to meet him at the Galle Face Hotel in Colombo, in order to remind him of an incident in which Woolf had dealt harshly with a headman. Woolf recalled: "I had only a vague, misty remembrance of him." The incident took place during the terrible outbreak of rinderpest. Woolf had received a message that there was a badly infected buffalo. He took a rifle with him to the spot and asked the village headman to drive the buffalo towards him so that he could shoot it. The headman, after venturing towards the animal, came back and reported that it was so badly infected he feared it would charge him. Woolf then gave his rifle to the *mudaliyar* (Wijesinhe) and told him that he himself would chase the animal and that the *mudaliyar* should shoot it. And so it transpired. But then—and this is what irked Wijesinhe—Woolf told him he intended to try the owner of the dead buffalo for not tethering an infected animal. "To my amazement I was told that the owner was the village headman standing hangdoggedly before me. As police magistrate I tried the headman and fined him ten rupees for not tethering an infected animal. As assistant government agent I then tried the village headman for breaking the law by not reporting the offender and fined him ten rupees."

While Wijesinghe was recounting all this ancient detail, Woolf suddenly remembered the incident and saw the scene again: the sweltering heat, the waterless tank, the dead buffalo swarming with flies, near a village called Angunakolapelessa. "I have only to murmur to myself Angunakolapelessa and it brings to me from 50 years ago quite clearly the vision of that small Sinhalese village; I can feel again the whip of heat across my face from the village path; I can hear again the hum of insects across the scrub jungle; I can smell again the acrid smell of smoke and shrubs."

When Wijesinhe had finished, he fixed Woolf with "a beady and a baleful eye" and said: "Was it just, sir ? Was it just? The village headman paid the ten rupees which you had fined him as police magistrate, but he could not pay the ten rupees which you had fined him for not carrying out his duties as headman. I had to pay it for him. Was it just, I say—was it just, I ask you sir?" According to Woolf, he replied: "He had committed two entirely different offences . . . Yes Mudaliyar it was just." But he also confessed to his autobiography: "I was not entirely comfortable about it, and I'm quite certain that fifty years before in 1910 when I stood in the village tank, faced by the *mudaliyar* and the unhappy *vidane* [headman], I had the same ambivalent feeling. This ambivalence with regard to law and order and justice in an imperialist society was one of the principal reasons for my resigning from the civil service."

Wijesinhe's January 1962 article made other criticisms of Woolf. He had apparently reminded him in 1960 of a day in the jungle on which they had narrowly escaped from three elephants and he had failed to shoot a leopard. According to Wijesinhe, the leopard had been in clear sight. But Woolf did not shoot and said afterwards he did not have the heart to kill the animal. However the headman who was actually with Woolf laughingly gave Wijesinhe his own version of the encounter: Woolf had raised his gun but "his hands shook so much that the barrel hit the sides of the 'ambush' and the leopard disappeared into the jungle." Perhaps the truth was a mixture of both stories. Woolf's hand tremor may have forced him to pause, then, seeing the leopard's magnificence, he became unwilling to shoot even when the tremor abated.

That Wijesinhe was not a wholly reliable witness is shown by the way he refers to *Growing* to support his case against Woolf. In particular, he says that in Jaffna Woolf waved his riding crop in front of Mr Sanderasekara's face "as an imperialistic warning against a brown man's right to use a horse in the presence of a 'white ruler'." But as Woolf described that unfortunate incident in *Growing* (as mentioned in our chapter on Jaffna), this was what Sanderasekara *thought* had happened, whereas the truth was nothing of the sort. Wijesinhe also claimed that Engelbrecht, the game ranger in Yala, displayed "simple, good-natured, honest and friendly behaviour." Wijesinhe would appear to have been alone in this belief.

Wijesinhe's article—and a second article by him in February alleging that Woolf's real reason for leaving the Ceylon civil service was a problem with his superiors—incensed Woolf enough for him to write a rejoinder in a letter to the *Ceylon Observer*. He said:

> I do not know why he should pursue me with these libellous lies. There is hardly a word of truth in Wijesinhe's article. It is untrue that I was 'forced to leave Ceylon'. . . There is not a word of truth in his account of his 'adventures' with me in the Hambantota jungle 50 years ago or in the Galle Face Hotel two years ago. I have always had and still have the greatest affection for Ceylon and its inhabitants. It is slightly depressing, therefore, to find that an old man like Wijesinhe can be so silly and so malignant.

The attack opened the way for a few other newspaper articles in Ceylon condemning Woolf as an arrogant imperialist—as might be expected in any post-colonial country. Their writers were in a distinct minority, however; there were far more articles in praise of the one-time assistant government agent. One of these described Woolf as a humane observer of life, unlike the current civil servants in Ceylon, who were nothing but bureaucrats. With the simultaneous publication of *Diaries in Ceylon*, another article in the *Ceylon Observer* in January 1962 took a completely different view from Wijesinhe and stated, "Woolf had a great love and affection for the people over whom he ruled. He obviously understood them very much more than any of his *mudaliyars* did." Indeed, asserted the writer, the *mudaliyars* were the more objectionable, since they worked with the British to oppress their own people. Anyway, the sins of the imperialist system could not be laid at the door of the individual. The article urged readers to read Woolf's *Growing* to get an accurate picture of him and not to draw their conclusions from Wijesinhe's account.

Woolf's warm reception in Ceylon in 1960—as a result of his tireless work as a colonial administrator, his literary contributions about Ceylon and his political lobbying for its self-government—supports the view that Sri Lankans have at least one imperialist who can be embraced as part of their history and culture. What may be even more enduring is how Woolf has become part of the folklore of a very small area, the Magam Pattu division of the Hambantota district—as we shall see when we go in search of the 'real' village of Beddagama in the Epilogue of this book. But first, let us revisit Woolf himself, and try to sum up what kind of human being the preceding chapters about his time in Ceylon, along with his subsequent life in England, reveal him to be.

10

Should We Be Afraid of Leonard Woolf?

> For just as, though I believe passionately in the truth of some things,
> I believe passionately that you cannot be certain of the absolute truth of
> anything, so too, though I feel passionately that certain things matter
> profoundly, I feel profoundly in the depths of my being that in the last
> resort *nothing matters.*
>
> LEONARD WOOLF, Sowing

A HUNDRED YEARS HAVE now passed since Woolf arrived in Ceylon and spent nearly seven formative years on the island. That colonial world of 1904 was incredibly different from today's world. In 1904, Lord Curzon—imperialist-in-chief—was viceroy of India, the 'jewel in the crown', and the British Empire and the imperial way of life shaped the destinies of dozens of countries and the lives of hundreds of millions. In 2004, all the colonial empires have gone, and some of the formerly colonised regions and peoples—India included—look set to play a dominant role in the twenty-first century.

I lived through this great transformation. I was born and raised in a small colony; educated in the heart of the empire; made my way in business in a white dominion; and then returned to live in a country which had lost its empire. Reading Woolf's fascinating autobiography as it appeared from the Hogarth Press in the 1960s, while I was living and working in Canada, and then rereading it while researching this book, I came to realise that my experience was a sort of echo of his: I travelled in the opposite direction to Woolf, yet we ended up in the same place. Woolf's friend and Hogarth author T. S. Eliot compresses the complex feelings aroused by the experience in his famous lines:

Portrait of Leonard Woolf by Vanessa Bell, 1940.

We shall not cease from exploration
And the end of all our exploring
Will be to arrive where we started
And know the place for the first time.

Woolf explored *himself* when he worked in Ceylon. In going there, and abandoning England, he gave up much of what was dearest to him: academia, close friendships with gifted men, and a large family circle. Then, in returning to England and marrying Virginia Stephen, he gave up most of what was dear to him in Ceylon—not only its physical beauty and the Sinhalese people but also his emotional ties to their way of life, since Virginia had no interest in Ceylon. At last, in later life, he returned there and saw the changes that had taken place in that ancient and diverse culture, as I have done in later life. Following Woolf's tracks has undoubtedly helped me to see my birthplace much more clearly, almost as if for the first time.

Yet, though I have read Woolf's books carefully and visited his old haunts in Sri Lanka, still I do not feel I really know Leonard Woolf. The five volumes of his compellingly readable autobiography are highly informative, appealingly frank and remarkably objective about himself, but their author remains to some extent enigmatic. He lifts the social carapace protecting his inner world and lets the reader in, but he leaves some of its corners in deep shadow (such as his feelings about Virginia's antipathy for 'darkies', already mentioned). Woolf's own view of himself was that he had remained essentially unchanged since he was a young child; but even if we accept this self-assessment, there can be no question that his experiences as a young man—at Cambridge and in Ceylon—shaped his personality and hugely influenced his adult career.

His comment on the wide gap between the public image of Virginia Woolf and the woman he lived with for 30 years, in volume four of his autobiography, seems relevant here:

> she was not a bit like the Virginia Woolf who appears in many books written by literary critics or autobiographers who did not know her, a frail invalidish lady living in an ivory tower in Bloomsbury and worshipped by a little clique of aesthetes. She was intensely interested in things, people, and events, and . . . highly sensitive to the atmosphere which surrounded her, whether it was personal, social, or historical. She was therefore the last person who could ignore the political

menaces under which we all lived. *A Room of One's Own* and *Three Guineas* are political pamphlets belonging to a long line stretching back to *Vindication of the Rights of Women* by Mary Wollstonecraft.

Leonard Woolf's public image has tended to suffer from the opposite problem to that of his celebrated wife. He is seen principally as a man of the world, chiefly the political world, and his inner life and introversion are underplayed or even ignored.

A melancholic streak was there in him from an early age. In the 1880s, every summer the Woolf family would leave London for a holiday in the country. On returning to London one September, and finding the garden he loved flowerless, grimy with soot and full of spiders in their webs, the adult Woolf recalled being overwhelmed with melancholy as a boy. In Ceylon, melancholy shadowed him, especially at the beginning. The flatness of the landscape around Jaffna inspired melancholy, and at the pearl fishery in Mannar melancholy deepened into suicidal depression.

There is evidence of it too in Virginia Woolf's diary. After a disillusioning party and a week spent with the Apostles in June 1924, Leonard allegedly again contemplated suicide. His dark side, and his disappearance from 'civilisation' to the tropics, intrigued Virginia. She was aware of it before their marriage from her brother Thoby's descriptions of his friend. In a reading to the Bloomsbury Memoir Club in 1928, Virginia described how she had been told about a Jew who trembled all over, the reason apparently being his violence and misanthropy. One night he had dreamt he was strangling a man and woke up to discover he had pulled his own thumb out of joint.

Along with the melancholy went a certain social unease. Woolf's phenomenal official success in Ceylon enabled him to conceal this fact but he was never able to make himself into a clubbable man, especially in the social milieu of imperial Kandy. He always had to make a conscious effort to be a 'good fellow' in Ceylon and to suppress his intellectual superiority, which undoubtedly struck some of his colleagues (such as the government agent for Hambantota district) as arrogance. And it appears that he usually succeeded. Quentin Bell, Virginia's nephew, wrote: "it would be wrong to think of him as one so cerebral in his approach to life as to be quite separated from his fellows by a 'superior' Cambridge arrogance. If he ever had that quality he lost it in Ceylon." But at what cost to himself?

Another defining characteristic of Woolf was his rationality. In the first volume of his autobiography he says that he never truly worried about anything, because he could endure the cruel blows of fate with amused detachment, since he believed that ultimately "nothing matters". His analytical detachment was evident from his time at Cambridge, where he and Strachey devised a psychological technique they named "the method". The two of them would grill a victim with the intention of revealing his true nature to everyone. The hope, according to Woolf, was that "by imparting to all concerned the deeper psychological truths, personal relationships would be much improved." They once applied this method to Saxon Sydney-Turner—but the result was not a greater openness, rather a greater determination in their friend to conceal himself more carefully in the future.

'The method' was more than a mere Cambridge caprice. Woolf said he trained it on himself in Ceylon and attributed to it a measure of his success there. In a letter to Strachey from Jaffna in 1905, he mentioned how he had passed his law exam in record time and that people commented on how he already ran the province—all of which he put down to his persistent use of the method. Of course his success may have been due to his belief in the method rather than to the method itself. (Woolf also had a keen, and insufficiently critical, belief in Freud—whom he published—and the efficacy of psychoanalysis.) Whatever the source may have been, the method seems to have given him added confidence in dealing with people, which, combined with his relentless hard work, intelligence and administrative skills, proved to be an excellent route to success in the civil service.

Irene Coates, possibly Woolf's most unsympathetic critic, in her book *Who's Afraid of Leonard Woolf?*, accuses 'the method' of having far more sinister consequences. She writes: "When Leonard returned to England in 1911, he brought back with him a psychological weapon that he had concocted in Cambridge and perfected in Ceylon: a method of manipulating other people to his advantage." Coates believes that Leonard's love letters to Virginia and his marriage proposal were part of "a preconceived plan, which only Lytton knew about", to take Virginia off her sister Vanessa's hands. The basis for this claim relies on rather shaky interpretations of two letters. The first of these is from Vanessa Bell to Woolf saying that he was the only person she could imagine as Virginia's husband and that she hoped he would not go back to Ceylon. But of course this could equally well be seen as evidence of her genuine belief in

Leonard as the best choice for her sister. Secondly, Woolf wrote to Strachey on 2 June 1912: "Do you remember the year in which I was going to justify myself and my method of dealing with life? 1935 was it? I feel somehow that I've done it in 1912 or at any rate life's justified itself to me. Virginia is going to marry me." Whether Woolf's "method of dealing with life" and 'the method' of Cambridge days are really one and the same thing is a moot point. And even if they are, I do not find Woolf's comment particularly objectionable.

Coates, and also some other less unsympathetic critics of Leonard Woolf, object because they regard him as predominantly a gold-digger and social climber, who married Virginia Woolf for her money and class. And there is enough circumstantial support for this view to give it at least a semblance of respectability. It is obviously conceivable that Woolf consciously set about trying to marry Virginia as a means of securing his own position: he was indeed a "penniless Jew" (as she called him) and Virginia was certainly of a higher social class and of independent financial means. To marry her would consolidate his position among the artistic and intellectual elite he had met in Cambridge who were becoming the Bloomsbury group. He was certainly an ambitious man. In Ceylon, he had demonstrated this with his fast promotion and record-beating collection of pearls, salt and census information. In England, he had literary ambitions too.

Yet after reading his love letters to Virginia, it is hard to imagine them as coming from a calculating manipulator. Woolf's letter to Strachey (who, let us not forget, had encouraged him to propose to Virginia after his own proposal had been turned down) continues: "I'm so happy that that's the only thing that I can say to you, simply that I am. Lord, it is difficult to put one's happiness into words and it was so damned easy to put the miseries of life into them from Ceylon." Surely, if Woolf were really a schemer writing here to a co-schemer, he would not have had so much difficulty in expressing the triumphant outcome of their scheme? Moreover, in relinquishing his position in Ceylon, Woolf had almost certainly abandoned a future governorship and knighthood in order to marry Virginia. Privately wealthy he was not, but his civil service job made him financially secure.

From January 1912 onwards, when Leonard first proposed to Virginia, his affection for her seems thoroughly sincere. He said he loved her not only for her beauty but for her mind and character too. In April he wrote to her: "It's true that I'm cold and reserved to other people; I don't feel affection ever easily:

but apart from love I'm fond of you as I've never been of anyone or thing in the world." He offered to go away for a while if it would help take the pressure off her, and also suggested she finish her first novel (*The Voyage Out*) before making a decision. Once they were married, the affection continues. In April 1913, he declared: "I love you and adore you and worship you Mandy ['Mandrill' was his pet name for Virginia; she called him 'Mongoose'] and I never want anything else in the world than you." In 1917, despite two years of strain during one of her major breakdowns, he wrote: "You don't know how many times a day I think of you and always with a longing to see you, talk to you, and kiss you." If ever they were apart, Leonard missed Virginia, even after ten years of marriage, and often wrote telling her so.

For her part, Virginia confessed to Leonard before they married that she had no physical feelings for him. She had been sexually abused by her two older half-brothers, Gerald and George Duckworth, and it is likely that this contributed to the lack of a sexual relationship in her marriage. When she was six years old, Gerald touched her but then left her alone. George, who was fourteen years older than Virginia, abused her when she was a teenager for several years after their mother's death, though her virginity remained intact. She described the first experience in "A sketch of the past", an essay published only after the death of both Woolfs:

> There was a slab outside the dining room door for standing dishes upon. Once when I was very small Gerald Duckworth lifted me onto this, and as I sat there he began to explore my body. I can remember the feel of his hand going under my clothes; going firmly and steadily lower and lower. I remember how I hoped he would stop; how I stiffened and wriggled as his hand approached my private parts. But it did not stop. His hand explored my private parts too. I remember resenting, disliking it—what is the word for so dumb and mixed a feeling? It must have been strong since I still recall it. This seems to show that a feeling about certain parts of the body; how they must not be touched; how it is wrong to allow them to be touched; must be instinctive. It proves that Virginia Stephen was not born on 25 January 1882, but was born many thousands of years ago; and had from the very first to encounter instincts already acquired by thousands of ancestresses in the past.

*Virginia Woolf's experience of being sexually abused by her older half-brothers
Gerald and George Duckworth appears in "A sketch of the past", which was published
posthumously.*

To complicate matters, Woolf confessed a terror of female virginity to
Strachey when he wrote to him from Ceylon. He appears to have been sexually
very active while in Ceylon, often visiting prostitutes, as mentioned in the
chapter on Jaffna. This experience in itself would have made for incompatibility
with Virginia, even without her own sexual problems. In Coates's words, "His
alienated lust and her terrified frigidity were at opposite ends of the sexual

spectrum." Coates details a comment by Gerald Brenan who was visited by the Woolfs in 1923. Leonard apparently told Brenan that when he tried to make love to Virginia on their honeymoon she got into such a violent state of excitement that he had to stop, believing her state to be a precursor to an attack of madness. On another occasion, either Virginia or Leonard must have confessed their difficult sex life to Vanessa, Virginia's sister, as a letter survives written by Vanessa to her husband in which she remarks how curious it is that Virginia gets no pleasure from sex.

In contrast with the open sexuality of many of the Bloomsbury group, there is not much evidence of sexual activity after marriage by either Leonard or Virginia, except for her three-year lesbian affair with Vita Sackville-West in the late 1920s. Many people have assumed that Leonard Woolf led the life of a monk. Frederic Spotts, the editor of Woolf's letters, claims: "Late in life he told Trekkie Parsons that he never had an affair with another woman. He said that even had he been so inclined, he would not have taken the risk, since, had Virginia learned of it, 'it would have sent her mad.'" He may not have had an affair but it is surely possible that he visited prostitutes. His tolerance of Virginia's affair with Vita Sackville-West could suggest that he had encounters of his own, or alternatively that Virginia knew Leonard had a sexual life of his own and was therefore carefree in sharing her own sexuality with Vita. Since Leonard Woolf was someone who rarely remarked on the sexual activity of his friends and barely discussed sex in the five volumes of his autobiography, we shall probably never know the truth. His natural discretion could have easily covered up any sexual activity. But it is equally possible that he led a largely sexless life throughout his marriage, having the strong-mindedness to sublimate his sexual urges in work. What is certain is that sex was not the main bond between Leonard and Virginia, other things were. "They were remarkably well matched. They shared the same values and ideals, obsession with work, simplicity of living, disdain for religion, disregard for money, love of independence and contempt for convention and bourgeois respectability," notes Spotts.

There is much more evidence concerning Woolf's attitude to his wife's madness. She was diagnosed as suffering from neurasthenia, a dated medical term describing headaches, irritability and fatigue related to emotional distress. Virginia's headaches would lead either to profound depression or to periods of mania when she was sometimes violent, would be unable to sleep, would talk incoherently for several days before falling into a coma, or hear voices.

She might imagine her dead mother to be in the room and start talking to her, or hear the sparrows outside her window talking in Greek. Very little was understood about mental illness and all doctors gave similar advice: enforced rest, plenty of food and milk.

Leonard insisted Virginia go to bed before eleven most nights and tried to impose a regime that would keep her stable and ward off any attacks. It could well be that if she had been given more independence she would have developed into a different person. But in doing what he did he was heeding the advice of the doctors. Criticism of him would have been far harsher had he failed to care for her or ignored medical advice. He was often in a situation where actions had to be taken in which the outcomes were not predictable. During her first major breakdown in 1914, Leonard found the strain of being Virginia's sole carer considerable—he had to watch her day and night without giving her the feeling of being watched.

Many thought him to have been entirely selfless in caring for his wife. Inevitably, Coates questions this assumption, as part of her case that Leonard manipulated Virginia for his own ends. Extreme though her view is, there are elements of truth in some of her assertions. She writes, in summary:

> Leonard Woolf's early and complete acceptance that Virginia had to be treated as somebody who was somewhat mad all the time, with bouts of overt insanity, locked her into a life that proved to be a forcing house for her writing but turned Leonard into her lifelong and, when he failed her, fatal support. By over-protection he denied her the possibility of the personal development that would have given her independence and taken her beyond the need for such a dangerous prop.

One disastrous incident was especially revealing of Leonard's attitude. He had gone out to visit Virginia's doctor when she took an overdose of Veronal and nearly died. Luckily her friend Ka Cox found her and her stomach was pumped. Leonard admitted some responsibility; in the chaos of moving house he had forgotten to lock the case containing the drugs. But as a rational man he said he felt no guilt, claiming that something sometime was bound to go wrong. He thought that whatever he did for Virginia during this time would never be enough and he was bound to make a mistake. While this was true, his lack of emotion is disturbing. Coates takes a typically extreme view and asserts that "he not only never admitted to feeling either guilt or remorse; he almost never accepted he was wrong or apologised." The ruthlessness of Woolf in Ceylon provides some support for this view, but on the other hand we must remember that we know about that ruthlessness—and about the details of Woolf's care of his sick wife—only because he himself chose to reveal them to us in his autobiography, while sometimes confessing his regret for his past actions.

✷ ✷ ✷

Virginia's illness was in part responsible for the creation of the Hogarth Press. Leonard thought that if she did an interesting manual job, printing, in the afternoons, this might stop her mind from dwelling on her writing and working itself into the state that led to a breakdown. They bought themselves a printing press and after a certain amount of trial and error produced their first book in 1917, *Two Stories*, by Leonard and Virginia Woolf. During the next three years, they published work by Katherine Mansfield, T. S. Eliot and E. M. Forster, among others. Although the Hogarth Press was never a full-time occupation for either of them, it still became phenomenally successful. Woolf attributed this to its near-zero overheads and its small size: by keeping it small they could concentrate on publishing only the books they really liked. In 1920, they expanded the press sufficiently to publish Virginia's latest novel, *Jacob's Room*. This avoided her work having to be submitted to Gerald Duckworth (her publisher and half-brother) and his reader for scrutiny, a process that, according to Leonard, "filled her with horror and misery". Throughout their marriage Leonard read Virginia's novels in manuscript and gave her valuable advice.

A further factor in their publishing success was that the Ceylon civil service had made Leonard into a very competent businessman. Compared with dealing in salt and other goods in the Hambantota district, running the business side of the Hogarth Press was child's play. Here Woolf also praised his former boss, the government agent in Jaffna, Price, for training him to answer correspondence on the day of its arrival. Thus Leonard combined literary judgement and a head for business as a publisher. The fact that the part-time nature of the Hogarth Press left him free to pursue his own writing, and his journalism and literary editing for magazines kept him in close contact with contemporary writers, put him in a virtually ideal position to turn the literary talent of the Bloomsbury group, and of dozens of other writers, into a profitable cottage industry.

However some assistance was needed and there were tensions between Leonard and his publishing colleagues throughout the early decades of the Hogarth Press. He admitted in his autobiography: "I have never been an easy person to work with. My experience in the Ceylon civil service proved that I got on much better with subordinates than with equals or superiors in business. In practical affairs I am in many ways a perfectionist—a character for which in the abstract, or when I see it in other people, I have no great admiration." Woolf was a man who liked to be in charge—whether of his publishing business or of his wife's illness.

The 1920s were marked by success for the Woolfs: the Hogarth Press, Virginia's novels, blossoming personal friendships and personal happiness. The following decade was less happy for them. In 1932, Lytton Strachey died of cancer, a real loss for the Woolfs, and his death was followed by the deaths of Dora Carrington, Roger Fry and their nephew Julian Bell, killed in the Spanish Civil War in 1937, and lastly Leonard's mother Marie Woolf in 1939.

Then there was the deteriorating international situation, which directly concerned Woolf through his work for the Labour Party and his political journalism. (In 1938 he even wrote a play, *The Hotel*, about the war that was coming.) In 1935, the Woolfs decided to see things for themselves by driving through Germany on their way to Rome, despite having received official advice from the Foreign Office recommending Jews not to go. Someone with inside knowledge had assured Leonard he would be perfectly safe, provided he avoided Nazi processions. To ease his way, Prince Bismarck, counsellor at the German Embassy in London, wrote a letter of recommendation for the Woolfs to present to German officials.

In the event it was Woolf's love of animals that helped him more than the letter from Prince Bismarck. At this time, he was looking after a marmoset called Mitz for some friends and decided to take her with them. By mistake their car, with Mitz in it, got caught up in Nazi processions for mile after mile—the very situation Leonard had been advised to avoid. But the car and its occupants received a very warm reception because of Mitz. First the Nazis saluted Mitz, then Virginia and him. Woolf wryly recalled: "It was obvious to the most anti-Semitic stormtrooper that no one who had on his shoulder such a 'dear little thing' could be a Jew." But it was hardly an enjoyable journey, with gigantic signs outside villages declaring that Jews were not welcome. Woolf found the Germany of 1935 "sinister and menacing".

The year 1940 arrived with the strong likelihood of an invasion of Britain by the Nazis, which would have quickly overrun the Woolfs' house in Sussex not far from the south coast. The best Woolf could expect as a Jew was a beating. He and Virginia made a suicide pact: should Britain be invaded they would kill themselves in their garage by gassing themselves with carbon monoxide—Leonard kept petrol reserved for this purpose. Other friends took similar precautions, preferring suicide to surrender. Writing about the Germans and the war in the final volume of his autobiography Woolf said: "I feel the hatred welling up in myself, and yet I hate the hatred, knowing it to be neither rational nor objective."

On 28 March 1941, Virginia Woolf committed suicide alone. In his autobiography Leonard described the run-up to this event as the most terrible and agonising period of his life. Looking back, he naturally questioned whether he could have foreseen the suicide but he remembered feeling that her mind was more stable than usual and her spirits happier. She had suffered from a severe bout of depression for ten days in January 1941 but had then seemed to recover. The day before her death, he had driven her to Brighton to see her doctor Octavia Wilberforce, who was also a friend, and he had afterwards (as a German bomber flew low over the house) discussed her condition with the doctor in private. They both knew that the wrong method of treatment could be disastrous. Whatever their decision the risk was acute. Woolf wrote in his last volume of autobiography, "I knew . . . that a wrong word, a mere hint of pressure, even a statement of the truth might be enough to drive her over the verge into suicide."

On the morning of 28 March, Leonard was in the garden and assumed Virginia was in the house. But when he went inside for lunch he found her deeply moving suicide note to him on the mantelpiece:

> Dearest, I feel certain that I am going mad again. I feel we can't go through another of those terrible times. And I shan't recover this time. I begin to hear voices, and I can't concentrate. So I am doing what seems the best thing to do. You have given me the greatest possible happiness. You have been in every way all that anyone could be. I don't think two people could have been happier till this terrible disease

came. I can't fight any longer. I know that I am spoiling your life, that without me you could work. And you will I know. You see I can't even write this properly. I can't read. What I want to say is I owe all the happiness in my life to you. You have been entirely patient with me and incredibly good. I want to say that—everybody knows it. If anybody could have saved me it would have been you. Everything has gone from me but the certainty of your goodness. I can't go on spoiling your life any longer.

I don't think two people could have been happier than we have been.

V.

Leonard searched for Virginia and found her walking stick on the bank of the river. After further searching he informed the police. He knew with some certainty that she had committed suicide, and on the evening of her disappearance he wrote to Vita Sackville-West telling her what had happened. Virginia's body was found floating in the River Ouse three weeks later.

Irene Coates, whose book on Leonard Woolf has the subtitle, *A Case for the Sanity of Virginia Woolf*, thinks that Leonard deliberately plotted her death. "With his 'secret and sinuous psychology' and thirty years watching his potential victim, he knew exactly how to drive Virginia to suicide." For, "if Virginia succeeded in killing herself he would have received sympathy and practical help from everyone, while inheriting her money." An annulment or a divorce would not have suited Leonard, claims Coates, as he would have lost control of Virginia's money.

But if Leonard was so eager to be rid of Virginia, why did they spend so much time together, and why did he care for her so persistently, even if at times that care may have been smothering? His affection and regard for her are transparent not only in his letters but in his autobiography, written more than two decades after her death. No sane person can read the autobiography without being persuaded that his feelings for her were genuine.

There were two great elms in the garden of Woolf's house in Sussex, with their boughs interlaced. The Woolfs called them Leonard and Virginia. Virginia's ashes were buried under one in 1941, Leonard's beneath the other after his death in 1969.

✳ ✳ ✳

During the last three years of the Second World War, Woolf became "intimate friends", as he put it, with Trekkie Parsons and her husband Ian. Woolf had known Trekkie's sister, Alice Ritchie, who worked as a sales representative for the Hogarth Press and was also published by them as an author. Alice died of cancer in 1941 and some time later Trekkie wrote to Woolf asking him to come and see her. Ian Parsons was in the air force in France and Trekkie often stayed with Woolf in Sussex during the final year of the war. Although Woolf denied it, it seems fairly certain from his letters to Trekkie that they had an affair. In 1943, at the age of 63, he wrote to her, "I don't think I'm really romantic, though if I am about you, I have a good excuse. It is not romantic, though it may be dangerous, to love anyone like you as much as I love you."

At the end of the war the Parsons moved to a village two miles from Woolf's house at Rodmell. They also shared a house with him at Victoria Square in London. Ian Parsons was a director of publishers Chatto and Windus and it was through their friendship that Hogarth Press formed a partnership with Chatto and Windus in 1946. While Hogarth retained its independence and editorial control, Chatto took care of production, sales and accounts. Parsons and the other directors of Chatto shared the same view of publishing as Woolf, and so the partnership was a good one. Woolf remained a director of Hogarth and of Chatto until his death in 1969, visiting the Chatto office once a week.

His relationship with Trekkie Parsons also continued until his death, although she remained married to Ian Parsons. It was she who accompanied him on a trip to Israel in 1957 and, as we know, on his return visit to Ceylon in 1960, where an interviewer in Hambantota noted how Woolf would frequently glance at her while speaking.

That year marked the publication of the first volume of his autobiography, *Sowing*, followed by *Growing* in 1961. The third volume, *Beginning Again*, appeared in 1964 and won the W. H. Smith literary award. *Downhill All the Way* was published in 1967 and the final volume, *The Journey Not the Arrival Matters*, appeared in 1969 just after his death. The autobiography meant that, in his eighties, Woolf at last began to receive the acclaim he deserved. Malcolm Muggeridge spent three days with Woolf at his house in 1966, interviewing him for a television programme. He said: "The great quality in Woolf as an autobiographer is his utter truthfulness—rarer in this genre of literature than one might suppose . . . Woolf has to a notable degree that passion for truth which is perhaps the most admirable of all human qualities". Around the same time he was given an honorary doctorate by the University of Sussex, which now holds a large fraction of his papers.

His political labours continued into his last years. He had worked tirelessly since the time of the Great War on political matters, and his involvement with the Fabian Society helped sow the seeds of the thinking that brought Labour to power in 1945. But Woolf was characteristically ruthless in assessing his own contribution. He calculated that on politics he had expended over his lifetime between 150,000 and 200,000 hours of useless work—useless because, he said, the world would have been the same had he played ping-pong for all those hours instead of sitting on committees and writing books and memoranda. "Happy the country and era—if there can ever have been one—which has no politics," he wrote in *Downhill All the Way*—a striking and unexpected observation from so politically engaged a man. Yet he also stated: "in a wider context, though all that I tried to do politically was completely futile and ineffective and unimportant, for me personally it was right and important that I should do it . . . 'It is not the arrival, it is the journey which matters.'" (The title, of course, of the last volume of Woolf's autobiography, taken from Montaigne, who Woolf regarded as "the first civilized modern man".)

Shortly before his death on 14 August 1969, Woolf summed up his life rather well in this last volume. "*Sub specie aeternitatis*, in the eye of God or rather of the universe, nothing human is of the slightest importance; but in one's own personal life, in terms of humanity and human history and human society, certain things are of immense importance: human relations, happiness, truth, beauty or art, justice and mercy." Always honest to a fault, he does not mention love. And neither did Virginia Woolf in her suicide note to him. Should we be afraid of Leonard Woolf? Perhaps we should be, a little, even while we cannot help but admire his steadfast integrity and civilized humanity.

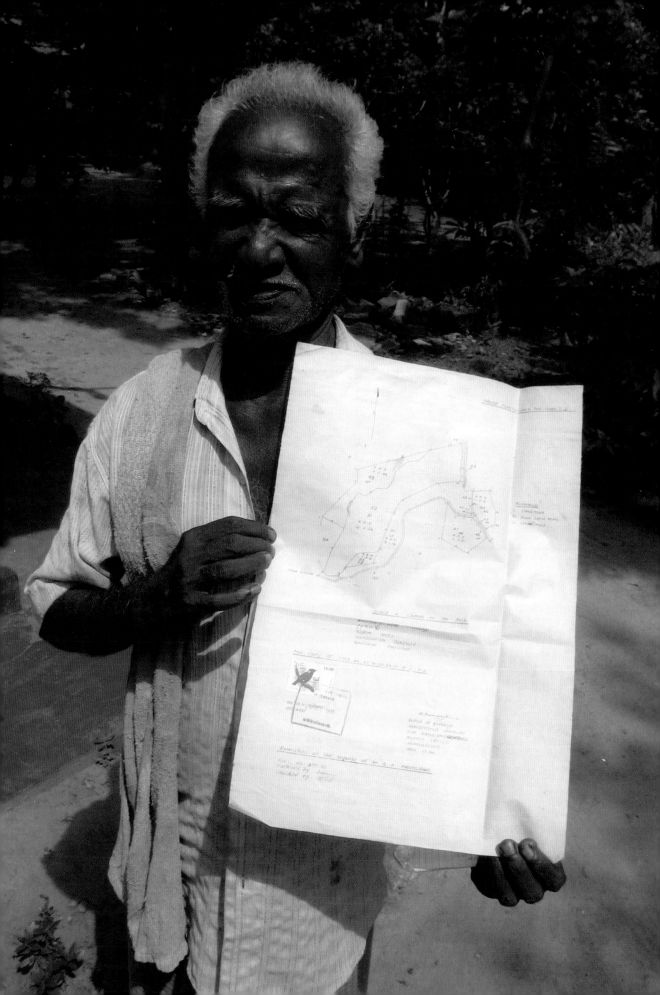

EPILOGUE

In Search of Beddagama

> During my absence on circuit there has been a most cold-blooded murder at Malasnegalwewa which Mr Willett came down especially to enquire into as police magistrate . . . In this case the *vel-vidane* deliberately shot the acting *vidane arachchi* from behind and then walked a mile to shoot the ex-*vidane arachchi*, the acting V. A.'s father. He found the old man digging in his garden and shot him dead. He then went to the *mudaliyar* and gave himself up.
>
> LEONARD WOOLF, *Diaries in Ceylon*, 13 December 1910

W HEN I LEFT SRI LANKA in March 2004, I left behind some unfinished Woolf business. Was there or was there not a 'real' village in the jungle which formed the basis of *The Village in the Jungle*? While we were travelling in the Hambantota district, several villagers assured us that there was such a village—although everyone agreed that it was not called Beddagama, as it is in the novel. So in December, I returned to Sri Lanka to see what, if anything, I could find out about this mysterious village.

Literary scholars may scoff at the desire to locate the factual reality behind works of fiction, but there is no denying the fascination of this quest—as the countless visitors to the Baker Street address of Sherlock Holmes, the crowds of tourists who flock to walking tours of 'Dickens's London', or indeed the scholars who pore over the details of Dublin's geography as imagined in Joyce's *Ulysses*, clearly attest. Every major work of fiction—especially if it has been made into a movie—provokes passionate interest in the concrete details of the places it portrays. Such is the power of great literature that it can make a fictional place seem more real than its original.

In the case of Woolf's novel, the appeal to 'location spotters' is particularly seductive, because Woolf is known to have been a stickler for accuracy, who

S. A. Amarajeeva holds a land plan of the Malasnegalwewa property.

kept a detailed official diary of his work in the Hambantota district. As already remarked in the chapter on "The Literary Woolf", there are many strong resemblances between passages in the diary and passages in the novel. Why should there not have been a real village, too, which closely resembled the Beddagama depicted in the novel?

The most intriguing of his diary reports, seen from this angle, is the one quoted above. In December 1910, Woolf noted that while he was away on circuit there had been a double murder in Magam Pattu, the area in which he would set the double murder in the novel when he began writing it less than a year later in London. In real life, a *vel-vidane* (a headman in charge of irrigation) had shot a *vidane arachchi* (chief headman) in the back, then walked some distance to shoot the headman's father (a former chief headman), and had then surrendered himself to a *mudaliyar* (district government official). In *The Village in the Jungle*, Silindu shoots the headman Babehami in the back in the fields, then walks back to the village and shoots Fernando, the moneylender, and then gives himself up to a district government official. In both real life and fiction, the two murders are committed in cold blood.

Woolf says no more about the incident in his diary, which was investigated not by him but in his absence by Willett, a colleague acting as police magistrate. But we can be absolutely confident that he would have discussed Willett's findings with him and would have formed his own view as to the circumstances and motive behind the double murder. It strains credulity to believe that such a rare incident as a cold-blooded double murder in Magam Pattu did not form the basis of the novel's murders. I am convinced that it did.

This link does not of course mean that the village of the actual shootings, named by Woolf as Malasnegalwewa, is the basis for the fictional Beddagama, but inevitably the parallel events piqued my curiosity about this place. When I now visited Malasnegalwewa with my travelling companions Raj and Lucky— joined by the playwright Ernest Macintyre, a friend of my sister in Colombo, with a strong interest in Woolf's novel who was sceptical yet curious about Beddagama's 'reality'—we encountered some very interesting new evidence.

Finding Malasnegalwewa was a task in itself. In March, while looking for 'Beddagama' in Magam Pattu near Migahajandura, a place mentioned more than once by Woolf in his diaries, we came across a jungle retreat for Buddhist monks, which local people said was not far from Woolf's 'Beddagama'. Returning to this retreat in December, we were lucky to meet an old man seated outside the monks' refectory. Amazingly, when Lucky started to question him, "We are making inquiries about a former government official ...", the old man cut short the question by saying "Leonard Woolf." Then he told us that 'Beddagama' was nearby. His name was R. A. Samarapala and he was the voluntary co-ordinator of the meals served to the monks. Since lunchtime was still some way off, he offered to help us in any way he could.

Excited, we got back into our vehicle with Mr Samarapala and drove about a mile and a half down a barely motorable track. He then asked us to get out and look at a jungle setting some two or three hundred yards in front of us. I pulled out my much-thumbed paperback of Woolf's novel and read the following passage while studying the view:

> Below the huts to the east of the village lay the tank, a large shallow depression in the jungle. Where the depression was deepest the villagers had raised a long narrow bund or mound of earth, so that when the rain fell the tank served as a large pond in which to store the water. Below the bund lay the stretch of rice-fields, about thirty acres, which the villagers cultivated if the tank filled with water, by cutting a hole in the bund, through which the water from the tank ran into the fields. The jungle rose high and dense around the fields and the tank ...

The description tallied with the view.

This in itself did not prove much, since such a configuration was standard for villages in the Magam Pattu jungle. But then we moved forward for a closer look. At this moment, a young man came out of the jungle, approached us and wanted to know what we were doing on his family's land. Mr Samarapala explained the reason for our interest. The young man became more relaxed and friendly and introduced himself as Ajith Siriwardena. He said that this piece of land had come into his family in the days of Leonard Woolf. According to his family tradition, it was on this land that a man called Silindu had killed a headman and a trader who had come from a town, in a time long before Woolf arrived in Hambantota as the assistant government agent. Ajith's great-grandfather had told Woolf about the killings, and Woolf had rewarded his great-grandfather by allocating the piece of land to him. Ajith also mentioned that his great-grandmother was called Babunhami—and I was interested to note the name's resemblance to the names of two characters in the novel, Babun and Babehami, the headman.

The story seemed attractive but a bit too good to be true. For a start, I doubted if Woolf was the sort of man who would have given a grant of land in exchange for an old story, however interesting the story might have been. Secondly, couldn't the story in the novel, which is well known, have influenced the family tradition about the history of their land? Ajith, however, had some legal documents to support his claim.

He took us to meet his uncle Mr S. A. Amarajeeva. He led the way to him on a light motorbike while we followed in our vehicle. On the way we passed a neat-looking school set in the jungle, with healthy-looking students playing in the grounds, and also a decent-looking roadside eating house. The home of Mr Amarajeeva—who had to be called out of his paddy field by Lucky wading in knee-deep muddy water—was made of brick and cement with a fine tiled roof; its sitting room was comfortably furnished, including an up-to-date hi-fi and television set. I was finding it difficult to square the reports of poverty and lack of change in the jungle districts since Woolf's day, quoted in my chapter on Hambantota, with the modern reality of agricultural life in Magam Pattu.

We settled down, over tea, to study the government land records. The most intriguing entry was dated 4 February 1911 (in other words, when Woolf was

R. A. Samarapala points to posts marking the site of 'Silindu's hut'.

in charge of land registration). It referred to the "mortgage of 24 kurunies" of land—that is 240 perches—to Don Bastyan Siriwardena of Malasnegalwewa, "for Rs 75 as security for the due performance of duties as police officer and division officer of Malasnegalwewa by the grantor."

The entry was a mere two months after the double murder recorded in Woolf's diary in December 1910. This seemed to me to be far more than a coincidence. In my view, it looks very likely that Don Bastyan Siriwardena was granted his land by Woolf in exchange for acting as a local policeman and government representative—presumably to deal with the aftermath of the double murder which had removed the source of authority (the acting headman and the former headman) in the village. This was just the kind of good reason Woolf would have needed to make a grant of land to the Siriwardena family.

To the present-day family, however, who clearly were unaware of the historical murders of 1910, the land grant has a more legendary quality and refers to murders committed in an earlier, 'pre-historic' time. The murders occurred, but they predated Woolf. This local view seems to me a good example of how powerful myths, including novels, grow out of facts. There is no way

Ajith Siriwardena shows us where Silindu supposedly tied his cattle.

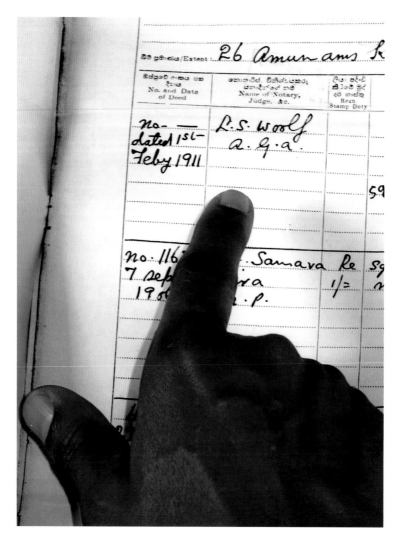

Above and opposite: Documents dated February 1911 give details of land grants by Leonard Woolf to Don Bastyan Siriwardena.

to be sure which view—mine or the Siriwardena family's—is the truer one.

What is certain, though, is that the people of the area accept the link between Malasnegalwewa, a double murder and Woolf's novel about a double murder in Beddagama. Indeed, when the Government's Irrigation Department, some four years back, came to dig a channel to supply water to the tank from a government reservoir and began to dig up part of Ajith Siriwardena's land with a bulldozer, Mr Amarajeeva persuaded the irrigation workers not to obliterate the spot where the family believed Silindu's hut to have stood. Instead, the workers planted four posts there and a signboard in Sinhala on

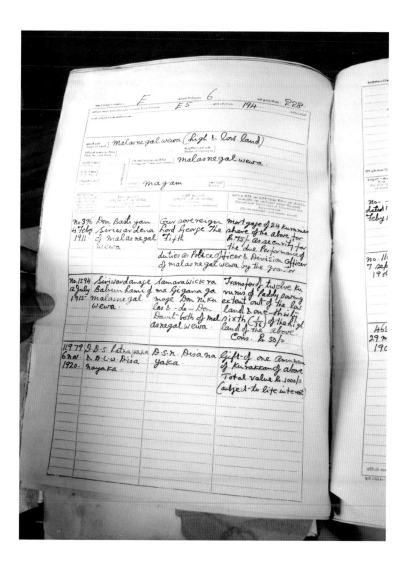

a nearby tree which reads as follows: "This is where Silindu tied his cattle". The bulldozer even unearthed a clay pot containing an assortment of old things, which the family believes to be the remnants of Silindu's home.

In 2002, this belief reached the national press. Mr Amarjeeva showed us an article in the *Sunday Times* of Sri Lanka, headlined "Still a village in the jungle". Its author, Kumudini Hettiarachchi, commented:

> As we stare at the four pillars marking the place where Silindu, one of the main characters in Woolf's *The Village in the Jungle* or 'Beddagama', lived a life of fear, of evil and deprivation, we are transported back in

time to the early twentieth century. It was an era when the jungle ruled the lives of the humble peasant as it does even now in remote villages scattered across the country . . . The belief in the area is that 'Beddagama' was based on the lives, loves, hates and ordeals of villagers in Pallemattala clustered around the Malasna Palugalwewa. Even the shooting of the headman and a money-lending *mudalali* by Silindu had apparently taken place here.

I share this belief, if for reasons different from the 'legend'. It seems highly probable that Woolf based his novel on Malasnegalwewa and its violent events in 1910, and then elaborated his powerful story from these initial sources using his profound knowledge of other villages in the area. This idea does not contradict his statement, quoted earlier, that "*The Village in the Jungle* is not based on any single village in Ceylon. It is really a composite picture of a number of villages north of Magam Paituwa [Pattu] in the Hambantota district." Rather, it deepens the interest of the novel.

*   *   *

That Woolf and his novel still matter in Sri Lanka, not only locally but nationally too, was emphasised by a remarkable conference held at the University of Ruhuna (the name of the old southern kingdom) in Matara in December 2004. Entitled "Culture and Society in a Colonial Context: Leonard Woolf Memorial International Conference", it was called to celebrate the centenary of Woolf's arrival in Ceylon in December 1904. Scholars from an astonishing range of disciplines took part: literature (both English and Sinhala), naturally, but also agriculture, anthropology, history, medicine and sociology.

Virtually all the participants were Sri Lankans, however, whether based in Sri Lanka or in universities in the West. This fact in no way diminishes Woolf's significance, but it does beg the question, what is Woolf's importance outside Sri Lanka? One can easily imagine a conference on Leonard Woolf in England or the United States, but one may be sure that only one, or at most two, of the papers would deal with Woolf in Ceylon.

Interestingly, the *Encyclopaedia Britannica* gives almost as much space to Leonard as to his wife Virginia Woolf, with a photograph for each of them. But whereas Virginia's entry concentrates on her literature and contains a substantial bibliography of scholarly writing about her, Leonard's is mainly biographical and offers only two bibliographical references, one of which is about his politics, the other about his relationship with Virginia. The entry calls him a "British man of letters, publisher, political worker, journalist, and internationalist who influenced literary and political life and thought more by his personality than by any one achievement."

This personality, as expressed in Woolf's marvellous autobiography, is likely to become even more fascinating with the passing of time. Empire is out of fashion now, but the interpenetration of disparate cultures that Leonard Woolf epitomised is more than ever alive in our post-imperial world. He is a key figure in the Bloomsbury group, which was at the very centre of English culture, but he is also, uniquely, at the centre of Sri Lankan culture. A lone Woolf by nature—but a man who managed to be an insider in two exceptionally different worlds. This was his extraordinary achievement.

Sources of Quotations

Quotations from books and academic articles are referenced here; for the sources of most quotations from newspaper reports, articles and reviews, see the Bibliography.

Leonard Woolf is abbreviated as LW, while Virginia Woolf is spelt out in full.

Introduction

p. 15   **In so far as anything** LW, *Growing*: 25

p. 15   **It dispelled** Quoted in Morris, *Pax Britannica*: 27

p. 16   **The infatuated** Morris, *Pax Britannica*: 99

p. 17   **how to induce** Ibid: 144

p. 22   **This was the imperial class** Morris, *Farewell the Trumpets*: 28

p. 22   **carapace** LW, *Sowing*: 56

p. 23   **Looking back I can see** Ibid: 169

p. 23   **unconscious imperialist** LW, *Growing*: 25

p. 23   **an embryonic feeling** Ibid: 16

p. 24   **relations between Europeans** Ibid: 17

p. 24   **they were very ordinary** Ibid: 12

p. 24   **of some intelligence** Ibid: 13

1   Arrival in Ceylon

p. 29   **To be born again** LW, *Growing*: 11–12

p. 30   **Caressed by warm waters** *Handbook for the Ceylon Traveller*: 1

p. 36   **an immense hotel** 16 Dec. 1904, in LW, *Letters*: 67

p. 36   **I'm partially drunk** Ibid.

p. 37   **There was something extraordinarily** LW, *Growing*: 21

p. 37   **as though it were** Ibid: 22

p. 39   **short and cynical** Ibid: 23

p. 39   **ordinarily lacking** Quoted in Wright: 80

p. 39   **which in the late morning** LW, *Growing*: 23

p. 39   **the English are hell** 20 Dec. 1904, in LW, *Letters*: 68

p. 39   **either Gods or animals** Ibid: 69

p. 39   **I have never felt** 17 Dec. 1904, in LW, *Letters*: 68

p. 39   **Do you feel my isolation** 20 Dec. 1904, in LW, *Letters*: 69

p. 39   **There has never been a lower depth** 29 Oct. 1905, in LW, *Letters*: 105

p. 41   **heaven** 20 Dec. 1904, in LW, *Letters*: 68

p. 46   **In the daytime** Ibid: 69

p. 47   **The powers of the civil service** Introduction to LW, *Diaries in Ceylon*, xii

p. 47   **the unifying bonds** Ibid: xiv

p. 48   **I did not want to return** LW, *Growing*: 247

p. 48   **He had no involvement** Jayawardena: 152

p. 49   **I was only a little child . . . the closed hand.** LW, *The Village in the Jungle*: 91–92

p. 50   **We are to be sent** 28 Dec. 1904, in LW, *Letters*: 69

2   Journey to Jaffna

p. 53   **To Anuradhapura** LW, *Growing*: 23

p. 53   **like that of the lagoons** Ibid: 32

p. 54   **fail to feel enchanted** Cave: 75

p. 56   **I once in Anuradhapura** LW, *Growing*: 160

p. 60   **Nothing in the universe** Ibid: 28

p. 63   **an athletic** Ibid: 24

p. 64   **We were grand** Ibid.

p. 64   **The result was that** Ibid: 26

p. 69–70 **with even justice . . . because of this worship** *Mahavamsa* (W. Geiger trans.) quoted in Farmer: 11

p. 70   **pre-colonial** Nissan and Stirrat: 24

p. 70   **I left Anuradhapura** LW, *Growing*: 30

p. 70   **unending ejaculations** Ibid: 29

p. 70   **I have just endured** 5 Jan. 1905, in LW, *Letters*: 70–71

p. 71   **Each time that the rolling** LW, *Growing*: 30

p. 74   **Consideration should be given** LW, *Letters*: 416–17

p. 79   **As we approached** LW, *Growing*: 30

3   Jaffna

p. 83   **It was characteristic** LW, *Growing*: 50

p. 83   **The *kachcheri*** Ibid: 52

p. 86   **The Portuguese had built** Ibid: 50

p. 89   **Europe has made** Ibid: 48

p. 89   **These *cadjan* fences** Keble: 103

Colombo pedestrian.

p. 90   Everywhere the lone LW, *Growing*: 34

p. 93   curious mixture Ibid: 21

p. 94   an appalling ex-army [captain] Ibid: 36

p. 94   A bloody unwashed Ibid: 63

p. 94   The 'society' of this place 23 Jan. 1905, in LW, *Letters*: 74

p. 95   In England Charles LW, *Growing*: 39–40

p. 96   Silence fell upon Ibid: 40–41

p. 96   H.E. is, I think 3 Sept. 1905, in LW, *Letters*: 101

p. 97   the same incongruous LW, *Growing*: 46

p. 97   He was extremely Ibid: 45–46

p. 97   I didn't ask for much Ibid: 48

p. 98   His roots began Ibid: 66

p. 98   Sah! Sah! Ibid: 67

p. 98   The whole incident Ibid: 68

p. 99   so queer Ibid: 74

p. 99   O Pen dear Ibid: 43-44

p. 99   I hope you kissed Ibid: 43

p. 99   miserable wretches Letter to Lytton Strachey, 8 Jan. 1905, in LW, *Letters*: 73

p. 99   an arrogant LW, *Growing*: 56

p. 100   you have no conception 27 Jan. 1905, in LW, *Letters*: 75–76

p. 100   the most astonishing 25 Mar. 1905, in LW, *Letters*: 84–85

p. 101   beneath the façade LW, *Growing*: 12

p. 104   My unpopularity in Jaffna Ibid: 111

p. 104   The amount of spitting Ibid: 111–12

p. 105   It shocked me Ibid: 113

p. 106   It seems entirely possible Personal communication from Michael Holroyd (Mar. 2005)

p. 108   only serious dressing down LW, *Beginning Again*: 167

p. 108   Very few have worked LW, *Growing*: 109–10

p. 109   I can never forget Letter from K. Naganath to LW, 17 Apr. 1913, in Special Collections, Leonard Woolf Archive, University of Sussex

p. 110   We give a drowned man LW, *Growing*: 77

p. 110   The hospital consists 23 Apr. 1905, in LW, *Letters*: 86

p. 111   A violent dispute 9 Apr. 1905, in LW, *Letters*: 85

p. 111   I expect that . . . Jaffna peninsula 21 May 1905, in LW, *Letters*: 90

p. 111   Can you see it all? 11 Feb. 1905, in LW, *Letters*: 77

p. 112   Which almost certainly saved LW, *Growing*: 82

p. 113   Sir, we heard Ibid: 83

p. 113   It was obviously Ibid: 86

4 *Pearls and Swine*

p. 115   The pearl fishery camp LW, *Growing*: 86–87

p. 115   It really was as though Ibid: 87

p. 115   When they ran Ibid: 88

p. 117   The Tamil treated Ibid: 94

p. 118   the Arabs will do 4 Mar. 1906, in LW, *Letters*: 114

p. 119   I sometimes wonder 21 Mar. 1906, in LW, *Letters*: 115

p. 124   I do not know why I am so fond LW, *Growing*: 100

p. 124   cosmic strangeness Ibid: 100–01

p. 125   platonically Ibid: 102

p. 125   Among other things 19 May 1907, in LW, *Letters*: 128

p. 125   whenever I suddenly LW, *Growing*: 102–03

p. 125   Thus were the graves Ibid: 121

p. 126   As the rainfall for day after day Ibid: 117

p. 126   I suppose I shall 24 Mar. 1907, in LW, *Letters*: 127

p. 126   passions and prejudices LW, *Growing*: 62

p. 127   She was so lovely Neruda: 100

p. 127   one of the best books Ibid: 93

p. 128   You hear it coming LW, *Growing*: 117–18

p. 144   What a soft liquid gentle Sinhala word Ibid: 132–33

p. 146   At one moment Cave: 82

5 *Kandy*

p. 149   I certainly LW, *Growing*: 158–59

p. 150   wanton, arbitrary Mills: 157

p. 151   war was being undertaken K. M. de Silva: 229

p. 152   a conspiracy hatched Ibid: 230

p. 152   Like all Kandyans Mills: 160

p. 152   wanted a king Quoted in Mills: 160

p. 152   absolutely essential Quoted in Mills: 98

p. 153   Here are tall people H. A. I. Goonetileke: 201–02

p. 154   far the best stable companion LW, *Growing*: 134

p. 155   until his marriage LW, *Letters*: 584

p. 155   a symbol and centre LW, *Growing*: 135

p. 156   I suppose, Woolf Ibid: 137

p. 156   For five days 25 Aug. 1907, in LW, *Letters*: 131

p. 158   positively ugly LW, *Growing*: 141

p. 159   The courtyard is crammed Quoted in Bradnock: 196

p. 162   It all passed off LW, *Growing*: 145

p. 162   If my memory is correct Ibid: 144

p. 162   if one must have a religion Ibid: 159

p. 162   anthropomorphic Ibid.

p. 163   recognises that different people Ibid: 161

p. 163   The folk religion Sarachchandra: 2

p. 163   That horrible insistence LW, *Growing*: 163

p. 164   Like the esoteric Buddhism Ibid: 164

p. 164   the only real Buddhist Ibid: 159

p. 164   I am enmeshed 8 Apr. 1908, in LW, *Letters*: 137

p. 165   they played like demons LW, *Growing*: 146

p. 166   extraordinarily romantic Ibid: 151

p. 166   it so happens that 17 Nov. 1907, in LW, *Letters*: 134

p. 166   liked her very much LW, *Growing*: 153

p. 166   sometimes I think really 17 Nov. 1907, in LW, *Letters*: 134

p. 166   the undiluted female mind LW, *Growing*: 151

p. 167   gentler, more sensitive Ibid: 152

p. 167   We had slipped Ibid: 155

p. 168   mile after mile Ibid: 156

p. 168   According to the Ceylon Govt 8 Apr. 1908, in LW, *Letters*: 136

p. 168   You'd better marry Letter from Bella Woolf to LW, 27 July 1909, in LW, *Letters*: 148

p. 171   working for hire Quoted in Moxham: 172

p. 172   The price of foodstuffs Moxham: 179

p. 174   They were typically LW, *Growing*: 156–57

p. 175   Suddenly he said to me Ibid: 110–11

p. 176   Kandy was a lovely place Ibid: 166–67

p. 176   the flogging of a man Ibid: 166

p. 176   The first two were hanged 29 Sept. 1907, in LW, *Letters*: 133

p. 177   The prisoners were confined LW, *Growing*: 169

p. 182   I believe it is the only way 15 Sept. 1907, in LW, *Letters*: 131–32

p. 182   sturdy Kandyan Keble: 147

p. 182   I was up above LW, *Growing*: 158

p. 183   the fate, the whole life even Ibid: 171

6 Journey to Hambantota

p. 185   As dawn was breaking LW, *Growing*: 156

p. 187   Julia Jackson LW, *Sowing*: 160–61

p. 189   I saw the sun rising Quoted in Keble: 296

p. 194   a phony French nobleman Neruda: 95

p. 194   Shall I ever forget that morning De Mauny: 16

p. 198   There are plenty of people Keble: 278

p. 198   the last outpost Williams: 444

p. 199   the town of Tangalla LW, *Diaries in Ceylon*: 147

p. 200   If I had to show anyone LW, *Growing*: 71–72

7 Hambantota

p. 203   All the year round LW, *Growing*: 176–77

p. 205   Yet it was Magam Pattu Ibid: 176

p. 206   As the night goes on Ibid: 197

p. 207   I liked the complete solitude Ibid: 211–12

p. 207   One could grow 23 Oct. 1908, in LW, *Letters*: 139

p. 208   I work, God, how I work 2 Oct. 1908, in LW, *Letters*: 137

p. 208   Lord of ten million blacks Quoted in LW, *Letters*: 131

p. 209   completely immersed LW, *Growing*: 225

p. 209   After two or three years Ibid: 172

p. 209   In the last half of my time Ibid: 232

p. 209   In the evening rode Hatagala LW, *Diaries in Ceylon*: 151–52

p. 210   I worked all day LW, *Growing*: 180

p. 210   the colossal laziness LW, *Diaries in Ceylon*: 182

p. 211   Even in a remote village LW, *Growing*: 242

p. 211   I told the women Ibid: 241

p. 212   arrogant and offensive Ibid: 223

p. 212   not an end in itself Ibid: 181

p. 212   Most women naked 25 Nov. 1908, in LW, *Letters*: 142

p. 213   I have never worked so hard LW, *Growing*: 187

p. 213   It was the only time Ibid: 191

p. 214   In the Ceylon jungle village LW, *Beginning Again*: 100

p. 216   The enormous empty lagoons LW, *Growing*: 176

p. 216   Great mobs of snowy pelicans Keble: 275

p. 217   I am going to walk on to Tissa LW, *Growing*: 185

p. 218   Looking back it seems to me Ibid: 187

p. 218   A delightful place 28 Oct. 1908, in LW, *Letters*: 140–41

p. 219   extremely nervous LW, *Growing*: 220

p. 220   He behaved to the Sinhalese Ibid: 202

p. 221   He is a white man Ibid: 203

p. 225   I hope the Kataragama god LW, *Diaries in Ceylon*: 166

p. 225   one could actually say Wirz, *Kataragama*: 16

p. 227   Everybody who stays in Kataragama Ibid: 44

p. 228   It was these kind of strange LW, *Growing*: 229

p. 228   an authentic, spontaneous explosion Ibid: 231

p. 228   The stars blazed Ibid: 192–93

p. 230   it almost seems as if a Sinhalese Wirz, *Exorcism and the Art of Healing in Ceylon*: 208

p. 232   These were sophisticated disputes LW, *Growing*: 239

10 *Should We Be Afraid of Leonard Woolf?*

Epilogue: In Search of Beddagama

Bibliography

Select Books by Leonard Woolf

An Autobiography, 1 : 1880–1911, Oxford: Oxford University Press, 1980 (contains *Sowing* and *Growing* with an introduction by Quentin Bell)

Beginning Again: An Autobiography of the Years 1911–1918, London: The Hogarth Press, 1964

Diaries in Ceylon 1908–1911: Records of a Colonial Administrator, London: The Hogarth Press, 1963

Downhill All the Way: An Autobiography of the Years 1919–1939, London: The Hogarth Press, 1968

Growing: An Autobiography of the Years 1904–1911, London: The Hogarth Press, 1961

Imperialism and Civilization, London: The Hogarth Press, 1928

The Journey Not the Arrival Matters: An Autobiography of the Years 1939–1969, London: The Hogarth Press, 1969

Letters of Leonard Woolf, Frederic Spotts ed., New York: Harcourt Brace Jovanovich, 1989

Sowing: An Autobiography of the Years 1880–1904, London: The Hogarth Press, 1960

Stories of the East, London: The Hogarth Press, 1921 (republished in *Diaries in Ceylon*)

The Village in the Jungle, pbk edn, Delhi: Oxford University Press, 1981 (introduction by E. F. C. Ludowyk)

Select Articles by Leonard Woolf

"After fifty years", *New Statesman*, 23 Apr. 1960

"Economic imperialism", London: Labour Publishing Co., 1921

"Mandates and empire", London: League of Nations Union, 1920

"Sanctuary", *Times of Ceylon Annual*, 1910

"Why so malignant?", *Ceylon Observer*, 22 Feb. 1962

Related Books

Bradnock, Robert and Roma, *Sri Lanka: Handbook*, London: Footprint, 1998

Cave, Henry W., *Ceylon along the Rail Track*, 2nd edn, Colombo: Visidinu Prakashakayo, 2002

Coates, Irene, *Who's Afraid of Leonard Woolf ?: A Case for the Sanity of Virginia Woolf*, New York: Soho Press, 1998

De Mauny, Count, *The Gardens of Taprobane*, Bernard Miall ed., London: Williams and Norgate, 1937

De Silva, Chandra Richard, *Sri Lanka: A History*, 2nd edn, Delhi: Vikas, 1997

De Silva, K. M., *A History of Sri Lanka*, London: Hurst, 1981

De Silva, M. C. W. Prabhath, *Leonard Woolf: A British Civil Servant as a Judge in the Hambantota District of Colonial Sri Lanka (1908–1911)*, Colombo: self-published, 1996

De Silva, R. K.:

   Early Prints of Ceylon (Sri Lanka) 1800–1900, London: Serendip, 1985

   Illustrations and Views of Dutch Ceylon 1602–1796, London: Serendip, 1988 (with W. G. M. Beumer)

   19th Century Newspaper Engravings of Ceylon—Sri Lanka, London: Serendip, London, 1998

Farmer, B. H., *Ceylon: A Divided Nation*, London: Institute of Race Relations/Oxford University Press, 1963

Buddhist priest, Anuradhapura.

Glubb, John, *The Fate of Empires; and, Search for Survival*, Edinburgh: Blackwood, 1978

Goonetileke, H. A. I., *Images of Sri Lanka through American Eyes: Travellers in Ceylon in the 19th and 20th Centuries*, Colombo: Embassy of the United States of America, 1976

Handbook for the Ceylon Traveller, Colombo: Studio Times, 1974

Hollup, Oddvar, *Bonded Labour: Caste and Cultural Identity among Tamil Plantation Workers in Sri Lanka*, Colombo: Charles Subasinghe and Sons, 1994

Keble, W. T., *Ceylon Beaten Track*, pbk edn, Colombo: Sooriya, 2001

Mills, Lennox A., *Ceylon under British Rule 1795–1932*, London: Frank Cass, 1964

Morris, Jan:

    Farewell the Trumpets: An Imperial Retreat, London: Faber and Faber, 1978

    Pax Britannica: The Climax of an Empire, London: Faber and Faber, 1968

Moxham, Roy, *Tea: Addiction, Exploitation and Empire*, London: Constable and Robinson, 2003

Nelson, W. A., *The Dutch Forts of Sri Lanka: The Military Monuments of Ceylon*, Edinburgh: Canongate, 1984

Neruda, Pablo, *Memoirs*, Hardie St Martin trans., London: Penguin (Twentieth-Century Classic edn), 1978

Ondaatje, Christopher, *The Man-eater of Punanai: A Journey of Discovery to the Jungles of Old Ceylon*, Toronto: HarperCollins, 1992

Ondaatje, Michael, *Running in the Family*, Toronto: McClelland and Stewart, 1982

Sarachchandra, Ediriwira, *The Folk Drama of Ceylon*, Colombo: Department of Cultural Affairs, 1952

Spater, George and Ian Parsons, *A Marriage of True Minds: An Intimate Portrait of Leonard and Virginia Woolf*, New York: Harcourt Brace Jovanovich, 1979

Strachey, Lytton, *The Letters of Lytton Strachey*, Paul Levy ed., London: Viking, 2005

Williams, Harry, *Ceylon: Pearl of the East*, London: Robert Hale, 1950

Wirz, Paul:

    Exorcism and the Art of Healing in Ceylon, Leiden: Brill, 1954

    Kataragama: The Holiest Place in Ceylon, Doris Berta Pralle trans., Colombo: Stamford Lake, 1996

Woolf, Virginia:

    The Diary of Virginia Woolf, Anne Olivier Bell ed., London: The Hogarth Press, 1977

    The Letters of Virginia Woolf, Nigel Nicolson ed., Vol. 1, London: The Hogarth Press, 1975

    Moments of Being: Unpublished Autobiographical Writings, Jeanne Schulkind ed., London: Chatto and Windus, 1976

    Virginia Woolf and Lytton Strachey: Letters, Leonard Woolf and John Strachey eds, New York: Harcourt, Brace, 1956

Wright, Arnold, ed., *Twentieth Century Impressions of Ceylon*, London: Lloyds Greater Britain Publishing Company, 1907

Related Articles

Ackroyd, Peter, "Guardian of Bloomsbury", *The Times*, 1 Mar. 1990 (review of *Letters of Leonard Woolf*)

Clarance, William, "Woolf and Bandaranaike: the ironies of federalism in Sri Lanka", *Political Quarterly*, 72:4, 2001

Clarke, Arthur C., "Who's afraid of Leonard Woolf?", in his *Greetings, Carbon-Based Bipeds!: Collected Essays 1934–1998*, New York: St Martin's Press, 1999

De Silva, Mervyn, "Random reflections on Leonard Woolf", *Daily News*, 14 Feb. 1960

Gooneratne, Yasmine, "A novelist at work: Leonard Woolf's *The Village in the Jungle*", *Journal of Commonwealth Literature*, 18:1, 1983

Goonetilleke, D. C. R. A., ed., "Leonard Woolf: a symposium for the centenary of his birth", *English Bulletin* (of the English Association of Sri Lanka), 4, Dec. 1980

Hettiarachchi, Kumudini, "Still a village in the jungle", *Sunday Times*, 29 Sept. 2002

International Commission of Jurists, *Ethnic Conflict and Violence in Sri Lanka: Report of a Mission to Sri Lanka in July–August 1981* (by Virginia A. Leary), Geneva, 1983

Jayatilaka, Dayan, "The mystery of the missing intelligentsia", *Weekend Express*, 10–11 June 2000

Jayawardena, Kumari, "Leonard Woolf, a background note", in *I Want to Speak of Tenderness: 50 Writers for Ann Ranasinghe*, Gerard Robuchon ed., Colombo: ICES, 2003

Mathmaluwe, M. B., "*Jungle Tide*—after 60 years: another look", *Island*, 3 Apr. 1990

Nissan, Elizabeth and R. L. Stirrat, "The generation of communal identities", in *Sri Lanka: History and the Roots of the Conflict*, Jonathan Spencer ed., London: Routledge, 1990

Punchihewa, Gamini, "On the trails of Village in the Jungle", *Daily News*, 14 July 2004

Ratnaweera, Karel Roberts, "Swings to swing on, houses to visit", *Sunday Observer*, 13 Apr. 2003

Roy, Anindyo:

"Metropolitan civility, Bloomsbury, and the power of the modern colonial state: Leonard Woolf's 'Pearls and Swine'", *Journal X*, 3:1, 1998

"'Telling brutal things': colonialism, Bloomsbury and the crisis of narration in Leonard Woolf's 'A Tale Told by Moonlight'", *Criticism*, spring 2001

Samaranayake, Ajith, "Drought and stagnation in the village", *Sunday Observer*, 5 Sept. 2004

Thwaites, Jeanne:

"The voice of colonization", *Lanka Guardian*, 1 Dec. 1995

"Leonard Woolf should be shot!", *Lanka Guardian*, 15 Jan. 1996

Wijesinhe, E. R.:

"Reminders (not so gentle) of the GA author", *Ceylon Observer*, 14 Jan. 1962

"Woolf of Hambantota", *Ceylon Observer*, 11 Feb. 1962

Overleaf: Elephants in the Mahaweli Ganga with their mahout.

Index

Numbers in *bold italic* refer to illustrations. Works by Leonard Woolf (LW) are indexed by genre under 'Leonard Woolf: writings', e.g. autobiography, or novels. Woolf's relationships with individuals appear under the individual's name, e.g. Strachey, Lytton, or Woolf, Virginia.

Villager and jak fruit, outside Kandy.